OVER THE CIRCUMSTANCES

Over the Circumstances

Lawrence Hoyle

Terra Nova Publications

First published by Terra Nova Publications Ltd, 2003

Published in Great Britain by
Terra Nova Publications Ltd
PO Box 2400, Bradford on Avon, Wiltshire BA15 2YN

ISBN 1 90194 922 2

Printed in Great Britain by
Bookmarque Ltd, Croydon, Surrey

Contents

Dedicated to the memory of

Colin P.L. Oliphant

1948 – 2000

Good friend and fellow-worker

Foreword

Many noted leaders questioned the wisdom, if not the sanity, of Lawrence Hoyle when he began the task of transforming Lamplugh House into a conference centre. Its location, though beautiful, was hardly strategic and its size would permit only a limited number of guests.

That he was convinced that his wisdom was inspired by God was evidenced in the way Lawrence and Margaret persevered against all the odds. The vision came into being and I was happy to support and encourage the Hoyles by speaking at one of the initial series of conferences that suddenly put Thwing on the charismatic map!

Little did I realise then that Kingdom Faith would in due course lease Lamplugh House, make it into a teaching centre and even establish a new congregation there!

It is a cause of great rejoicing that over the years many people have met with God at Lamplugh in life-changing ways. People have come to salvation, received the baptism in the Holy Spirit, have been healed and experienced God's miracle working power in other ways. Often they have been totally unaware of the story of how this place of meeting with God came into being, or the cost involved in the lives of the original pioneers.

Lawrence is a man who has always said it as it is. He never dresses up mutton to look like lamb! So it is refreshing to hear his candid reaction to events, not only concerning the house, but also the other aspects of his ministry, especially his concern to see the Church come alive in the power of the Holy Spirit.

I trust this book will not only cause you to reflect on what has been, but will also prompt you to consider issues that are raised by implication —issues that constantly have to be faced by the Church in order to be effective in obeying the call to be not only relevant in today's society, but the instrument in God's hands to effect His purposes.

Colin Urquhart
Kingdom Faith

Prologue

On March 31st 1989, at the age of sixty one, for reasons of ill health, I retired early from active ministry and the leadership of Anglican Renewal Ministries. I had been the Co-ordinator and then first Director since the inception of ARM in 1980–81. After twenty years of hard, pioneering work, often against great odds, to establish Lamplugh House, the former rectory of Thwing, East Yorkshire as a renewal and conference centre, out of which emerged Anglican Renewal Ministries in the early 80s, the effects were becoming evident, and I was showing the classic signs of stress related illness. Hypertension, diabetes, and the first indications of angina were apparent; at times I was losing concentration and the ability to think straight, and I knew I was heading for some sort of breakdown. At the same time, my wife, Margaret, who was very much involved in the work, was suffering increasingly from an arthritic hip, which was to be replaced at the end of 1989.

It was of great concern to me that there was no one working alongside me who, in the event of my leaving, could carry on running the show. Inevitably the work had been very much moulded in my image and I knew that I had not been the easiest person in the world to get on with. Several attempts to appoint a suitable assistant were unfruitful, and this did nothing at all to ameliorate my growing health problems. Consequently, acting on medical and pastoral advice, I became convinced that my time was up and I should go as soon as possible.

At the 8th Annual Conference of ARM, held at Swanwick in September 1988, I announced my decision 'to return to the obscurity from which I had emerged', indicating that I would retire from Anglican Renewal Ministries six months later, giving the trustees time to find a suitable successor. They were very helpful and supportive—possibly they were also relieved—and forthwith set about finding my replacement, but more about that later.

Throughout the following six months, Margaret and I were totally overwhelmed by the appreciative letters we received from people all over the country, representing the whole spectrum of denominations, clergy and laity, including some bishops, one of whom had himself recently retired, who kindly said I had more to show for my ministry than most! Even I thought that a little over the top. However, we were able to subdue temptation to pride, secure in the belief that what had been achieved was the work of God, to whom was due all the glory. Though very conscious of our own weaknesses and failures, at this period when we felt bruised and weary we appreciated this kind and loving acknowledgement that our work had been of profound significance in many people's lives down in the grass roots.

At the time of our departure, many people, especially some who had been involved with us in prayer and support from the early days, and who knew of the way that God had guided us through formidable obstacles, suggested that I write a book about our experiences. I instantly dismissed this suggestion; my response was, 'let God be his own witness; if all this is of him, then he does not need me to prove it.' Also, I had always hated writing, and being naturally undisciplined I doubted that I could apply myself to it anyway. Remember also, that I was unwell and heading for eventual quadruple coronary bypass surgery. All I wanted then was to get off the scene knowing I had made the right decision. At that time, testimony books were appearing like blossom in spring and I was not a little disillusioned by the way things seemed to be going on the renewal scene. My reasons for this apprehension will be explained later. Rightly or wrongly, I had always believed that the Renewal, as one had understood it, was to release the power and love of the Holy Spirit in the local church congregation. It seemed now that this aim was being compromised. I was relieved that I was now free of all this as we disappeared 'below the parapet' and eventually found ourselves in the peace and beauty of the South Hams, the most southerly part of Devon. There, it seemed, the only 'renewal' people were aware of was that which was necessary each year for television licences and motor insurance!

So why did I contemplate writing this book after so many years? The logical reason is that, at the time, both Lamplugh House and Anglican Renewal Ministries were still going strong, each with its own aim and purpose. Perhaps it was time to record the story of the early days before they were forgotten. It was Margaret who first caused me to reconsider my original decision, after a phone call from a person currently involved with Lamplugh House, who wanted information from me as to its beginnings in the early 70s. He was preparing a leaflet to inform a new generation now using the place as to its origins and the vision behind it. Margaret insisted that if anyone should write about it, it should be me. I was still reluctant, though I did not dismiss the possibility, which I then pondered for several months.

I am a light sleeper. Usually I sleep soundly for three or four hours and then lie awake thinking, or sometimes reading. It is in these times that I often find I can meditate, talk to God and listen to him —more so than in specific prayer times. Over the years I have found many occasions when, during the night, after wrestling with important decisions and problems, the answer has come to me, literally in a flash. When this happens I have often experienced an immediate release of the burden and an enthusiasm to pursue the objective.

Whether these instances represent a true inspiration from God can only be proven by the ensuing results.

Over the years we had learned that whenever God seemed to be showing us the way forward we were required to be obedient, and it was not for us to question his purposes. Experience taught us that it was useless to prepare human plans and simply ask God to bless them. After all, that was what had been wrong in my earlier ministry, before I came into a new experience of the Holy Spirit. It is ludicrous to question whether God's plans are humanly possible. Usually they are not; he asks for obedience and, when that is forthcoming, he provides the means for fulfilment —that is God's way. We cannot make excuses to the Holy Spirit; there is only one way forward —his way. The wonderful thing is, that when we say 'yes' to God, then all his infinite resources for that project are provided: the resources of the kingdom for the work of the kingdom.

Early in 2000, in such a manner, I believe I received inspiration and became convinced that I should indeed put index fingers to word-processor and write the book. Excited at the prospect, I realised nevertheless that it would be a difficult task, as I had kept no records to fall back on. On my retirement I had been determined to be free of everything; I felt bruised and battered and found it was a liberating experience to clear my desk, cancel my subscription to the church newspapers, and 'ride off into the sunset'.

Everything was in my memory, much of it forgotten; however, that night when the inspiration came to write the book, a host of memories were released into my mind. I arose from bed, made a mug of tea and began writing down everything as it all came flooding back. Later, Margaret produced a dog-eared cuttings book, in which she had placed letters, newspaper articles and photographs —which I had forgotten about. Earlier, I had apparently asked her why on earth she needed to keep all that stuff! Maybe it is for the old men to dream dreams and for the old women to be practical.

Why was the book given its title? My experience in the Church over many years of parochial, teaching and conference ministry suggests that much Christian activity is conditioned by circumstances which often inhibit a satisfactory outcome, so any success might be described as having been achieved 'under' the circumstances. But such a description would be inappropriate for this record. The story of Lamplugh House—and of Anglican Renewal Ministries, which was a direct outcome of the vision that developed there and took shape over a number of years, when we witnessed the leading of the Holy Spirit, and the triumph of faith over adversity—can only be described as having been *over* the circumstances.

It is clear to me that in church affairs many plans and judgements are made purely on the human level. We make our plans and then ask God to bless them, failing to see that if they are not in accordance with his will, we can pray until we are blue in the face, but they will receive no blessing. We constantly forget that the church, though peopled by humans, is not a human institution. It is God's instrument for bringing his kingdom to the world, and is not constrained by man's parameters. God has his own agenda, which we have been given in Scripture, and it is revealed by his Spirit; only those who are open to his Spirit really hear his voice. If to make such a statement immediately opens me to the charge of 'fundamentalist' from the theologically liberal unbelievers, then I will be such.

It has been necessary to write of the opposition we experienced as the work began. There is often a failure on the part of some to recognise the work of the Holy Spirit when things happen that seem to be outside recognised structures. It is that attitude which drove from the Church of England those who were despised as 'dissenters' or 'enthusiasts'; which drove out the Methodists; and, in recent years, some modern day charismatics, who then formed the 'house church' movement. Such opposition as we experienced was responsible for turning the vision we had been given, of Lamplugh House as an Anglican centre for spiritual renewal, founded in the parish and linked with the local church, into something which in the end was to move beyond that initial vision into a non-denominational charismatic ministry. The purposes of God continued to be fulfilled under the commendable stewardship of Kingdom Faith Ministries. Any who opposed us, I forgive completely, as we must all do if we ourselves are to receive forgiveness.

This record is of how we perceived events, and how we sought to obey the guiding of the Holy Spirit. Most of us, particularly clergy, have a love/hate relationship with the church as an institution, and this book contains a good deal of implied criticism, which is intended to be constructive. Nevertheless, I believe it is important to note that when, as church members, we do offer criticism, in the last analysis we are criticising *ourselves*. We cannot stand away from the institution in indignation, whether righteous or unrighteous. There is corporate strength in the witness of true believers. As the late Geoffrey Paul memorably observed in his sermon, when being instituted as Bishop of Bradford, "We must learn to love that collection of saints and fatheads who make up the Holy Catholic Church!"

About two thirds of the book was completed by August 2000, but I then gave up on it for a time, chiefly because of the need to move house for health and family reasons. However, at the beginning of 2002, I was hearing of problems concerning the future of Anglican Renewal Ministries. By March a decision had been made to end its operations. The letter advising me of this, and the following public announcement, contained conflicting euphemisms as to the reasons for the closure, which seemed to me like Downing Street–type 'spin', to which I reacted with unease and not a little anger. I concluded that there was little left of the vision for ARM, which had emerged so dramatically twenty years earlier, and decided that I must finish the book and put down my 'four pennyworth' for posterity. This I have now done —but, I hasten to add, not before repenting of the anger and bitterness that I realised was part of my motivation! Wrong decisions can be made sincerely, and ostensibly 'wrong' decisions can sometimes, with hindsight, come to be seen as the right ones. The leadership was faced with the need to arrive at a difficult decision. If the result proves in time to have been of God, then we will see what he in *his* timing will replace it with. I recall that the Fountain Trust was replaced by ARM. What remains true is that the impetus for renewal in the Church of England, which Anglican Renewal Ministries was called into being to encourage, is still very much needed. My positive hope is that the work of the Holy Spirit will flourish in local churches, empowering them for witness and evangelism.

It is the Holy Spirit who convicts us of sin and draws us to the cross of Jesus Christ; it is he who calls us to repentance and discipleship, and who opens the Scriptures to us, creates in us his fruit, and equips us with his gifts, for witness and ministry. The need for openness to his work is as great as ever. My hope in writing this book is that it will encourage others to learn of the way he strengthened and used those of us involved in an exciting period of Renewal, despite our many human weaknesses, and despite the mistakes that all Christians make, for which we stand in constant need of the grace and forgiveness which flow from our Lord Jesus Christ.

One

Over the Circumstances

Given the circumstances of my background, my early education, and its limitations because of wartime conditions, I would not have believed it possible that I should one day enter the ordained ministry of the Church of England and then have such wide ranging experience, nor that I would have been entrusted with a ministry of encouragement for Anglicans seeking to move in the power of the Holy Spirit. It is a humbling thought, and it could be said that my background suggests I have much to be humble about —not that I could claim any personal credit for what was to happen. I believe that God must have had his hand upon my life from the beginning.

In retrospect, when I consider how my outlook, ideas and faith developed until I was ordained (in 1955), it would seem that it was 'over the circumstances' rather than under them that all this happened. I was to owe much to the help and encouragement of many Christian friends when my faith began to mature in my early twenties. Several years of traditional (and sometimes disappointing) parochial ministry were to prove invaluable when I found myself engaged in the renewal-teaching ministry that was to emerge some twenty years later.

I was born in Barnsley, Yorkshire. In those days it was a grim, dreary place, not just in appearance but also because of the Depression of the 1930s, which particularly hit the coal mining industry. Many miners were unemployed or on short time work and there was much poverty and distress. At school in the years preceding World War II, I was able to appreciate that many children of my age, and their families, had a very hard life. Some children literally had no boots, so they were provided by the local authority. Not everyone was affected, though. My family was comparatively well off for those days. My father held a full time job at the Post Office, driving a mail van, and had many opportunities of working overtime; in addition, he had come out of the Royal Artillery as a reservist, so he received a helpful monthly pension. I remember that we always went away for a summer holiday each year; we had a small car, and were able to move into a brand new house in 1933.

Amongst the historic events I remember from the 1930s was the opening of the new Town Hall in Barnsley by the then Prince of Wales. This was a great occasion; we had watched for months the construction of the monumental, white stone edifice as it grew on its hill, from where it shone over the dingy blackness of the rest of the town. I became more acquainted with that building, as the father of one of my school mates was the resident caretaker. This meant that sometimes, after the offices were closed, some of we school-boys would go and play there, skating and running along the seemingly endless corridors and playing in the lifts. Happy days! The Silver Jubilee of King George V and Queen Mary was remembered for the commemorative tins of toffees given to all the school children! Then followed the Abdication — no tins of toffees then, but a few scurrilous verses about a certain Mrs S. were all the rage at school. The Coronation of 1937 was a great time; the tins of toffees appeared again, together with a splendidly illustrated book about the Coronation and the Royal Family. Later in that year, the new King and Queen actually visited Barnsley, though to me it seemed that they simply drove through the town very quickly. Who could blame them? All the schoolchildren were crocodiled to vantage points along their route and, after much excited waiting, we caught a fleeting glimpse of the royal couple as they sped by in a closed but well-lit limousine.

The following two years were full of talk about forthcoming war with Germany. There were various political crises, and preparations for when we were all to be bombed and gassed as we schoolboys ominously predicted. However, this did not prevent us from having great fun playing in newly erected air raid shelters near the school. The reality of it came home to us on 1st September 1939, when my father was called up to rejoin the Army. Then, two days later, my mother, sister and I listened to the Prime Minister declare war on Germany. My mother was quite tearful. She still remembered the Great War, but to me it was very exciting — and the added bonus was a school summer holiday extended by several weeks. My schooling, for what it was worth, ended in 1941, when we moved from Barnsley to Bradford. This move meant that I left school early and avoided going to a new one, as I ought to have done, for three or four more terms. Instead, I obtained my first job, as an office boy at a well known worsted manufacturer's mill nearby. There I was the general dogsbody. I made the tea and dealt with all the post. I found the mill a very interesting place, which I had the run of, so to speak, as long as I looked busy and had a piece of paper in my hand! Eventually, I was promoted to less menial activities. It was a fascinating place, full of many old fashioned Yorkshire characters (now a rare breed). It was a pleasant and enjoyable four years. I made many friends and often enjoyed weekend hikes with them in the Yorkshire Dales.

Even during the stringency of wartime clothes rationing, it was possible at times, on surrender of the appropriate number of clothing coupons, to buy suit-lengths of the finest Yorkshire cloth quite cheaply at periodic sales held for the staff. There were many Jewish bespoke tailors in the town who, for a reasonable cost, ensured that even the office boys attended Saturday night 'hops' attired in almost Savile Row fashion. But that was in the days before jeans and stylish scruffiness all but ruined a great industry. This brings to my memory an amusing incident when, years later, after it had become known that I was leaving to train for ordination, I attended the annual ball, where all the directors and staff dressed up for the occasion. I found myself in a group that included a Jewish director, and also the little tailor who had made suits for me over the years. Maurice Levy, the director, introduced me to a friend saying, "Lawrence is going to be Archbishop of Canterbury one day."

Sammy Drazen, the tailor, piped up, "Yes, and I will make his uniform!" As it happens, it turned out not to be an authentic prophecy!

In July 1945, having reached the age of eighteen, I was conscripted into the Royal Air Force. My civilian job ensured that I would be employed on clerical duties and, after a few weeks of training, I was posted, first, to India where I worked in New Delhi for the Air Priorities Board for a while, before being posted to Singapore, where I was to spend the rest of my service, until I returned home in April 1948.

It was in Singapore that I was confirmed, in 1946, at St. Andrew's Cathedral, by Bishop Wilson, who had been imprisoned by the Japanese in Changi jail. Sometimes I would attend the Station Chapel on Sundays, now with a heightened sense of being a full church member. I believe that I had acquired Christian values and moral understanding both from my upbringing and through the more or less accepted standards of the time —standards that had begun to erode during the war years and would rapidly decline further as time went by. However, as I know now, I was not a committed Christian in the true sense, but as far back as I can remember I believed in God, and knew who Jesus was. I was always able to take on board what I was taught, without any problem. Although churchgoing was never on the agenda for my family, my younger sister and I were sent off to Sunday school, as was then the custom. This was in the 1930s and we lived opposite the parish church where, though I was quite young, I would on occasion go alone to a service, out of curiosity. I understood very little, but I was fascinated by the atmosphere and the mystery. At school I learned that Jesus was very special. This awareness came through an excellent religious instruction teacher, who had a wonderful ability to tell contemporary stories with a Christian message, and who spoke about a boy who got into many dangers and difficulties, but in the end Jesus saved him from them by the use of a special 'password': 'John 3:16'. That was the first biblical text I ever learned and it became imprinted on my mind at a very early age.

In my teens in Bradford, in pre-service days, I had been a member of the local parish church youth club and joined the 'heavy gang' on Sunday nights, chatting up the girls at the back of the church during Evensong. Following my confirmation, I became a sporadic communicant, until I came home in spring of 1948 and went back to work at the mill office again, where I became responsible for working out and preparing the wages for several hundred people. This was before the days of computers and electronic calculators, so all the sums had to be worked out the hard way. This was good experience for the future. I became quite adept at figures and mental arithmetic, and acquired good experience of administration in the mill office and through having a variety of jobs during my service career, so acquiring further abilities that were to prove very useful in years to come.

A close friend, a Roman Catholic, unwittingly was instrumental in my religious education, as we seemed often to have deep discussions, which meant I had to defend the Church of England against the dogmatic claims of 'the one true church' of a brand of Catholicism that was strong in Bradford, due to a large population of people of Irish origin who had come to work in the textile mills during the years of poverty in Ireland. My friend was well versed in the dogmatic and simplistic certainties purveyed by the Irish priests who, in those days, still exercised a remarkable dominance over their flock, but whose understanding of the Church of

England and the Reformation often left much to be desired.

Admittedly, at that time I was prejudiced, through my upbringing, against the Roman Catholic Church. It was not until several years later, when I began to associate with Roman Catholics who were more philosophical and intellectual about their beliefs, that I was more able to respect their ideas, if not to share them myself. I began to read more widely, and became more informed about Anglicanism and its claims to be a true part of the catholic church, both catholic and reformed, holding a healthy balance of word and sacraments. I began to understand and to love the Book of Common Prayer and the liturgy of the Church of England. At the same time, I had begun to worship regularly at Bradford Cathedral. At my Confirmation in 1946, I suppose that, like so many others, I had committed myself to the church, rather than personally to Jesus Christ. I started off by going to Holy Communion on Sundays at 8.00 a.m. – thereby not needing to listen to sermons! I did not go every week initially, but after a time I began to realise that if I did not go then something seemed to be missing in my life, and I became a weekly communicant. Eventually, I would attend the main Sunday morning service, which was usually Morning Prayer but once a month it would be Choral Communion. There was an excellent choir and a large congregation. The churchwardens would wear formal morning suits on special occasions, such as civic or special services, or when the Bishop was there.

At this time, the cathedral, which was the fine old parish church of Bradford before the formation of the diocese earlier in the century, was beginning to get delusions of grandeur and was seeking to adorn itself with pseudo Gothic extensions. Though it was a cathedral, it still remained the parish church of Bradford, and the original patrons, the Simeon Trustees, appointed incumbents to this important living, who functioned primarily as Vicar of Bradford, but who also held the post of Provost, with the duties of a dean. Consequently, successive incumbents were of impeccable evangelical stock, of a kind which is now, sadly, almost extinct. I consider myself very blessed to have had the privilege of listening to good biblical preaching over a long period. John Tiarks, who was later to become Bishop of Chelmsford, was Provost, and I listened week after week to his sermons and his applied scriptural teaching, until soon it began to have an effect on my thinking and my lifestyle — so much so that I began to see that I was something of a split personality, in that during my weekday life from Monday onwards I was quite a different person from the one I purported to be on Sundays. Like water dripping on a stone, God's word was beginning to have an effect on me: good biblical preaching, unlike so many pitiful little homilies that pass for preaching these days, and which move nobody, except out of the church! If the Church of England seeks revival, let it once more preach the gospel about Jesus Christ and the need for salvation, and challenge people to convert. That includes consciously turning to Jesus Christ and being led by him. In those days there was, and probably is still to this day, a disconcerting little text in the cathedral pulpit awaiting every visiting preacher preparing to deliver his finely scripted offering. As he arranges his notes in front of him, he sees the words, 'Sir, we would see Jesus!'

During this period, after successfully hiding behind a pillar for two years, I became more involved in the life of the congregation and fellowship, and I made friends there, many of whom had a deeper spiritual awareness and testimony than I had. There was a very good supportive staff who, with other responsibilities, conducted all the youth work and sought to lead people to full commitment to Jesus Christ. They were an approachable, friendly team, people who believed personal evangelism to be a vital part of their work. They were not afraid gently to challenge individuals as to their personal relationship with the Lord Jesus Christ, and were used to setting firm foundations to the lives of many young people. Looking back, I believe that in those early post-war years the Spirit of God was at work through the gifted and dedicated team at Bradford Cathedral. Many young men came forward for ordination, and many others, men and women, went out into full time Christian ministry and service.

My own personal commitment was greatly helped by one staff member in particular, John Gaunt Hunter, as a result of which I no longer experienced a division between Sunday and the rest of the week in my spiritual life. I did have a problem with the assertion that one becomes a Christian upon making a personal commitment to the Lord Jesus. Is this the moment when one is 'saved', or is it a milestone, albeit a very important one, in a process? The word 'conversion' speaks to me of an encounter with Jesus at which there is repentance for one's sins, and one acknowledges him as your only Lord and Saviour. Certainly, that moment marked, for me, a new, significant and important stage of my spiritual growth, and it represented a major turning point in the direction of my life, but I was conscious that God had always been there, and I do not recall ever not believing in him. What was happening, however, was the emergence of faith and repentance, upon which the efficacy of baptism depends. Christians in general, and Anglicans in particular, have held varying interpretations of Scripture on this point. In any event, for me, turning to Jesus Christ was a real and significant moment, from which I was quickly led forward.

It was twenty years later that I was to reach another major milestone experience, when I received what is called baptism in the Holy Spirit, a term with which some traditional evangelicals have difficulty, but less so than used to be the case. That experience was another definitive moment, from which came the major calling and direction of my ministry and for which, it would seem, the preceding years and experience had been a preparation for what was to come.

From this point I became actively involved in a parish visiting scheme, which sought to minister to people in the Victorian slums that formed a large part of the Cathedral parish. This entailed regular visiting of these back-to-back houses by members of the congregation, who went out in pairs. Many became involved in this, including quite a few of the younger members of the church, who entered into it prayerfully, willingly and with enthusiasm. Whether it did much good for the people who lived in those slums, I do not know, but it was certainly good experience and training for those of us who participated as visitors. At this time I found myself entertaining vague notions that I would like to go into the ordained ministry, but such thoughts I quickly dismissed as a vain dream. Given my educational and social background, it seemed impossible and quite ridiculous even to consider, and I told no one of this recurring aspiration. I continued to enjoy fellowship with Christians who were seeking together the Lord's direction for their lives, and I was finding more confidence in myself as a result.

There was a flourishing young people's group, consisting of students and late teenagers and those in their early twenties, like myself. We would meet after Evensong for talks and discussion on topics serious and not so serious, usually led by one of the Cathedral staff. This consisted of the Provost, who seemed an awesome, remote figure, two curates and a 'lady worker', as she was quaintly described. Afterwards, as an exercise in 'witnessing' or a little light relief, a group of us would descend to a huge cleared space in the city centre that had become a Sunday night 'Hyde Park Corner' where all kinds of nutters and cranks held forth on soapboxes. Among these was a notorious atheist and freethinker, a very earnest preacher from an independent conventicle in the town, plus the Catholic Evidence Guild, where a man with a rich Irish accent belaboured the protestants. Our little group would appropriately heckle them. I remember one occasion when a person in our group was heckling the Roman Catholic and hurling texts at him. Then the speaker said to him, "Would you just give me your Bible a second?"

So the fellow handed over his large King James Version and the speaker opened it at a certain page. "What does it say there then?" he asked.

Our heckler replied, "St Paul's Epistle to the Romans."

The speaker said, "Now you show me the Epistle to the

protestants, and I will believe you!"

As my church commitment grew, I found that I was now distancing myself from several activities and relationships that had developed upon my return home from Singapore and RAF service when I resumed my job in the textile industry. I developed several other interests, along with my love of walking in the Dales. For a year or two I was in an amateur dramatic society, and enjoyed playing roles in various productions, as well as the social life that went with it. However, after a time I became disillusioned with that activity; there was so much backbiting and bitchiness amongst these self-styled thespians, who took themselves and their imagined talents far too seriously. A friend and I had joined the society together. We must have been very innocent in those days, because it took some time for us to realise what was going on 'behind the scenes' by way of deviant and immoral behaviour amongst some members, though not all by any means. My friend was on the point of getting married, and I was becoming more involved in church matters, so, much to the detriment of the West End stage of the future, we left and had no more to do with it.

Another activity I gave up was the Young Conservatives. I had joined that not so much for political reasons as social ones, though that was the time when the post-war Labour years were coming to a close, and the Conservatives were scenting victory. However, like Tony Hancock, I drank much beer, enjoyed the parties and dances and played table tennis for the cause. My growing Christian awareness revealed its superficiality, and I was now making new friends who had a different outlook on life. I mention these activities in order to establish my growing awareness of the weakness and fickleness of human nature, and how it always seemed to sabotage the best and most worthy intentions or ideals. I was seeing the great difference between godly people and those who could not thus be described. It was new to me, and I was for the first time experiencing Christian love in friendships where I realised I was being affirmed and encouraged by people who were not motivated by a self-seeking agenda. My earlier life experience as a child and teenager was of being diminished or 'put down' as they say —the classic ingredients of the 'I'm not good enough' syndrome. Having low self-esteem is a great problem for many Christians, as I was later to discover. In my maturing spiritual awareness, I was seeing how natural human life needed a Saviour, the Lord who had now become personal to me in a new way, and whom I knew had saved me from my sins —good old evangelical truth, of which I am neither ashamed nor embarrassed. On churchmanship, a later teacher, whose name I have forgotten, said, "You may go up the candle as far as you like, as long as you begin at the evangelical and biblical base." I was to learn in later years that the church is not *either* 'evangelical' or 'catholic', but both —and that it is intended to be pentecostal also. Bishop Lesslie Newbigin was to write a prophetic book *The Household of God* on that theme in the 1950s, but it was in the charismatic renewal which began in the 1960s that so much began to happen to bring about a transformation.

During that period, the Cathedral staff were very friendly to me, helping me in my growing faith. I must have been somewhat of a nuisance at times because I was constantly seeking answers and explanations. John (or Gaunt, as he is variously addressed) Hunter, Raymond Fountain, the Succentor and his wife-to-be, Anne Hall, the Almoner at one of the local hospitals, together with Beatrice Kennedy, the Lady Worker formerly of the Lee Abbey community in Devon, seem to have singled me out at the time as someone with a potential to be encouraged. One day, John Hunter asked me if I had ever thought of being ordained. Of course I had, but I had dismissed it as impossible and told him of this. From then on I was encouraged to pursue the possibility. I began to wonder if this approach was an indication that I was having this mysterious 'call' from God, which people spoke about; it seemed that it was being confirmed.

Although aware of my lack of academic qualifications, I was not without intelligence. I read a lot, including a daily newspaper —reading a good newspaper over the years can instil much useful information into the memory. I was quick-witted and had a sense of humour, which I had found to be an effective social tool. At the same time, I continued to have that low self-esteem, especially in spiritual matters. 'I am not good enough.' The truth I needed to learn was that the heavenly Father knows all our weaknesses and has made provision for us to come to him through Jesus, be filled with the Holy Spirit, and be equipped with his gifts to do his work. It was many years before that particular penny dropped for me, and I was released from this failing —one so common in the church that it inhibits many from doing the work of God's kingdom. In later years this was to become a main plank of my understanding and teaching about renewal in the Holy Spirit. God is seeking from us not so much our ability as our availability, and our willingness to depend on him and receive his gifts, his tools, which we need in order to be used in his service. I have always been grateful for the grounding in faith that I received through the pastoral care of the staff at Bradford Cathedral. From those days, Canon J.G. Hunter recalls:

During my time at Bradford, Laurie appeared in our midst, quite unexpectedly and quite without warning. Suddenly he was just there. He could not be ignored; he was big, and he was more mature than most of our 150 strong Youth Fellowship, so much so that we did not quite know what to make of him. Would he vanish as quickly as he had emerged? He didn't; he just gently dug himself in, with his sense of humour, and his shrewd view of life —of the world and of the church. During his time with the Cathedral he continued to mature and grow in confidence, and this was due not only to the splendid biblical sermons of the Provost, but also the rounded experience that the Cathedral provided, with its fine worship and genuine fellowship of the congregation —but also the Youth Fellowship, which not only provided thought provoking programmes, but real friendships for the youth of the church right across class barriers. Then there were the opportunities for outreach beyond the congregation, in particular the Parish Visitors.

The Cathedral parish consisted of some 5000 people living in back-to-back stone built properties immediately above the Cathedral up the hillside along Otley Road. It was solid working-class, 90% were loyal to the Church of England, but largely non-practising. Yet the parish provided lots of children for the Sunday School, the Boys' Brigade and the Guides, even the choir. Their parents might be found in the Men's Fellowship—a tiny group—or the much more lively Mother's Union, run by the Provost's wife. They were, however, not to be seen in church—a social habit—except for the Family Pew service in the autumn, when the Cathedral would be packed. Many of these local folk kept in touch with the Cathedral staff throughout their lives, and even after the slums had been demolished and replaced with tower blocks and they themselves had moved out to Ilkley, or the Bradford suburbs. The friendships then made seemed very real, and the visitors appeared to find the challenge of this house-to-house visiting an encouraging and deepening experience.

Despite my academic deficiencies, I was encouraged to pursue this apparent calling. I was sent to see various clerics and then the Provost himself, who, as I said before, seemed an awesome figure, but proved to be quite human at close quarters. His first reaction was that I should think about entering the Church Army, but this did not seem to fit my aspirations and I said I would like to pursue the possibility of ordination. I was encouraged by these encounters and through them learned of what would be required of me to be ordained. It seemed that, following the war, the church had altered its requirements for those seeking ordination. In the past, bishops had usually looked for people with a university degree who would be required to take a two year course in theology, but now men were coming back from the forces seeking ordination, for whom a new system was required. Obviously many had missed out on further education but had a genuine call and needed to be helped. The Church's Advisory Council for Training to the Ministry (CACTM) was established. This body set up three-day residential Selection Boards every few months, at which about twenty men would be questioned and interviewed by several clergy and one leading layman, including one who was an academic. They assessed the calling and academic possibilities of each applicant, and would then inform the sponsoring bishop whether or not his nominee was recommended for training. Some bishops, who preferred the old more autocratic ways, rejected this, including Dr. Alfred Blunt, Bishop of Bradford, whose fame is chiefly due to his sparking off the Abdication crisis ('Alfred the Kingmaker', as he was described by a friend in the Youth Fellowship!), who without doubt was one of these, and to whom, therefore, I was not sent. Instead, the Provost arranged for me to see the younger and more progressive Bishop of Wakefield, who did support the new system. The outcome was that if I was accepted by CACTM, and if I managed to get through theological training, he would ordain me to a title in his diocese.

All this thrilled me and I had a resolute conviction that I was being called, and that somehow God would help me through the difficulties. The church had devised the 'Church Preliminary Examination' for such as myself, designed to help older men to reach the old School Certificate standard in basic subjects, thereby to get them into a studying and learning mode, to equip them to study for the General Ordination Examination (GOE). The GOE usually required a three-year residential course at a theological college. In 1951, by now earnest in my objective, I was advised that I could probably help myself by doing a Wolsey Hall correspondence course, that would help me whilst I awaited further developments. I did so during the following year. I forget now which subjects I took, but they included English Language and Literature. I think it helped me a good deal. I was informed that I would need to apply to a theological college for admission, should I be recommended for training. In fact, this decision was settled for me.

John Tiarks was involved with the 'Parish and People' movement in those days, and I was encouraged to attend its conference at The Hayes, Swanwick, from Whit-Monday of that year. Little did I realise that one day that place would become almost our country home! One of the speakers was Canon W. M. F. Scott, (Gerald, as he was popularly known), who in 1950 had been appointed Principal of St. Aidan's College, Birkenhead. He had a reputation as a preacher and broadcaster, and as an evangelist, but above all as a gifted biblical teacher. He brought new vision, new thinking and readjustment to the requirements of post-war clergy training, and endeavoured to break down the prejudice and bigotry which still existed between many evangelicals and anglo-catholics of their respective old schools. John Tiarks introduced me to him, and I will always remember the two hours or so I talked with him as we walked around the grounds in the magnificent spring weather. I was very impressed by his attractive character, his friendliness, and the keen interest he showed by his apparent sympathy with my situation. His top front teeth were so arranged that he appeared to be wearing a perpetual smile. This was a disconcerting feature at times, as I later discovered that he could be quite firm, and admonish when circumstances so required.

The college had fallen back before he was appointed, so that at that time it needed as many students as it could get and Gerald had a vision that it should provide for men of all ages, backgrounds and churchmanship, and include graduates and non-graduates alike. The outcome of this meeting was that he would bend the rules and allow me to start at St. Aidan's before I had actually attended a Selection Board, the idea being that I could concentrate initially on the Church Preliminary Exam and be helped along with it by the teaching staff of the college. This was wonderful, and I went home rejoicing at how things were working out for me, and that my hopes were being fulfilled. The financing for that first term from September 1952 came from my own savings, until later I qualified for funding by CACTM. I soon settled down to college life. Having had the experience of corporate life in the RAF, and being unmarried at the time, I was free to throw myself into it and to enjoy the tremendous fun and fellowship that went with a disciplined spiritual regime, together with a strenuous academic programme.

In November I went, apprehensively, to a Selection Board in Cheltenham. Much to my surprise I enjoyed it very much and most of the interviewers seemed to be a little unsure themselves of what they were supposed to be doing. I recall that the lay member of the Board seemed to be at a bit of a loss as to what he should ask me, but he showed great interest in a hitch hiking trip I had done that summer, from Bradford to Copenhagen and back, and just wanted to hear of all my adventures on that expedition. He seemed very impressed with my initiative, but whether that was accounted to me for righteousness I shall never know. In due course I learned that I had been conditionally accepted, which meant that I needed to pass the Church Preliminary Exam —which I did, thanks to the special help I had been given during that first term.

At last I was on my way, thanks to the discernment and pastoral help I had been given. Looking at my background and the events that had led me thus far, it was truly 'over the circumstances' that I had reached this stage. During my future parochial ministry I remained constantly on the look-out for people whom God might be calling to full time service, and who might need the kind of help and encouragement that I had been given through Bradford Cathedral.

Two

'What Hath God Wrought?'

St. Aidan's College, Birkenhead was founded in 1847 through the vision of Dr. Joseph Baylee, an Irishman who was the first incumbent of Holy Trinity, Birkenhead. His vision was prompted by the spiritual needs of the growing industrial population of Merseyside and the North of England. It was aptly named after the great seventh century 'apostle of the North' and Bishop of Lindisfarne. A former Principal of the college, Canon F. B. Heiser, wrote of him,

> St. Aidan was more than an evangelist, he was a builder also. He formed a school at Lindisfarne, and later at other centres, where he maintained twelve English youths and trained them to become ministers to their own people. This was the original St. Aidan's College. And to it he brought not only that fire of the Gospel which inspired the ancient Celtic Church to write so glorious a chapter in the history of Christian missions, but also that tradition of sound learning which through all Western Europe was the acknowledged heritage of his Church.[1]

'What Hath God Wrought?' were the words I saw inscribed over the main entrance when, in September 1952 at the age of twenty five, I began my training at St. Aidan's College; I am sure they were not intended to be ironic, otherwise more appropriately they might have read, 'What Hath God Brought?' — especially looking at the diversity of the student body to which a few more 'freshers' and I were added that term.

We students occupied two corridors of the three-storey accommodation block, and the top storey was used as a residence for about ten secular students studying at Liverpool University, to which St. Aidan's was attached. Not only did it bring in extra income for the College, it was supposed to keep we 'theologs' in touch with the world! —a charming thought, considering that most of them were eighteen year olds and still wet behind the ears: we no doubt could have taught them a thing or two. There were about twenty five theological students of a wide age range, from early twenties to at least two in their fifties; and they were of a variety of backgrounds and church tradition, in line with the policy of the college under Gerald Scott. There were two or three former army officers, a dentist, people from industry and commerce, graduates from various universities, including a Dutchman from Utrecht, and a Nigerian priest doing a one-year refresher course. Rodgers Bara Hart eventually became Bishop of the Niger Delta. Most of them were great characters and personalities, except for one who seemed to have little personality of his own, but would, to much amusement, constantly mimic members of staff, visiting speakers and other students.

The spiritual discipline of the place was almost monastic: Morning Prayer in chapel early in the morning was followed by a silent 'quiet time' for half an hour before breakfast. Before lunch, an informal intercession period was conducted by the students, and Evening Prayer took place before formal dinner in the evening. Students took a part in all these services and the Sunday morning Choral Eucharist. On Sunday afternoons and evenings we were sent out to various churches in the area, in order to help with services and pastoral work —and, hopefully, to acquire some useful experience for the future. Lectures were held throughout the morning and early evening, whilst afternoons were free for leisure, sport or working on the grounds. The period between eight and ten o'clock in the evening was devoted to private study. It was indeed a disciplined way of life, difficult at times, but for the most part I enjoyed it immensely. It took time for me to get used to study and to the writing of weekly essays, but the staff constantly encouraged me. My first year was not easy academically; I failed my first set of exams and had to sit them again with those of the second year, which I passed successfully, so that by the third year I sailed through with no problem.

The quality of teaching was good, but that provided by Gerald Scott himself was excellent. His scriptural exposition made the Bible come alive, and his doctrine lectures were first class. The attractiveness of his character and the quality of his teaching had a profound effect on the lives of many St. Aidan's men. I certainly remember him with great affection, respect and gratitude. Sadly, during my third year he was suddenly struck down with a tumour on the brain and was away for several months. Although he was to return as Principal, it was only for a short time. Continued ill health necessitated his retirement in 1958, and he died the following year, still in his early 40s. In his few short years as Principal the reputation of St. Aidan's grew, and in due course so did the applications for entry to the college.

Gerald Scott's progressive views on liturgy and the need for an expression of word and sacrament that might embrace a broad spectrum of Anglican predilections were seen in his re-designing of the Victorian college chapel. On his retirement, Michael Hennell, the Vice-Principal, wrote the following in the College magazine:

The present interior of the chapel, with its spacious dignity and majestic simplicity, is further evidence of a new approach.... Canon Scott was able to have the chapel rebuilt in order that the Holy Communion might be celebrated facing the people across the table. Gradually over the last seven years, the 'St. Aidan's Rite' has been built up under the Principal's vigilant eye, and a serious attempt has been made to give that equal emphasis to Word and Sacrament that was integral to his convictions and teaching. This order of worship has won its way into the hearts of all of us in the college and has impressed many visitors.

An innovation in the church following World War Two was the setting up of Industrial chaplaincies, in an attempt to bridge the gap between the church and the industrialised workers. At the same time there was news of the French Roman Catholic 'worker priests' movement, and the book *Revolution in a City Parish* about St. Sulpice, Paris, appeared. Part of the advanced outlook of St. Aidan's College was the introduction of a two-year Industrial Course, as it was named, which became part of the curriculum but was not a subject for examination. The Vice Principal, Michael Hennell, directed the course with enthusiasm. Michael was a charming person but he appeared to live in something of a time warp. His subject was church history, but his heroes were the early evangelicals, whom he researched diligently. He wrote a book entitled *John Venn and the Clapham Sect* and other notables of the same period. It seemed that he approached the industrial subject with academic rather than practical vigour. His great hero was Canon Ted Wickham, who had established the 'Sheffield Industrial Mission', and who wrote a large book on it, and later became a suffragan bishop. He came to speak to us: whether he had ever actually done any work in industry I don't know, but he looked quite scruffy and wore shoes that seemed uncleaned and perhaps oil-stained. One gathered that the primary object of this endeavour was not actually to convert people to Christ but somehow to 'influence' them. No angler would be satisfied with merely influencing fish; he would hope to catch a few! I venture to suggest that the Holy Spirit coming upon the parish of St. Thomas, Crookes in the 1970s did far more for the spiritual life and needs of people in Sheffield than the liberal theology of 'industrial mission' ever did. The course entailed listening to Christian businessmen of the standing of George Goyder, and to trade unionists, and visits were made to various factories and industrial undertakings around Merseyside (they still had them then) —places like the Lever Brothers empire at nearby Port Sunlight. Those students like me who had come from industry were mildly sceptical, but we went along with it all and enjoyed the outside visits and the good lunches that went with them.

An annual activity was the 'College Mission'. Each year, during the summer vacation, a group of students and some staff would descend on a suitable 'industrial' parish where we would conduct meetings and visit places and people and seek to evangelise or 'influence' them, depending upon the cut of one's jib. There was usually a measure of success, but each 'mission' would result in at least one student finding his life's partner, though we were discouraged from marrying until after ordination. I had to wait until my first curacy before I was to find mine. I went on two such missions, one to a parish in Oldham. Whilst we were there, early one morning some of us, together with the college chaplain were waiting for a bus where several boiler-suited men were also waiting to go off to their jobs. David Anderson, the chaplain, who was a quiet, cultured southerner, and to whom this whole exercise was a severe trial, spoke to one of the workmen saying, "Are you off to business then?"

The man disdainfully replied in a pronounced Lancashire accent: "We call it work here, mate!" —a suitable commentary on industrial mission, I thought.

Recently, I read for the first time the life of William Haslam *From Death into Life.*[2] He was the vicar in Cornwall famously converted by his own sermon, thus eliciting the cry from a member of his congregation: "The Parson's converted!" How in the nineteenth century did he (and, in the eighteenth, Wesley and Whitfield, to say nothing of the early Anglican evangelicals) have such success in reaching not only the rural but the industrialised masses of their time? I am sure that it was nothing to do with any intellectualised techniques that they used, but the content of the message that they delivered. They preached a gospel of salvation that led to personal repentance and turning to Jesus Christ. Haslam had been a convinced 'Puseyite' as followers of the new Oxford Movement were called, and pursued with vigour what seemed not so much a search for God, but for a church; and many of its followers, especially those not encumbered by wives and families, went over to Rome. At Baldhu he had built up a new and seemingly flourishing congregation. He says, "I entered upon my work here with renewed energy and sanguine hope. I had of course gained more experience in the various duties of my ministry, and had, moreover, a clearer perception, as I thought, how sacramental teaching, under the authority of the Church, ought to work. I preached on holy living, not conversion, for as yet I knew nothing about the latter."[3] Haslam's ministry was transformed after he became converted, and though it was very successful so far as the work of God's kingdom was concerned, he was not all that popular with many bishops and church leaders. Alas, it was ever thus. I am sure there are many people today involved in spiritual or renewal ministry who would say to Haslam, "welcome to the club!"

St. Aidan's firmly imbued in me a vision of a Church of England that held a firm balance of word and sacrament, and was, I believed, God's true lampstand to give light to this nation. Those three years at the college were among the happiest of my life. I enjoyed the friendships and the fellowship and I learned a lot. Through it, I felt that my vocation had been confirmed and affirmed, and I was enthusiastic and ready for the great adventure. F. B. Heiser's words could have described my aspirations. "...It is only in the spirit of St. Aidan that this fair land of England can once again be won for Christ. The message is the same as thirteen hundred years ago, and the messenger? What part may not the College play which bears his name if all its sons are truly 'St. Aidan's men?'[4] I left in the summer of 1955, having successfully passed the General Ordination Exam. I had been nominated to attend a very interesting three week long World Council of Churches Ecumenical Study at the Chateau de Bossey, Geneva, during August. It was made more interesting through meeting many other ordinands of all denominations from all over the world. They included two Germans from South America, who might well have been sons of escaped Nazis. That short study helped me to a wider vision of the complexities of the worldwide Church, its differences in doctrinal emphasis, ways of worship and traditions. The experience was intellectually stimulating, and through it one learned to respect and understand the theological and cultural reasons for the differences between the denominations. Nevertheless, there was an underlying unity and fellowship of people who shared a common vision of the world's need of the gospel. This was enhanced by the fact that, at the same time, a Big Four meeting of the Cold War powers was taking place in Geneva.

I was made Deacon in Wakefield Cathedral at Michaelmas that year and went to serve at All Souls, Halifax. I was soon to experience a dampening of my enthusiasm and a shattering of my illusions. The parish of All Souls, Haley Hill owed its existence to a certain Edward Ackroyd, a wealthy, nineteenth century industrialist who built the church, and near to it a model housing estate, suitably named Ackroydon, for his work people, and graded as befitted their pecking order in his employment. His huge Victorian mansion and its grounds were to become the Bankfield Museum and park. The church itself was an architectural masterpiece, designed by Sir Gilbert Scott. It was built in grandiose Gothic style with a very tall spire and was almost a miniature of Salisbury Cathedral. It was elaborately ornamented both inside and out, high and spacious with many stained glass windows. Regrettably, his expertise did not run to an assessment of the durability of the white Italian stone with which the church was built. Though it looked very impressive, having been imported specially for the purpose, it was unable to withstand decades of the polluted air of industrial Halifax and was dangerously crumbling by the mid 1950s, and at close quarters looked a sorry sight. Several years later, despite expensive repair work, it became too dangerous to use and the congregation moved into the church hall, which was re-designed for the purpose of worship and was more practical than the old building.

The parish extended for a mile or so up a steep hill towards Queensbury, on the outskirts of Bradford. The top end of the parish consisted of run down, nineteenth century, workers' housing, typical of the industrial West Riding of Yorkshire. Up the hill was a small, rather tatty, daughter church, St. Edward's Mission, self-contained with a schoolroom beneath. In the days of the Victorian glory of All Souls, it would have served the hoi polloi of the parish, whilst the carriage trade went to the parish church under the benevolent eye of Edward Ackroyd. There was an air of dereliction at the top end of the parish, and one of faded glory at the bottom, where the parish church dominated.

I soon discovered that this faded glory applied equally to the inside of the church and its activities. It represented a dull, traditional conservative evangelicalism, devoid of attraction or vitality. However, it proudly bore all the essentials necessary to qualify for a Church Pastoral Aid Society grant, i.e. no stoles or vestments, no candles and the ludicrous practice of standing at the north side of the table to celebrate Holy Communion —a misunderstood rubric of the Book of Common Prayer. One could have accommodated all that, were it not that there seemed to be little of the vital gospel message supposed to accompany such deprivations. The result was a boring, predictable annual pilgrimage through the church calendar, interspersed with various social and money raising functions.[5]

The Vicar had spent several years as a travelling secretary for CPAS, and obviously was considered to have all that was needful to train a curate. I gathered that he was apprehensive about taking me on, as he had had difficulties with a previous curate. I never learned the reasons for this, but I think I was to confirm his apprehension over the two years I was there. Whether it was the curates who were chiefly at fault is another matter. The relationship was cordial, rarely warm, and sometimes a bit strained. The contrast between my expectations and the reality of my first experience of parish life was shattering. I had to wait until my second curacy before I was to be convinced that I was not being naïve and immature in my reactions. I was put in charge of the mission church, and was well supported there by a devoted little band of stalwarts, to whom others were added eventually. The first few months were particularly depressing, because I was in poor health with some sort of painful viral or bacterial infection.

Like many other clergy, it seems that the vicar had found a system, or carved a niche, whereby he could, as he thought, successfully do his job, holding together the various factions in the church, encouraging the faithful with little apparent expectation of progress or growth. If he was not cynical toward my ideas and enthusiasm, he certainly expected that a good dose of parochial reality would temper them. Once we were discussing problem people and troublemakers. He said, "You will soon find that the Church is the gathering ground for the world's malcontents." His recipe for advancement in the Church was to be well known to a bishop or other influential worthy, keep your nose clean, and go along with the trend; he meant, 'don't rock the boat' —and he must have followed his own advice because, many years later, he became an Archdeacon.

By 1956 I was back to good health, finding my way a bit, and had settled down to finish my term with as good grace as I could. I suggested to the vicar that we might set up a parish visiting scheme like the one at Bradford Cathedral that was still successfully in operation there. He agreed to this, and in order to try and put it across to members of the congregation we invited the Cathedral to send a team of visitors to talk about it. David Barrett, the chaplain, brought half a dozen people to address some of our folk in the church hall, to try to awaken interest in them to do something like it. Nothing came of it. However, that meeting was not without purpose in God's good plan. The team of speakers included a smartly dressed blonde young woman, who was introduced as Margaret Terry. Although she was involved at Bradford, she lived and worked in Halifax as assistant personnel officer at the huge John Crossley's carpet factory. I had never met her, nor spoken to her, but as I sat in the audience, looking at the team on the stage, I just knew that here was the person I was going to marry! Although she had a flat in Halifax and worked in the town, she had attached herself to Bradford Cathedral, partly because of its reputation and partly because she was acquainted with one of the new members of staff there whom she had known in SCM circles at Cambridge —though she always insisted she had no designs on him.

The next day was my day off, and later that night I went home to Bradford on the bus. On the bus was a girl I knew from my earlier Bradford days, and who was one of the team of speakers. I did not realise that she was a particular friend of Margaret, but I pumped her for more information about her and succeeded in getting her address and telephone number in Halifax, and I contacted her on my return. To cut a long story short, I persuaded her to transfer her allegiance to All Souls, and by the end of the year we were engaged to be married. Our courtship during the rest of my time there alleviated my loneliness and occasional depression, and she worked enthusiastically with me to set up a youth fellowship that met on a Sunday evening. Several of the members became committed Christians, including one, Melvin Oakes, who was to join the Church Army and was eventually ordained.

Although relations with the vicar could have been better (and I realise that any blame was mine as well as his), I set to, with Margaret's help and encouragement, somehow to be useful to the Lord in that place. We made several friendships, one of which has remained close and life-long. Beryl Gaukroger, a young woman who had a husband, Geoffrey, and two small boys, came along one evening to a weekly group meeting. She and Geoff became firm friends, joining us in our efforts at the mission church. Later, they became godparents to our children. Sadly, many years later, in 1979, Geoff was to die suddenly. Beryl remains a strong Christian and belongs to St. George's, Ovenden, a renewed parish in Halifax.

Our wedding, on a miserable, rainy 21st September 1957, was the end of my time in Halifax. It was in the middle of the Asian flu epidemic, which meant that many guests were unable to attend, and I had a mild form of it during our honeymoon in Torquay, before moving to our next parish. A few months earlier I had received an invitation for an interview for a possible second curacy at Bromley Parish Church, Kent. The Vicar, Canon Murray Walton, had approached St. Aidan's College for recommendations and was given my name by the Principal. Consequently, accompanied by my wife-to-be, I went to see him and the parish, and he said he would be happy to take me on. We were very impressed with what we saw, and in due course I indicated that we would like to begin in September, after our wedding.

Unhappily, this was not to the liking of the Bishop of Wakefield, Roger Wilson, who had it in mind that I should stay in his diocese and go to Penistone, and he tore a strip off me for wanting to leave the North, "where the need was". I had to go and see the Vicar of Penistone, but he did not want me when he saw that I was reluctant and had set my heart on Bromley. I had become convinced that the call was right and that I would benefit from the experience of a lively parish after my experience at Halifax. I went to see the Bishop again and I stuck to my conviction. He also thought that Margaret, who came from Shropshire, would prefer the more salubrious South, and was influencing my decision. Margaret was livid when she learned of this. In fact she loved Yorkshire, and anyway was prepared to go anywhere that seemed right for us. When I told him we had thought seriously and prayerfully about the options, he accused me of "rationalising my decisions." I was beginning to identify with the words of the psalmist: 'Do not put your trust in princes, in mortal men, who cannot save'[6] —even if these are 'princes' of the church! The following year, he was translated to Chichester. A few months later, I actually met him in London, coming out of Westminster Abbey after the consecration of Mervyn Stockwood as Bishop of Southwark. He recognised me, of course, and passed the time of day. I managed to refrain from asking him whether he had 'rationalised his decisions' when he left the North 'where the need was', to go to Chichester. It turned out that most of my ministry was actually to be based in the North of England.

We went straight to Bromley from our honeymoon, into a special youth weekend organised by Philip Gardner, the curate who was moving the following week to his first living. We stayed at the vicarage for a few days until our furniture and belongings arrived. We had purchased quite a bit of furniture from a store in Halifax, with savings and wedding gift money. It was a local family firm, and they generously transported all of it to Bromley, free of charge, together with our bits and pieces from our respective flat and digs. Our first home was the ground floor flat of a three storey, Georgian house, with a pleasant garden, on top of Martin's Hill, a local park and beauty spot, from where there was a fine view over the Ravensbourne valley. We were warmly welcomed to the parish and soon felt at home. Many of the people were 'something in the City', many with deep faith and intellect. Not a few had been brought to faith through the various Billy Graham revival meetings of the early fifties. It was a refreshing change from Halifax, to have fellowship with so many who were serious about their faith and sought to put it into practice. It was stimulating, and though the work was demanding and my new vicar was a hard taskmaster, I realised this situation fitted with my earlier aspirations on leaving theological college.

The church had been totally destroyed in the blitz, apart from the tower, and was now approaching the completion of its rebuilding after several years of using only the rebuilt nave. The consecration of the new building took place two months after our arrival. It was large, new and attractive, with a huge congregation, a fine choir and a lively, go-ahead vicar, of the old school. Canon W. M. F. Walton, or 'Murray' as he was usually named, was a very energetic and well-known personality in his day. Before the war he had been a CMS missionary in Japan, where he had pioneered a form of newspaper evangelism, and he was a fluent Japanese speaker. He was on the CMS Council, and was involved with other missionary bodies. He had a good reputation for his training of curates, and for his organisational and administrative abilities. Everything was well organised; he had a huge card index system, with a card for every house in the parish, and he was keen on visiting, so that every visit had to be recorded on its respective card, together with any relevant matter emerging from the visit. The curates were expected to produce the cards of their visiting forays, which enabled him to see that we were visiting diligently. Sometimes one would see that a card bore a tiny inscription in Japanese, presumably recording what was considered to be confidential information. A mathematician by training, he was amusingly methodical in the way he recorded everything in his tiny writing; even the date of purchase was put on every light bulb. The church vestry contained a huge book with the illuminated title 'Book of Strange Preachers' —not to insult a preacher who did not match up to expectations, but in line with some ancient canon or directive. He was a Cambridge man and, though in his late sixties, he retained all the freshness and enthusiasm of his younger days.

Murray Walton was loved by many and respected by all, though he often exasperated people, as may be imagined, and he was often the butt of affectionate jokes. When he was made a canon of Rochester Cathedral, the churchwardens had presented him with a huge, black, wide-brimmed, canon's hat, with its black rosette on the front. He was a familiar figure, wearing it as he cycled along Bromley High Street, all over the place, while the big, red London buses swerved to avoid him. He was no better when he drove his car. It was often said that he was never closer to the Lord than when at the wheel of his car. A fellow-curate, Bob

Torrens, who had now joined the staff, and I, were passengers in the vicar's car as he drove us to Rochester for the Diocesan Conference. It was a hair-raising experience as he drove along in an erratic, almost reckless fashion. If we had not known it before then, we certainly learned the value of prayer! Bob was a motorcycle fanatic, and thereafter I would ride on the back of his powerful bike to go to such affairs; it was much safer.

The parish church provided chaplaincy services to the local hospital and two maternity units, and we all took our turn visiting each week. When Margaret was having our first child, Susan, I was able to combine my regular visiting with seeing Margaret at the same time. Murray approved: I was not wasting time unnecessarily.

In due course, Murray baptised our new member of the family, and we had a happy party afterwards on the lawn. Life progressed and we were happy enough. Some of the locals were not too keen on me. Being a Yorkshireman, I was not versed in southern finesse, and I have always been blunt and, I hope, straightforward. Bob Torrens was very much the smooth man of the team, whilst I, like Esau, was definitely the hairy man. Charterhouse and Trinity College, Cambridge followed by Ridley Hall, was his background. Different as chalk and cheese, we nevertheless got on quite well. We both had a keen sense of humour, a vital qualification for working under Murray Walton, and we were once described as representing the difference between the music hall and the West End revue. I was due to move on after two years, and in the summer of 1959 Bob was due to get married, and would need to have the flat where we were then living. Our second child was due in September of that year, so we needed to be settled in a new parish reasonably before that event. Consequently, I was offered the parish of St. Ambrose, Widnes by the Bishop of Liverpool, through the agency of Murray Walton, and we moved there in a very hot summer (as Margaret well remembers). Jane was born at Widnes, fourteen months after Susan. There were no more children to follow.

We had spent a memorable time at Bromley, and we never regretted our decision to go there. For me, it had seen the healing of my negative reaction to my first curacy; but nothing is wasted —negative experiences can bring forth positive alternatives: 'God's knitting' has always been my description of how he can bring good things out of bad, and it was all part of a varied experience of different kinds of parishes which was to be such a great benefit to me in my later travelling ministry. Murray, and his wife Myra, remained good friends thereafter. It was his habit always to pray for his former curates on Wednesdays, and by then there were many indeed. He came to Widnes to baptise Jane, and he visited us at all the different places where we were to serve, until his death in 1980, at the age of ninety. We also visited them during their retirement whenever we were in their part of the country. I thank God for that time, and for all I learned from him. The Bromley experience had restored my vision, confidence and enthusiasm for the future. I had been given a rich experience in two totally different parishes, north and south, and now I was to embark upon a new chapter, this time as the vicar, and at liberty to do things my way. I was soon to realise that as vicar of a parish you have to take all the flak that can come thick and fast at times. Curates, especially if they are young, tend to be indulged somewhat by the flock, and are rarely disliked by the parishioners; moreover, they do not, as a rule, have to carry the blame for things that go wrong.

Notes
[1] *The Story of St. Aidan's College 1847–1947* F.B. Heiser.
[2] Adam Gordon Christian Reprint No.1A.
[3] ibid. p.29.
[4] ibid.
[5] Ironically, twenty years and two vicars later, All Souls experienced a measure of charismatic renewal.
[6] Psalm 146:3

Three

Doing It My Way

What a contrast from Bromley! It could not have been greater. Widnes was a grim place, its main industry being chemicals, and there were several huge chemical works and an asbestos factory. Very often the air was full of fumes, depending upon the direction of the wind, but we were not to experience this fully until we moved there. My heart sank when I first saw the place. St. Ambrose Church and its ancillary buildings, including the vicarage, were all built in dingy redbrick, on the junction of two busy main roads. The church itself was dark and cavernous. It had a stained glass east window, but the rest of the windows were made of small panes of bottle-green glass, and were bulging out in many places; also, there was dry rot in some of the timbers. However, it was a lively and well-attended church, and we found it to be the centre of the activities of the community (for those who were not Roman Catholics, who comprised almost half of the population.) I met the churchwardens, who were warm and friendly. They acquainted me with the parish set-up, and seemed keen for me to take it on. The Bishop of Liverpool offered me the living, but I wanted Margaret to see everything before a decision was made. I went back to

Bromley, and in due course we went up to stay with Margaret's parents in Shropshire, and then visited the parish together. It could be said that we were pushed by the circumstances. It was definitely 'under' the circumstances, not 'over' them, because of the new baby due in September and the need to vacate our flat in Bromley. Widnes did not seem quite so grim on the second visit. The large numbers of people, and the vitality of the church life, impressed us, so we accepted the invitation to go there. At our wedding in 1957 we had sung the hymn with the words, 'Not forever in green pastures, do we ask our way to be.' The Lord certainly took us up on that one!

Before our arrival the parish installed central heating and re-decorated the vicarage for us. The church was full for my Institution and Induction by the Bishop of Warrington, under whose jurisdiction we came, and the congregation included both the Mayor and the local Member of Parliament. In true Lancashire fashion—Widnes had not yet been moved into Cheshire—a lavish spread was laid out in the church hall and, following the service, a reception was held to welcome us. We trusted that we were where God wanted us to be. Surely the people mattered most, not the place. During the industrial development of that part of the country, the Church of England had managed to identify with the working class population, and Anglican parish life was quite strong around St. Helen's, Widnes and Warrington. The congregation of St. Ambrose consisted of artisans and white-collar workers and their families. It was a real family church and there were literally hundreds of children in the Sunday school, choir and numerous uniformed organisations, so that on 'parade' Sundays it was standing room only in the church.

They were, for the most part, kindly and friendly people, though inevitably the congregation had its share of the 'malcontents', of whom I had been warned at Halifax. The Sunday services followed the pattern that was traditional in most non anglo-catholic churches: 8 a.m. Holy Communion, Matins at 11, (but once a month Choral Eucharist) and Evensong at 6.30. Most Sunday afternoons there would be several baptisms. Life was hectic, not least because of the number of baptisms, weddings and funerals, with the attendant visiting and preparation. There was a Church Army sister, Marion Reavill, who was a big help in this area, and she was also responsible for some of the children's work and women's groups. With two small children to care for, Margaret was not able to be much involved in parochial activities, but she did her bit, especially constantly answering the door and the telephone when I was out. I was eager to do things and make my mark, and doubtless I was full of my own importance as the new, young vicar. I endeavoured to be challenging and radical in my approach, though I soon learned that these people could be led but not driven. Inevitably, I made mistakes and upset a few people along the way, but there was positive progress.

The great event of each year was the 'Rose Queen' parade, which was the St. Ambrose version of the Whitsuntide 'walks' which used to be popular in many northern parishes. All the Sunday School children would be dressed up and bedecked with flowers, and would walk around the parish in procession, led by the Boys' Brigade brass band. There would then follow a huge tea in the church hall. There was much rivalry and competition when it came to dressing up the children, and the whole affair was taken very seriously indeed. It was a reflection on how deeply the life of the parish still centred round the church.

Much energy was spent on money raising activities, and the parish was struggling financially with the burden of expensive repairs. It was about that time when people were hearing about the American 'Wells Organisation', which had begun operating in England and was transforming the financial scene for many churches with its 'stewardship campaigns'. The PCC agreed to examine the possibility of such a scheme for our parish. We were staggered at the amount of work and the cost it would involve—a large fee, plus expenses—but we were assured it was possible to have a successful scheme, and to my surprise the PCC agreed to do it. The campaign was launched the following spring, in

1960, and lasted several weeks. The campaign was a huge success, not only financially but also spiritually. It was spectacularly courageous of the PCC to undertake this measure; especially as such stewardship campaigns were quite new on the scene. As a result, weekly offerings increased over tenfold. Thus the finances were placed on a sound footing, and so we were able to go ahead with necessary work required on the church and hall. The first major improvement was to replace the windows in the church that were in such a poor condition. We finished up with clear glass panes instead of the green ones that darkened the place so much: now there was light, and it transformed the appearance of the interior.

After a very tiring and hectic first twelve months, we were ready for a holiday. We took up a long-standing invitation from Kay Harper, a teacher who had retired from Bromley to Penzance, where she had a small cottage on the seafront, the upper floor of which was made into a holiday flat. The long trip by road was an adventure in itself, but we were able to break the journey to Cornwall, at the home of Margaret's parents, and at my parents' home in Tiverton, Devon. We had a pleasant, relaxing holiday, then made the long journey back to Widnes. I must say my heart sank when the distant view of factories and the canopy of industrial gloom, which was permanently over the whole area, appeared over the horizon. A year later, that link with Cornwall was to prove significant for the future direction of my ministry.

The following year was not very pleasant. In the spring of 1961 we had a motor accident on a country road in Cheshire. It could have been more serious, but by the grace of God we got off lightly, apart from a severe shaking and some bruises. The car was damaged, and was off the road for a while for repairs. There was the additional worry of a court appearance, for I had missed a warning sign, though I found it to be partially covered by overhanging branches, and I was fined £15 for driving without due care and attention. That was bad enough, but it was made worse the following weekend, when the local newspaper appeared with its main headline: 'St. Ambrose Vicar Fined for Motoring Offence'. I was very embarrassed, and my pride suffered as a result!

Shortly afterwards, our vicarage was burgled while we slept. Not much was taken, other than Margaret's purse, the children's allowance books and their savings certificates. It is, as many will know, a ghastly experience when this happens, and the house had a feeling of having been violated. Despite fitting security devices to the windows, the same thing happened again, a few weeks later. We found that a back window had been forced, but the intruder had apparently been frightened off when a light upstairs was switched on for us to attend to Jane, then eighteen months old, who had woken up, crying. We felt very unsettled following all this. The surroundings were now getting us down, me more so than Margaret, who was busy looking after the house and children. Opposite the vicarage were a noisy pub and a busy fish and chip shop, outside which rowdy gangs of teenagers would gather. But more depressing was the realisation that our oldest child, Susan, had developed a persistent cough, which was developing rather than receding after medication. We blamed the polluted atmosphere for this condition. So polluted was the air, from all the chemicals, that struggling plants and flowers in our small garden would die off overnight. We had a privet hedge, and all the leaves suddenly turned purple in the middle of summer.

That summer, we went again to Penzance for our holiday— we needed a break and some clean air. Susan noticeably improved during that two weeks, but the cough returned after we got back to Widnes. Our friend in Penzance attended St. Paul's Church. We were introduced to her vicar, and he and his wife invited us to a meal at the vicarage one evening. Naturally, we shared with them our tale of woe, what had happened that year, and how depressed we were at the way things were turning out at Widnes. I thought he was joking when he said we should come down to Cornwall. I responded by saying, "Oh that would be great, wouldn't it—exchange the Mersey Riviera for the Cornish one!" I could not think of a move after only two years, and was resigned to the fact that we ought to stick it out for a while longer. We ended our holiday, returned home, and settled back into the routine of busy parish life. I started a class for a confirmation service to be held at St. Ambrose in late October. It was my first one since going there, and there were eventually sixty candidates, including several adults, all from the parish.

Imagine our surprise when, a few weeks after our return from holiday, we received an impressive looking letter with the Prince of Wales' feathers crest embossed on the flap. It was from Sir Patrick Kingsley, the administrative secretary to the Duchy of Cornwall, inviting me to look at a vacant living in north Cornwall, that was in the gift of the Duke of Cornwall (and, in fact, had been since the Black Prince.) Apparently, this invitation had come about through the Vicar of St. Paul's, Penzance having been in touch with Sir Patrick for some reason, giving him my name. The parish concerned had the fascinating title of Lanteglos-by-Camelford with Advent. We quickly looked at a map and saw that it was between Bodmin Moor and the Atlantic Ocean, near romantic sounding places like Tintagel and Boscastle. Legend has it that Camelford was the Camelot of King Arthur; and within the parish was Slaughter Bridge, where he was reputed to have had his fatal last battle with Mordred. The ruins of his castle at Tintagel added to the legend, and the tourist trade thrived on it. Margaret was so excited when this letter came that she found a recipe for Cornish pasties and immediately made some!

As soon as it was possible, we made the journey once more to the far South West, to stay with my family at Tiverton. We left the children there for a day, and Margaret and I drove the sixty miles to Camelford to meet the churchwardens and to see the set-up. Camelford was then a small town with a population of 1500. It was proud to be a town and not a village, and it had an old town hall. In the days of the 'rotten boroughs' it had two Members of Parliament. The parish covered a large area and included Helstone, a village a mile to the west, and several hamlets, one of which, Lanteglos, was where the ancient parish church stood —in a secluded valley, one and a half miles away from Camelford, where most people lived. Just prior to World War Two, a small new church, St. Thomas of Canterbury, had been built in the town centre on land bequeathed for that purpose, which was large enough for a new rectory to be built in due course. Advent (or St. Adwena) was a sad little church, three miles out on the moor, with no heating or lighting and no access except by a footpath up a field. There was a small, scattered population of smallholders and hill farmers, who scratched a meagre living.

The original rectory was down at Lanteglos, and it was a magnificent, big building designed by Pugin (of Houses of Parliament fame.) The last incumbent had sold this place, and a temporary rectory, Inns Park, had been purchased, which stood on the main A39 road just outside the town. The old rectory, with its extensive grounds, is now a hotel and holiday park. We met the churchwardens, two delightful Cornishmen, one a farmer and the other the local undertaker. They showed us round everywhere, and introduced us to several other people. The temporary rectory was a nice house, and from the bedroom windows was a magnificent view of Bodmin Moor with its two highest points, Rough Tor and Brown Willy, visible in the distance. They wanted us to accept the post; it was a novelty for them to contemplate a young family in the rectory after many years of older clergy.

It all seemed too good to be true, and we returned home in great excitement. I immediately wrote to Sir Patrick Kingsley, and was invited to go and see him at the Duchy of Cornwall offices in London (at 1, Buckingham Gate, just opposite the palace.) I was somewhat overawed by all this, and was kindly received by the Duke of Cornwall's right hand man. I was shown the Prince's chair, large purple and gilt, where generations of Princes of Wales have sat to chair meetings of the Duchy Council. I was not invited to sit in it, but I was invited to take the living of Lanteglos-by-Camelford with Advent. I was to meet Sir Patrick again when he came to present me, on behalf of the Duke of Cornwall, to the

Bishop of Truro, at my induction, early in November 1961. The Widnes folk were somewhat shocked (and some were genuinely saddened) at the news of our impending departure. My final service at St. Ambrose was on a Sunday evening, and it was also the confirmation of the sixty candidates whom I had prepared since the summer. As it was my last appearance, the bishop said I should give the blessing at the end. When I did so it was a very emotional moment for me, and briefly I felt that I was deserting these kind, friendly folk. The time at Widnes had been an eventful and valuable, if short experience, and we had the conviction that we were doing the right thing. It seemed that the Lord was with us and was leading us forward to a new experience.

We moved to Cornwall in late October 1961, and had two weeks in which to settle down before my induction as the incumbent 'with all the rights, members and appurtenances thereunto belonging.' We soon discovered that life here moved at a slower pace than in our previous parish, and from the start I was determined not to rush things: I would take the services and get the feel of the place. There were three churches, but the pattern of services was not burdensome. The usual Sunday services would be 8 a.m. Holy Communion and 6.30 p.m. Evensong at St. Thomas's, the small new church in the town, with a mid morning Eucharist at the parish church. There were two distinct congregations, except for special occasions, at Lanteglos, mostly local Cornish families, and at St. Thomas's they were mainly people who had come to live in the area from 'up country'. Only one service a month was held at Advent — that would be in the afternoon, attended by a handful of people.

St. Thomas's was an attractive building with no structural problems. To save costs when it was built, a temporary north wall allowed for the eventual addition of another aisle, if and when it was necessary. Lanteglos Church, however, was in a poor state of repair. A few years earlier, the inevitable dry rot had appeared in strength, resulting in the removal of the old organ, which had been replaced with an 18th century chamber organ, magnificent with its inlaid mahogany casing, but totally inappropriate for its new setting. In addition, the dry rot meant that all the woodwork in the former side chapel had been removed, leaving an open space. The worst remaining problem was the state of the walls because of the ravages of damp. The church was in a hollow and, over the years, earth had piled up behind the walls, thus encouraging the water to rise. Although the outside had been excavated and drainage installed, the interior walls were a major problem. It seemed that my predecessor, having had all the bother of leaving the old rectory and moving into the temporary one, together with the problems at Lanteglos, soon moved on to a new parish when the opportunity arose, leaving the latter to be dealt with by whoever followed him. In due course I made an attempt to do this. We raised some money and also had a grant of £500 from the Historic Churches Preservation Trust. The whole amount was spent on restoring the walls, but it was not all that successful and still showed stains and blemishes.

Many of the Lanteglos folk resented St. Thomas's, wrongly assuming that it drew away resources from (their) church, so it was being neglected. This was also the attitude of many who never entered the church except for funerals. An amusing incident occurred in February 1963. An old Lanteglos supporter, Granny Button, died that month; she was quite old. She once was going on to me about St. Thomas's, and that it should never have been built. She said, "I would not be found dead in that place!" For the previous two months we had endured the terrible blizzards of that winter, when the whole area was covered in deep snowdrifts and was almost paralysed for several weeks. The narrow lanes were blocked to the hedge tops, and only one of the three churches, St. Thomas's, could be open and used for services. The other two were unapproachable from Boxing Day 1962 to mid–February 1963. About the time of the lady's death, the weather changed and a thaw set in. The family arranged for the funeral to be held at Lanteglos, and sure enough it became possible to get down the lane to the church.

On the day of the funeral, however, the weather suddenly become quite warm, so that all the snow quickly melted, resulting in a torrent of water rushing like a river down to the church and flooding it. There was only one thing for it; we held the service at St. Thomas's, into which her coffin was brought, and where she had been so determined not to be found dead!

There was a scarcely concealed rivalry and dislike between church and chapel. It was a cultural thing really. Many of the local people were in fact Methodists of various persuasions, as was general in Cornwall; the result of the revivals under Wesley and Whitfield in the 18th Century, when the alien and moribund Anglican Church had for the most part opposed that particular movement of the Holy Spirit — an attitude not unknown either in earlier days or in modern times. Not that there seemed to be much fire left in Methodism by then; it had become institutionalised and as complacently established in Cornwall as was the Established Church. Evidence of this was seen in Camelford, where there still remained three separate chapels, each following the traditional streams within Methodism that had united in the early thirties. One minister served them all, as well as many other small chapels in the various hamlets and villages. In the early 1960s, the joint unity discussions between Anglicans and Methodists were held. In Camelford we dutifully attended local joint meetings, and it was obvious there would be no unity forthcoming on the strength of those deliberations! Freemasonry was very strong in the area and had a subtle influence over much of local life, and some Anglicans and some Methodists were members. I was once informally approached to join them, but I refused. There was occultism and spiritual conflict over the whole area, but I was in no position either to identify its evil influence or to contend with it, until ten years later when we became involved in renewal ministry.

There were several committed people in our congregation and they were added to in course of time, but it was difficult to make much headway. Fred Rapley and his wife, Betty, were deeply involved in the church life, and Fred became a lay reader and was a great help. A few years later, he was to be ordained. Another young man, John Elford, became a friend and was later confirmed. Eventually he went forward for ordination and pursued a philosophical line, obtained a doctorate, and became largely involved in academic work in Manchester and Liverpool.

In Camelford there was a degree of resistance to suggestions of the need to be personally committed to Jesus Christ. The attitude was, 'If we wanted that sort of thing, we would go to the Methodists!' As time went on, several new people joined the church, but it was through personal friendships that we were able to add to the small group of loyal and dedicated people who supported and upheld us. We made many friends and, through these personal contacts, more people became connected with the church, mainly from amongst the professional and retired who had come into the community. They tended to be the people with ideas, who would help to run things, and the locals were happy for them to do so.

The large, new Sir James Smith's Grammar School brought many young teachers, some of whom joined us. There was a lot of social life, in which we enjoyed taking part. Our two daughters thrived: Susan's cough disappeared, and both were happy at the local primary school, where they soon acquired Cornish accents from the other children. When we took them to the nearby beaches and enjoyed the rugged North Cornwall coast, I sometimes thought of the contrast with Widnes.

Within the first year, the Archdeacon of Bodmin, who was on the Diocesan Board concerned with Parsonage Houses, advised me to make a start on preparations for the building of a new rectory on the land behind St. Thomas's. It took two years and six months before we were able to move into a brand new modern rectory. Inns Park, the house where we had been living, was sold to the local veterinary practice, and the proceeds went towards the cost of the new rectory; the rest of the money required was provided by the

Board and no fund-raising was involved. It began to dawn on me that a large part of my work was to do with building problems, here as had been the case at Widnes. Late in 1962 we had a crisis with Advent Church. The Diocesan Surveyor uncovered massive dry rot infestation. It was in the wooden floor, the pews, and under the plaster of the walls. We were ordered to remove and burn all the timbers and woodwork, thus leaving a bleak and sorry shell of a building. The Diocesan authorities indicated that they would like the church to be permanently closed and left to become a ruin. I understood the reason, for there was a very small congregation, the church had no particular architectural merit, and it was difficult to foresee much future for it, even if large sums were spent to restore it. I had no quarrel with this judgement; it seemed sensible. But the authorities would not effect the necessary legal moves, and avoided a firm decision because of the outcry that it would raise. Meanwhile, I was left to hold the baby and try to appease a growing number of demands for the church to be restored. At that stage they did not think that they themselves could do anything, but looked to 'They' and 'Them' to do something, whoever 'They' and 'Them' might be. There was a bit of ignorant talk about the Church Commissioner's 'millions'.

The Member of Parliament for North Cornwall was James Scott-Hopkins, and not only did he live in the parish, but was an honorary churchwarden, and he swiftly took up the cause of his angry constituents, which included me by that time. Together we ascertained the cost of treating the dry rot and basically restoring the church as simply and cheaply as possible. We eventually came up with the figure of £3000 —a huge sum in those days for a very poor, sparsely populated parish to raise. Most of this would be needed to treat the infection and re-plaster the walls. Still there was no move by the diocese, and I was fed up with getting all the flak and accusations of having no concern for Advent. A small 'do-it-yourself' committee was established from the community; and, having an influential person to help, I felt it was right to ignore the timid authorities and support the locals, who now realised that it was up to them if they wanted to save the church. We managed to get publicity in the press for an appeal for funds, and soon money began to come in, which was an encouraging sign. I went to London, to the House of Commons, and with James Scott-Hopkins, met Ivor Bulmer-Thomas MP, who was Chairman of the Friends of Friendless Churches. As a result we were given a grant of £500, worth ten to twelve times that amount in today's terms. The Scott-Hopkins family organised a gymkhana to raise funds, which was a huge success and became an annual event. There was soon enough money to get in the dry rot specialists and, when they had finished their task, a team of local farmers and labourers set to work to restore the floor. First they filled in the cavity with a suitable aggregate and then surfaced it with a coloured concrete. They made a good job of it and it turned out smooth, level and without blemish. I was not 'flavour of the month' so far as the archdeacon was concerned, when I told him what was going on. In the first instance I would have gone along with the authorities, I told him, but following their indecision I was going to support my parishioners. It was very exciting, and the interest grew. South West Television news came up from Plymouth and made a splash about Advent's self-efforts that caught the imagination of many, and the money came rolling in!

Soon the work was nearing completion and we were able to cover all the costs. To replace the pews that had been removed and burned, we bought a suitable number of wooden chairs, drapes to cover the vestry and entrance door, and other necessary furnishings, including new hymn and prayer books. By now the archdeacon showed an interest, but only to say that it must be painted in white, not cream. When I passed this on to our stalwarts, they said, "Tell the archdeacon where he can go", and they did not mean to Bodmin; then they promptly set about painting the walls in an almost Cornish cream colour. When all was finished, it looked really attractive in its bright and clean simplicity. When it came time for the re-dedication and opening, the bishop and archdeacon had no option but to come and officiate. The church was full and I was all too aware of what the congregation were thinking about the diginitaries!

The combined self-help and enthusiasm on the part of the parishioners resulted in a strengthening of the little congregation, and gave them a pride in what they had achieved. I have never visited Advent since we eventually left Cornwall, but it is still open, forty years later. Today there are brown 'heritage' signs on the A39 road to Wadebridge, directing tourists to Advent Church.

Soon after our arrival in Cornwall, we had become friends with Roy and Peggy Crosley, who lived in the next parish to Lanteglos, at St. Teath, where Roy was a Lay Reader and village schoolmaster, whilst Peggy taught at a nearby village school. They were involved in, and pioneered, many local activities, including amateur dramatics. In 1962 they were involved in the production of a 'Pageant of Cornish History' at the Royal Cornwall Show in Wadebridge, and prevailed upon me to help them out by doing a small 'walk on', non-speaking part, which I did, albeit rather reluctantly. I was dressed up as King Arthur, and all I had to do was to lead a procession across the arena, with a rather frosty-faced Guinevere on my arm. Roy and Peggy also played a leading role in the organisation of the annual music and drama festival, held each summer in the attractive parish church of St. Endellion, near Port Isaac. For the drama, Roy would produce a one-act play each year, usually with a Christian theme, and I began to take part in these activities, along with a few other people from our parish.

At some stage I had seen somewhere, possibly in York, a performance of part of the Wakefield Cycle of Mystery Plays, and had acquired a copy of *The True Mystery of the Passion*, which I showed to Roy and Peggy, suggesting the possibility of the group performing it. They immediately saw the possibilities, and the idea took off with great enthusiasm. It was far too ambitious for the usual small group to perform by themselves, but soon other people showed an interest in it, not least Kathleen Mackenzie, a writer of children's stories and a sister of the then Bishop of Gloucester. She lived at

North Hill, over Bodmin Moor towards Plymouth. She was most keen to produce it, and subsequently many more people were enrolled to take part, from all the villages around that area of North Cornwall. In order to present the plays, we called ourselves the North Cornwall Religious Drama Group: a name that remained long afterwards, when other productions were staged.

Eventually, over one hundred people were persuaded to take part, and enthusiasm spread as the venture caught people's imagination. It was a wonderful community affair, which included the most unlikely people. Farmers and their wives and families, teachers from Sir James Smith's school, some local clergy, as well as the Crosley family, and people from their church and village. There were Methodists and Anglicans, and others of no allegiance. Not all enrolled as actors; there were many other jobs and roles to play. It was a first class production, and Kathleen was most meticulous about costumes, their design and colour. Many women set to work dying cloth —to get the right shades—and making the vast number of costumes that were required. It was a monumental effort, almost like medieval times, when whole communities would do exactly the same thing; only they would perform the plays on the streets. Rehearsals and preparations went on for many months, until we presented it in Truro Cathedral for several days. It was a magnificent combined effort, and it turned out to be a huge success, as well as a wonderful witness to the community at large, and was free of any denominational bias. It was a spiritual experience for many of those taking part. Some who were not Christians came to faith through it, and for many others it created a deepening of their faith in the process. Although it did not begin as such, it proved to be an evangelistic activity, and not just for the audiences who watched it performed. All this happened in 1963, and was such a monumental event that it is still remembered today.

Towards the end of 1965, plans were put in hand to improve St. Thomas's by knocking out the temporary north wall, not to make a new aisle, which had been the original idea, but to incorporate a small meeting room and catering facilities. It was not to be completed during my time, but several years later I found that the work had been done, together with other improvements that had made it into a very useful, dual-purpose building.

I was now beginning to get 'itchy feet'. The church life was not growing and I felt that I was not achieving much. We had been happy there for five years, and it had been a novel experience of small town and rural life, in attractive surroundings, where we had made many friends. I hankered after a larger community in which to work, and now seemed to be the time for us to move on. Through the agency of the Duchy of Cornwall, I was invited by the Crown Appointments Secretary to look at the parish of Delamere in Cheshire, but as this was another mainly rural parish it seemed right to decline it. I was then invited to look at St. Cuthbert's, Wrose, in Bradford, my former home town, and we were to move there in the summer of 1966.

It was a large, suburban parish containing a council estate and pre-war and post-war, semi-detached houses. Many of these were occupied by people who had moved there from older parts of the city that were now occupied by the many Asian and other immigrants who had flocked to the area to work in the mills. The church building was, in fact, the first new one to be built following the war. The ageing Bishop Blunt was succeeded by Donald Coggan in 1956; he promptly began an urgent church building programme. St. Cuthbert's had been a 'conventional district' rather than a separate parish, and had a small church building, which became the parish hall when the new church was built, and was linked with it by a series of small ancillary rooms. A minimum size vicarage had also been built, so that the whole complex comprised a good parochial 'plant', as the jargon has it. It had all been built at as little cost as possible, and the old pews and furnishings from the former church building were plonked in traditional order into the new building and looked somewhat incongruous. There was a reasonable sized congregation and a large Sunday school; at my first Parochial

Church Council meeting I discovered that the band of leaders and teachers acted as a faction within the church. After the meeting, their main spokesman came up to me. It was evident that he thought that, as we had come all the way from Cornwall, we must be 'southerners'. He said, "You'll find out, Vicar, that we call a spade a spade up here."

My reply to him was, "Well, I come from Bradford too, and I call a spade a b . . . . . shovel!"

There was a choir, and an organist who constantly complained about the electronic organ and its limitations. Once, during a wedding, we actually heard police radio messages on it! This organ was in the chancel and so were the choir stalls. A year or so afterwards, my old college, St. Aidan's, and several other theological colleges, were being closed down or merged because of the reduction in numbers of ordinands at that time. I went to the final closing thanksgiving service, where I met again many old friends among the former students. It was a sad occasion and we were told that the buildings and site had been sold for housing development. All the fittings and furnishings were to be sold off —including the fine Walker organ up in its loft in the chapel. With the backing of the Parochial Church Council, I wrote to see if we could purchase the college organ and, if so, how much would it cost. I had a reply, saying that it was still available, and the College Council would consider my request. To my great delight, they offered it to us free of charge. The PCC agreed to have it collected, and for many weeks it lay in pieces all down the north side of the church. We expected it would be an enormous cost to re-assemble it, but we found an organ builder who lived in the parish, and he did it at a reasonable price. It cost altogether £700 to transport and place it in position. A large plot of derelict church land had been sold for building houses, so the necessary funds were available. Because it was so much bigger than the previous, electronic, organ, we installed the new one at the back of the church, and the church council were prevailed upon to move the choir stalls to the back of the congregation. There were some grumbles, but it was done. Not only was it a great improvement to the worship, it also meant that some members of the choir could not be seen talking during the service! The greatest advantage of all was that we were able to transform the open chancel. We built a central plinth for the communion table, and carpeted the whole floor in blue, so now we were able to conduct the Eucharist in 'St. Aidan's style', with servers and assistants using the whole chancel area. A large, beaten silver, processional cross was commissioned, and this was placed behind the table by the plain East wall (there was no East window). The whole effect was very striking, and a tremendous aesthetic and liturgical improvement.

Further improvements to the buildings were made with part of the proceeds from the land sale. A larger meeting room was re-decorated, carpeted, and furnished with comfortable chairs, and two smaller rooms knocked into one, incorporating improved catering facilities, and the dingy church hall was re-decorated. Once more, my time seemed to be occupied with buildings and their repair and maintenance. During all this time I tried, with little success, to encourage the congregation into deeper commitment, but for the most part they preferred social activities, upon which they had been reared in the past. We collected a few newcomers, who, as in previous situations, became friends and who did respond in a measure. All the time, however, there was constant bickering over trivialities, and again I thought of that comment made by my first vicar about the 'world's malcontents'. I was becoming aware of my failures, and how all my best efforts came to little or nothing. I had not yet learned that it was not 'my efforts' that were important: only that which was revealed as God's purpose would receive any blessing from him.

Another innovation in the life of the parish arose through my link with West Berlin, as it then was. A long-standing friend was Dietrich Bärend (whom I first met at Capernwray Hall in Cumbria, where I had taken a young people's group from Widnes, for a teaching weekend.) He was connected with a fellowship of young, evangelical Christians, who were called 'The Torchbearers', which the founder of Capernwray, a Major Thomas, had formed in Berlin, when he was stationed there after the end of World War Two. Dietrich had visited us several times at Widnes and in Cornwall, and we had visited him in Berlin. I had also become friendly with the Lutheran Pastor of the German church in Bradford, Christian Maechler. He had assisted with an Anglo-German wedding that was held at St. Cuthbert's. Out of these contacts came a link-up between our church and the Pauluskirche, Zehlendorf, where Christian had served before coming to Bradford. It resulted in exchange visits between Bradford and Berlin, for several years, involving groups of people of all ages. This was a good exercise in ecumenical and international relations, and at least two marriages came out of it.

By 1970 I was becoming more and more depressed by parish life and ministry. I knew that I had not been ordained to be either a tour operator or a clerk-of-works. It seemed to me that I had been in all these places, each one different, where I had tried to perform my tricks, as it were, but it always went sour. Somehow, I began to think, after all the hopes and enthusiasm I had at the beginning, that I was in the wrong job. I was not much of a pastor, and my preaching produced no response —except, perhaps, controversy. I often had a strange feeling that there was something inside me which would not come out —something I wanted to declare with conviction, but which seemed not to come. Of course, I knew about New Testament times; it was great for the apostles and the early disciples; they had a special outpouring of the Holy Spirit, which allowed them to preach boldly and to see signs and wonders as God blessed their ministry. Like all good Anglicans (and most other denominations) I had been taught to believe that all that activity was a special dispensation, so that when the church had set up bishops, PCCs and committees to run it, that power was no longer necessary. It seemed now we had to progress by our own schemes and cleverness. Of course we always asked God to *bless* what we were doing, but God only blesses things that are in his will, timing and purpose. Was this a caricature?

—indeed, but with more than an element of truth in it. I became so sickened that I would gladly have left the ministry had I not, with a wife and two children, been economically tied to it. I told the bishop and the Crown Appointments secretary (as patron of the living) that I wanted a move. As it happened, recently, at the age of eighty, Margaret's mother had fallen down some steps and was quite badly hurt. She was in hospital for a time but never fully recovered, and we began to think that it might soon become necessary for Margaret's parents to come and live with us. We were quite prepared for this, but the main problem was that our vicarage was obviously too small. I explained this and said we needed to go somewhere with a larger house. Eventually, I was invited to consider going to the parishes of Thwing and Wold Newton, two small villages, out on the Yorkshire Wolds, in East Yorkshire. That was the beginning of another story: the old pattern of activity, followed by disappointment and a sense of failure, was transformed to a new type of ministry, which was to be fruitful and significant.

Four

Away to Thwing

Come my love, away, away
onto the Wolds this wonderful day!
Let's go over yon hill to Thwing,
for yonder, see, green plovers fling
white breasts to the sun.
Let's away, with the blown lapwing!
Wind in our teeth snatches our breath,
tosses gulls like kites on strings,
tumbles the quilts of corn-green silk,
ruffles the sheep in turnip folds,
chases white poodle clouds over the Wolds.
So we laugh and loiter, enjoying the fun
of cloud and shadow, and wind and sun—
And we never shall get to Thwing.[1]

Clare Ellin

Towards the end of 1970, I was forty three years old and had
been in the ministry for fifteen years. I had served in five
different parishes, two as assistant curate, and three as vicar
or rector. The five posts were very different from each other,
and together they represented a wide spectrum of the Church

of England. I left all the the parishes where I had been incumbent feeling that I had been a failure. I was enthusiastic; I had worked hard; I believed that I was where God wanted me to be, and I thought I was doing all that was expected of me; but I never felt that I was making much progress in a spiritual sense. It appeared that most of the people in these congregations seemed to regard the church as something of a religious club, and worship was a complacent celebration of the status quo! If the church was not 'the gathering ground for the world's malcontents' it was certainly heading that way. What was very obvious was that I was unable to reverse the trend, and after thirteen years it was beginning to dawn on me that nothing was going to change. I could not do it, and so I thought I must be the wrong person for such a role. In spite of all the disappointments, I had not lost my faith— that was always real—but I blamed myself for my apparent failure. I seemed unable to fulfil all that God wanted of me, and to which I had given myself with such great willingness and enthusiasm. Even if I was in the wrong job there was no way now that I could escape from it. When the invitation came to take on these two little parishes in East Yorkshire, humanly speaking, it was going to be an escape from the almost fruitless endeavours of working in urban parishes and an opportunity to bury myself in the country where, as a rural vicar, I would fulfil the local expectations, which hopefully would not be so demanding, and I could enjoy looking after the garden, without being a radical world–changer. Whatever my thoughts were, God had different plans, and after twelve months they were to become clear. The first intimation of this came the first moment I set foot in All Saints' Church, Thwing.

The day that the letter arrived, inviting me to look at Thwing and Wold Newton, we were saying goodbye to a family of friends who had been staying with us. As it was August, and the children were on holiday from school, we had been planning a family outing somewhere. When we saw on the map that Thwing was only eight miles inland from Bridlington, we decided to have a beach picnic, and at the

same time we would have a sneak preview of the parish before we officially contacted the churchwardens, as the letter
advised. It was a pleasant day and we drove the sixty or so
miles from Bradford to find Thwing. We followed what is
called 'the scenic route' from York, which took us up
Garrowby Hill and over the Wolds to Sledmere. From there
we went on a 'B' road for a few miles, before we turned off a
narrow unclassified road signposted to Thwing. It was about
a mile to the village, amid wide-sweeping views towards the
North Yorks Moors. Thwing is a small village, dominated by
a delightful little Norman Church, to which we drove. We
did not see a single human being around. Two fields away
from the church could be seen a very large house, sur-
rounded by trees; we assumed that must be the home of the
local squire or someone like that.

The moment we opened the church door and went inside,
I felt a strange sensation come over me: it was like that
moment at Halifax, when I first set eyes on Margaret and I
knew that she was the person I would marry. Apart from
the fact that it was clean and obviously well cared for, I was
immediately aware that there was an awesome atmosphere,
and I was convinced—at that very moment—that we had to
come to this place! It is hard to describe, but it was almost
like walking into a warm embrace. I knew that God was with
us and we were still in his plans. Thwing Church is a special
place; there are places that somehow feel holy; someone
described such as 'having thin walls' between them and the
heavenly. Several other people were to remark on this. The
late Father Humphrey Whistler, of the Community of the
Resurrection, put it down to a saint having prayed there —
an observation more in line with his theology than mine. The
last English saint to be canonised before the Reformation
had been St. John of Bridlington, where he had been Prior of
what, since the dissolution of the monasteries, is known as
the Priory Church of Bridlington. As John de Thwing, he had
been born and lived in the parish and would have prayed
regularly in the church. An effigy of a medieval priest reputed
to be Robert de Thwing, the brother of John, is still to be

found there. There was no such atmosphere in the other little Norman Church in Wold Newton; rather the opposite, we would discover. We went straight on to Bridlington; we did not look for the rectory or the other parish, and we still did not see a soul. I was convinced that we were to go there before I even knew anything else about the situation. It was strange and it was wonderful, even if, humanly speaking, it was quite mad!

The next day I telephoned the contact churchwarden, John Burdass, and arranged for Margaret and myself to visit officially and meet the churchwardens of both parishes. John, a farmer, actually lived just over into the next parish of Kilham, but the Burdass family, possibly the oldest family in the area, had farmed a large part of it for over two hundred years. Both his father and his grandfather had been wardens of Thwing church. We had lunch with him and his wife, Mary, and then were joined by the other wardens from both parishes. We were shown around, and it was almost a shock to discover that the huge house we had seen in the distance was in fact the rectory! It was a brick–built, Victorian house, completed in 1871, and designed to reflect the wealth and status of the incumbent of one of the wealthiest benefices in the Diocese of York. In 1871 his income was over £700 a year, not quite as much as that of a modern football star, but at least equal to that of a 21st century City financial juggler! Needless to say, it had now come down in the world and was on a minimum stipend rate like everywhere else. There were people still living in the parish who remembered when the rectory had two resident servants, together with a groom/gardener who lived in the village and was paid one shilling a week more than an agricultural labourer. The former coach house was now the garage, and had an adjoining stable block and the ruins of pig houses at the back. Together with ten acres of pasture, there was a large overgrown orchard, a huge garden, and a dilapidated tennis court on the lawn. The rectory was approached by way of a long drive from the bottom lane, but a footpath over two fields led to the church. Thwing was described in the Domesday Book, as Thuenc, and it must have been of Scandinavian origin as there was much evidence of barrows and settlements in the area. It had remained an agricultural community, though now that farms were mechanised and less labour intensive, the population was declining. In 1970 it stood at two hundred, one hundred of whom lived in the village, and the rest in farms and hamlets over a wide area.

Wold Newton was two miles away, at the bottom of a hill. It was a village of similar size to Thwing, about a hundred and fifty people, and the rest spread through the parish. It was the more attractive of the two, and had a pond and a former hall, now converted into flats. The church, also of Norman origin, in contrast to the church in Thwing, was rather dark and depressing: it had nothing of the feeling of the latter. There also seemed to be a different atmosphere about each village. Thwing had more of a community spirit about it, for most of the people were families that had been there for a long time. Wold Newton, on the other hand, contained many people who had retired there and had a different outlook on life. Very often, 'incomers' to rural areas want to try and make them rather twee and suburban. There was also a slight resentment that Wold Newton, not having had its own vicar for many years, had to share an incumbent with Thwing, where he lived. There was an assumption that, consequently, they were neglected. As a matter of fact, though, both parishes were not very demanding, in a pastoral sense. I spent more time over Wold Newton, than I did over Thwing, during all the years when I was the incumbent. I discovered that my predecessor, in addition to his parochial responsibilities, was Spanish teacher at a school in Hornsea, fourteen miles away, which must have limited his pastoral activity. It seemed, therefore, that if I really wanted to 'get away from it all', there was no better place than this! However, because of that initial experience upon entering Thwing church, I had a strong feeling that something was going to happen at some stage, though I had not the slightest idea what that might be. I had no hesitation in accepting the invitation of the Lord Chancellor to take the living.

On a freezing evening, towards the end of November 1970, I was inducted by the Bishop of Hull into my new domain with its two churches, four hundred people and thousands of sheep. A jolly crowd from St. Cuthbert's, Bradford came along to see us in and to wish us well; they seemed to be something of a culture shock to the locals, who were a much quieter breed, not much given to the more sophisticated, urban exuberance of my former parishioners.

It was fun setting up in the vast rectory. We had been very blessed in that a friend at Bradford was disposing of his late mother's large, Edwardian furniture, and, knowing that it would not fetch much at auction, offered us whatever we would like of it. As a result, it all added to what we had already, and we were able to completely furnish the house. There was a huge, Victorian kitchen, complete with a set of bells, all in working order, with which the children had great fun. The diocese allowed us to purchase a secondhand Aga, which was duly installed and converted from solid fuel to oil-burning; it was to serve faithfully for many years to come, after the conference facilities were installed. During fairly frequent power cuts in (usually) severe winters, it was the only source of heating and cooking.

A few weeks after our arrival, the Christmas services at both churches enabled us to meet a few of the more peripheral members of the two churches. The congregations were quite small when compared with what we had been used to at Bradford. Thwing was the better attended of the two churches. There was an 8 a.m. Holy Communion, attracting about eight to ten people, and a Parish Eucharist at 11 a.m., where the congregation averaged twenty five. At Wold Newton there was just one service, Parish Eucharist, at 10 a.m., where the numbers would average twenty. There had previously been an evening service at Thwing, attended by three or four people, but that had stopped during the interregnum. As the small congregation was now accustomed to the 11 a.m. service, I thought it better to leave it that way. Each Parochial Church Council preferred to keep that pattern of morning services, so I usually had to dash from Wold

Newton during the last hymn, and to drive up the hill the two miles to Thwing, occasionally arriving after the five minutes grace I was allowed, sometimes to find one or two looking at their watches or shaking them. They were two quite separate parishes, the only thing they had in common being 't'parson', and joint services were very rare indeed.

Often, in a new parish, you find the parishioners comparing the newcomer to the last incumbent. In my case, however, it was the last incumbent but one. He was Stanley Linsley, a local boy made good, you might say. Not only was he a direct descendant of Thomas Lamplugh, Archbishop of York at the end of the 17th Century, who was born in Thwing and was a branch of the family of the village of Lamplugh in Cumbria, but he himself came from a local farming family, and as a boy went to Driffield Grammar School. There were other descendants of his in the area; I knew of one Lamplugh family, the others had different surnames. Consequently, Stanley Linsley knew everyone, and was extremely popular. A fine preacher, he had been a prebendary in the Worcester diocese, where he had worked too hard and had a breakdown; his appointment to the parish was for recuperative reasons. He was a good pastor and preacher and made a great impression on the parish, attracting many new people to the church from beyond the parish. Sadly for the parish, after only two years he was appointed Archdeacon of Cleveland, part of the diocese of York. His successor had difficulty following him, for his character and personality was quite different; he moved on after four years.

Stanley Linsley enthused to me about the quality of the local people: "solid, 'yeoman' stock," he would say; "decent and reliable people" —and so I found them. The whole area was given to farming, not only cattle and sheep, but that part of East Yorkshire is a great arable area too, producing wheat and barley, oilseed, and so on. The farmers, for the most part, were very likeable people, never full of enthusiasm, but stolid, blunt and straightforward. At harvest time, none would acknowledge that they were gathering in a fine or exceptional crop, but one realised that the word 'middling' indicated the highest category to which they would admit. I remember once visiting a farm at Airey Hill, near Filey. The farmer's daughter-in-law was organist at Wold Newton, and as she was there at the time I called in for some reason or other. It was a glorious late spring day; the sky was blue, with a few white clouds in it, and down below was the sweep of Filey Bay and the blue sea, white waves contrasting with the sky. I said, parson fashion, something like, "What a glorious day. It makes you feel good to be alive."

The farmer replied, "Aye, but t'barleys pappy!"

In front of every silver lining there's a cloud! This seemed to summarise the local agricultural philosophy. There were several farming families connected with Thwing Church, three of whom were Burdasses. A few had learned their religion at St. Peter's School in York. John Burdass who held the post of almost hereditary churchwarden, following his forbears, was very loyal, reliable and supportive.

There would be a few social activities throughout the year, to raise money. They usually followed a pattern: there would be sales, auctions, suppers: and one would get quite worried that nothing seemed to be happening, as the time drew closer and it seemed that this event would be a great flop. But no, they only did things in their time frame and, sure enough, at the very last minute there would be activity and everything would materialise, and usually be a huge success. So I gave up worrying about such things after that.

The regular church people were not demonstrative, and were very traditional in their beliefs; some were very faithful indeed, and there was a degree of spirituality that expressed itself in practical, helpful ways. In 1970 there was a wonderful community spirit in Thwing, coming I believe, from the way they had been taught in earlier days, when a much revered Canon Smallwood had been rector for many years, before and after the second World War.

Apart from the farmers and their families, and a few retired professionals, the village people were mainly farm workers, many now retired; they were not well-off financially by today's standards, but for the most part they seemed to be happy, contented people who were interested in the life of their rural surroundings. They were interested in the seasons, and the crops and their gardens. Few of them had cars, and the extent of their travels would be an occasional trip to Driffield, eight miles away —a pleasant market town, basking in its self-given title: 'The Capital of the Wolds'. For many of the locals, it was in fact the capital of their world, or Bridlington, also eight miles away, to where, in those days, there was a bus two or three times a week. If anyone was sick, particularly anyone living alone, there was no lack of ready help from neighbours and members of the community. If any were in hospital, in Driffield or Scarborough, car owners would rally round and provide a ferry service for relatives without transport to visit the patients. I believe that this came from a genuine caring and unsentimental loving, which was remarkable when compared with attitudes to be found in the larger industrial and urban areas. It ought to have been commonplace, but it was almost a thing of the past. Indeed it was a residue of Christian community life, alas now long gone.

It is all very different now, thirty years on. The older residents have died off, the younger ones have moved away, and the inevitable middle-class retired people and commuters, with their suburban outlook and ways, have replaced them. Before local government re-organisation in the mid 70s, there would be a representative from each parish on the local rural district council, whose local knowledge was invaluable when decisions were made about planning matters or the allocation of the council houses, initially built to provide housing for local farm workers. The change in 1974 meant that we now were part of a bigger area, to be known as the Borough of North Wolds, in Humberside, instead of the Bridlington Rural District Council in East Yorkshire. Consequently, small villages suffered through diminished representation.

One very noticeable result came in the allocation of council houses, when, instead of meeting local needs, the new masters would often place dysfunctional urban families in the villages, well away from the urban areas. Maybe they hoped they would upset only rural yokels who had few votes and provided little tax revenue.

But we are concerned with what happened in 1971 and the following years. Early in that New Year, it came to my knowledge that I was intended to be the last Rector of Thwing. The diocesan authorities had been minded to sell off the rectory and to link the parish with a group of several other villages in the area. It seemed that I was there as a stopgap until, following the appointment of a new Archdeacon of the East Riding, it would be possible to work out a suitable Pastoral Reorganisation Scheme. I gathered that, when my appointment was allowed to proceed, it was thought that I would not stay long, and would therefore hold the fort conveniently until they were ready. How wrong they were, and how beneficial for me, and the future developments, that I was given the freehold of the benefice,[2] which meant I could not be removed without my consent. Looking back on this, I am sure that it was God's handiwork, because it safeguarded the future of the vision that we were to receive in due course. God had plans for Thwing and for the rectory.

The newly appointed archdeacon, Donald Snelgrove, had been Vicar of Hessle, a large urban parish near Hull, and was now vicar of a small commuter parish near Beverley; these were still the days when such officials had a parochial living that gave them an income, and the diocese would provide the special expenses of office that they incurred. Later on, however, when the church began to identify with worldly business culture and developed a pretentious (and expensive) bureaucracy, archdeacons and others became fully paid diocesan officials with no parish responsibility. To me, the position which the hierarchy would take seemed to represent the age-old story of the reluctance of the church's senior leadership to recognise, let alone encourage, any work of the Holy Spirit that had not been planned by a diocesan committee.

The revelation that the diocese planned to dispose of the rectory, and the post of rector in due course, came as a shock to the parishioners. It came soon after the village school had been closed down, and it seemed almost like a concerted effort on the part of the powers-that-be to demote their village to the status of an unimportant hamlet. The closure of the school had been traumatic, especially as most of the people had been taught there by Miss Helen Broderick, who had, since the 1930s, been an excellent head. She had influenced many of the people, and she was held in great respect and affection. She was now retired and still lived in the village. I believe that her influence had contributed much to the communal ambience of the village, previously mentioned.

I brooded over the fate that was decreed for the parish, and I did not think that I was there simply as a short time stopgap. The leading church members, including Miss Broderick, were extremely indignant, and in the true York-shire way they were not going to take it lying down. They loved their church, they maintained it well, and they paid their way. I liked these people and admired their independ-ence, and I fully identified with them in their concern for the future of their parish. I began to think about how we might make some use of the rectory that would justify keeping Thwing as a separate parish.

By the spring of 1971, an idea began to form, prompted by my experience in other places. I had often taken groups of young people for residential teaching/evangelistic weekends, but often had difficulty finding a suitable venue that was not too big or too expensive. Why not adapt the rectory for such a purpose? It was big enough; the large bedrooms could be divided and other facilities installed, and we could still re-tain adequate living accommodation for ourselves. My en-thusiasm for this idea grew, and soon I was picturing just how it could be done; it seemed that the building was made for the purpose.

First, I called a meeting of the Parochial Church Council and outlined my proposals. We discussed mainly the ques-tions, 'How much will it cost', and, 'Will "they" pay?' —mean-ing the diocesan authorities. They agreed there was no harm in looking into it, especially if it was going to help make the parish viable and thus keep its own rector.

A small committee of several key people was formed, which would examine the proposal further. I was sure that it could work but, strangely enough, I did not for one moment equate this idea with any purpose for which God had brought us there. The Wold Newton people did not have quite the same interest as those at Thwing, but some thought it a good idea, notably a churchwarden, Miss Joan Burgess, an elderly but extremely active lady and a deeply committed Christian. She welcomed the idea, and immediately grasped the sense of using the rectory for a wider Christian purpose. Joan became a keen supporter from the start, and remained so over the ensuing years.

My next move was to go and see Stanley Linsley, the Archdeacon of Cleveland, whose area covered the northern part of the diocese of York. He was delighted with the idea, especially when I said that I proposed calling it Lamplugh House, after his ancestor! There was a Lamplugh window in the church and the parish possessed priceless communion plate[3] that had been presented to it by Thomas Lamplugh when he was Archbishop of York. He warned me not to expect any financial help from the diocese; they already had a debt on the Diocesan Conference Centre, Wydale Hall, and as ever, money was in short supply. He was all for keeping the independence of Thwing, and once more he enthused about the local people, particularly the farmers. He said, "Show them you mean business, show them the facts, be practical, and, when you have won them over, they will support you." He would help in whatever way he could, but warned me that I would need to deal with my new Archdeacon. Stanley Linsley's support did much to persuade our local people to go for it.

With this encouragement, I then wrote to the Archbishop of York (Donald Coggan) and asked if I might go and see him, briefly explaining the reason. I duly went to Bishopthorpe on a very hot day, where the archbishop (accompanied by his dog, Chad, named after the second Archbishop of York) grilled me. As we walked around the gardens, he asked me many searching questions and made several useful points, whilst he emphasised that I would need to present the scheme in detail through the Pastoral and Parsonage committees. Because of the commitment to Wydale Hall, there could not be any financial help from the diocese. I was nevertheless encouraged by his positive attitude. He had been responsible for the setting up of Scargill House in Wharfedale, and knew the value of such places.

My father-in-law, meanwhile, meticulously prepared architectural plans of the whole building, the measurements being accurate to the last fraction of an inch. He was fully qualified to do this, having been a regular engineering officer in the RAF, and then, until his retirement, chief maintenance engineer for United Dairies in Shropshire. He spent several days doing this, and it was as professional as anyone might wish. With these plans I was able to demonstrate how the large bedrooms could be divided, so that, with two large attic rooms in addition as dormitories, there would initially be room for 26–30 beds and bunks. We were thinking of accommodation for young people at that stage, so that the sleeping accommodation would be rather spartan. There was a room rather like a butler's pantry, immediately opposite the kitchen, and we planned to make a serving hatch through that to the dining room. To cut a long story short, with the help of a joiner and builder from Wold Newton, I was able to produce not only details of alterations, but also a reasonable estimate of the cost. We estimated that £3000 would cover it. We would need more money later, for furnishings and equipment, but I was sure that would come in eventually.

Our little committee met in what was still our dining room and they were staggered at the estimated cost. In 1971, £3000 was considered to be a huge sum. However, I had worked out a plan whereby we could finance a bank loan for the initial work. In those days, tax-free covenants lasted for seven years and, income tax being quite high, made such a way of giving very useful indeed. The group eventually arrived at an agreement that we should go ahead with the scheme on the basis of what I had outlined. Arthur Conner, a local farmer of considerable repute, and the senior person there, finally swayed their agreement. He had talked with Stanley Linsley about my ideas, and the latter advised him to back me up. Most of the people who were present at that meeting, including myself, banked at a suburban bank in Bridlington, where also the church accounts were kept. The manager, Guy Manson, was a friendly person and knew everyone concerned. It was before bank managers moved from the cupboard into a computer! He advised that he could give us a loan of £3000 for two years, on the strength of covenanted pledges. I made the audacious suggestion that we should start off with others and ourselves in the parish, making a covenant of at least £15 a year (equal to almost £200 today). Arthur Conner started the ball rolling and everyone else joined in. We publicised our aims, and many others came on board.

I was now in a good position officially to approach the diocese to ask for the necessary permission to proceed. It was also necessary to apply to the local authority for permission to change the use of the rectory, though it was still to remain as such, and would still be our home. The new archdeacon then came up to look around the house and to hear my views at first hand. He was friendly, but it was obvious that he was not going to back us and seemed determined that the pastoral re-organisation scheme must eventually proceed.

Sadly, the plans drawn up by my father-in-law were to be rejected, and it was insisted upon that I should obtain new ones, drawn up by the diocesan architect, before submitting them to the Parsonages Board. Dutifully, I did as I was told; the architect came to Thwing with his pencil and tape measure, and produced exactly what we already had. This time, however, we were presented with a bill for £80 from the architect for his unnecessary and unwelcome services, that had to be paid out of the donated funds. At every stage of seeking diocesan approval for the project there were difficulties. I 'kept my cards to my chest' regarding the promised bank loan: this was the ace with which to trump what I knew would be the main objection: that there was no money available for the scheme. How many people place money as the chief arbiter of progress! In years to come I would often say that the church does not have financial problems, it has spiritual ones, and when people become truly committed to the leading of the Holy Spirit, they will always give freely, often sacrificially, to further what is perceived as the work of God's kingdom: they are reluctant when it comes to supporting a top heavy bureaucracy, miles away from their first concern, that of their local church. I have often quoted David Watson's illustration of how this seems to work. He describes the proceedings of an average diocesan committee, which would typically start with the recitation of a collect: "Almighty and eternal God, **whose grace is sufficient for all things**...", and so on. Immediately after such a prayer, the chairman starts the business of the meeting, "Ladies and gentlemen, the situation at St. Agatha's is **completely hopeless** and nothing can be done about it!" —so much for belief in the power and grace of God.

We had some supporters in York, nevertheless, and when it became known that the parish was enthusiastically supporting me and that we now had the means of financing the initial structural alterations, the Board gave somewhat grudging permission to proceed, providing that, were I to leave, the rectory was to be restored to the condition in which I found it when I went there. This was indeed the joke of the century. Everything we proposed to do would not only enhance its ultimate value for selling purposes, but also would repair and rehabilitate the dilapidated and run-down building we had inherited.

Whether or not the diocesan people were in the habit of believing in miracles, I could not say: but if hard-headed, East Yorkshire farmers could support the scheme, and above all commit themselves to financing it, then here was a miracle indeed! I was very proud of them, and their trust and commitment proved not to be misplaced.

We went ahead with more detailed plans and preparations until later in the year, when the local authority gave 'change of use' permission, but that was not as simple as it might sound. The new fire regulations, with which we must comply, were coming in to force. This meant we must build an extra staircase from the first to the second floor, install safety doors on each floor between the two staircases, and in addition many of the existing panelled doors had to be made fireproof. Safety lights and fire alarms were required also. This was a blow, and it obviously meant that we would need more money for all the extra work. Several other major items presented themselves that had not been included in the original estimates. One of these was the condition of the roof over the second floor, which was of unprotected, bare slates. When examined from the loft, daylight was visible in many places, through which rain and snow came into the rooms below. A large sum was spent on a remedy involving the spraying of a rubber solution underneath the roof, that did the trick, making it safe and waterproof. This latter was a genuine dilapidations item, which should have been paid for by the diocesan board, but I thought it wise to keep a low profile and get on with it within the permission we had been given.

Life was very hectic during most of 1971, making plans, assessing costs, seeing various people and all the correspondence to and from the various diocesan committees who shuttlecocked us between each other. We then had to wait for their next meeting to take place; leaving us on tenterhooks as to what the outcome would be. My mind was almost totally occupied to the point of obsession with the formulation of details, timescales and future possibilities.

Meanwhile, volunteers from the village came in and helped to strip and clean the walls where necessary, particularly in the bedrooms, ready for their eventual redecoration, following the structural alterations. We were now getting a good deal of publicity in the local press and the Yorkshire Post, together with photographs and informative articles that I readily supplied. All this helped to put us on the map with our scheme for the rectory. As a result, we received more financial help to encourage us forward.

Throughout all this activity in 1971, I have to admit that I was still in the 'doing my thing' mode, just as I had been in my previous parishes. Even at this stage, I did not consciously relate our efforts to the belief that God had brought us here for a special purpose of his design. In true Anglican fashion I asked him to bless *my* efforts. The revelation that we were to be used by God in a special way was not to come until I had learnt the lesson that it was *His* work we were engaged upon, and to which we must be totally dedicated. That disclosure eventually came, and how it came was remarkable indeed.

Notes
[1] From *East Riding Heritage; Poems by Clare Ellin*. © Used by kind permission of Ridings Publishing Company, Beverley Road, Driffield, Yorkshire.
[2] An ancient right of life-long tenure, now legally diminished.
[3] Now on permanent display in York Minster, together with other Lamplugh plate from Bishopthorpe.

Five

"By My Spirit"

Joan Burgess, the churchwarden at Wold Newton, had several times invited me to go to 'The Wolds Fellowship', a prayer and Bible study group consisting of Methodists and Anglicans from several villages along the Wolds valley. The latter runs several miles from east to west, and separates the Yorkshire Wolds from the foothills of the North York Moors National Park. The meetings were held weekly on Thursday evenings, in different people's houses. Given my thoughts about Methodism in Cornwall, I was not too keen on going, but when I did meet these people I found them to be very different from the mental caricature of Methodists that I had taken on board! The Sherburn circuit of the Methodist Church included my parish of Wold Newton, but not Thwing, where the chapel congregation usually consisted of three or four people. When two of those died it was closed and converted into a house.

There had been something of a revival in the Sherburn circuit and several people, including some local preachers, had received a blessing of the Holy Spirit that had prompted enthusiastic evangelistic activity. What was happening to them was similar to what was happening in many areas of the country, not least at St. Cuthbert's, York, where David Watson had been vicar since the mid 1960s. A group of people at Malton Parish Church, including the vicar and his wife, had also come into this experience. All this sort of thing was foreign to me in those days; in fact I think I must have been totally unaware or uninterested in the spiritual renewal, or I had heard some stories and dismissed it as something rather odd!

As I was so full of my hopes and plans for Lamplugh House, I was not aware of what was going on so close to home — until I received an invitation from the Vicar of Malton, Ronald Treasure, to a one day event taking place in Malton Parish Church sometime in November. It was entitled 'A Day with the Holy Spirit'; the proceedings would commence with a celebration of Holy Communion, presided over by the Archbishop of York, Dr. Donald Coggan. There were two main speakers: Harry Cooke, Vicar of St. Matthias, Burley, Leeds, whom I remembered as a St. Aidan's man and a former curate of Otley Parish Church in the Diocese of Bradford; and Michael Harper, Director of the Fountain Trust, an agency which he founded to help Christians in the denominations discern the renewing power of the Holy Spirit.

We decided to go to this and, when we discovered that Joan Burgess was going, we all went together in our car. It was a very interesting and exciting day. We heard how Christians of many denominations and churchmanship were receiving a transformation in their lives and witness by an outpouring of the Holy Spirit, and that they were experiencing gifts and manifestations of the Spirit in many ways identical to what happened at Pentecost. Harry Cooke told of what was happening in his congregation in Leeds. Michael Harper spoke in depth about the scriptural basis for all that was taking place, in particular about the 'baptism in the Holy Spirit', which was a key feature of this renewal. I wondered if we were entering one of those periods in history when God apparently brings revival and new life to the Church. There was to be a rally and worship service in the evening, but we had to leave following the afternoon proceedings as the children were coming home from school. On our way home we discussed what we had heard. I said that I was not sure (theologically) about this baptism in the Holy Spirit, and how it related to baptism and Christian initiation. Joan Burgess told us that Ron Treasure was coming to the next Thursday meeting of the Wolds Fellowship to discuss that very point. I was intrigued by what I had heard, and wanted to know more about it.

Two or three days later I went to the meeting, while Margaret stayed at home with the children. On 17th November 1971, we gathered in the large living room of a farmhouse at Helperthorpe, a few miles away, the home of a farmer, Jack Sleightholme, who was a Methodist local preacher. This was to be a very significant day for me, which would prove to be a major turning point in my ministry. The room was full of people, including Ron Treasure, none of whom I knew, except for Joan Burgess; but many of them were to become good friends, supporters, and helpers of the Lamplugh House project.

Strangely, I again had that presentiment which I had experienced on other occasions, that this would be of great significance. Ron spoke of what was happening to people and to church congregations through this baptism in the Holy Spirit,[1] which was releasing a new power in people's lives and an experience of the presence of Jesus as Lord. It released a new sense of worship and joy, and through it God manifested his life and reality in a way which confirmed faith. The Holy Spirit bestowed spiritual gifts to enable Christians to serve God's purposes in his power and strength. Such gifts are seen in the New Testament when, after Pentecost and the giving of the Holy Spirit to the church, the apostles preached the word of God boldly, and God confirmed the word with 'signs following'.[2] These gifts of the Spirit now being manifested included such things as speaking in tongues, prophecy, healing, words of knowledge, and, around it all, a deep sense of love, which broke down barriers between people and established a new unity in the fellowship of the Holy Spirit.

Much of this we had heard at Malton, but there were people at this meeting who had not attended, and to whom it was all new. I was still excited to hear it, because I immediately recognised that what was being spoken of as happening today was, in fact, that New Testament dimension which I had always longed for but had never achieved. Of course it could not be achieved through human endeavour; it was God's doing in the giving of the Holy Spirit. It was like the reality of Pentecost, when the Holy Spirit fell upon the apostles and disciples, transforming them from a group of frightened, bewildered individuals into men who now boldly preached the news of salvation through Jesus Christ. Scripture tells us that God confirmed that Spirit-filled preaching by miraculous signs following.

Like all good Anglicans, I had been brought up to believe that such a concept of the power of the Holy Spirit coming upon the church, was a 'one off' event, necessary only until the church had bishops, churchwardens and parochial church councils to run it! It had been a *pro tem* dispensation. The way most churches seem to run would suggest that as being the general belief, anyway! I also knew that if this was really happening, and was available for today's church, it was that vital element which was always missing in the places where I had served and where I had felt myself to have failed. Of course I had failed, as most of the church apparently had failed, because in those days we had not learned that God's work can only be done God's way, by his power; that is, by the Holy Spirit.

It was fascinating to hear these testimonies of what the Holy Spirit was doing in our time. I took the opportunity to ask one or two questions. I asked, "How does this experience tie in with the promise of the Spirit in baptism and confirmation?" I knew that there were people within Methodism who preached 'the second blessing' as something over and above whatever might be inherent in Christian initiation (baptism in water, and confirmation.) My teachers had regarded this as a false idea. So I asked about this, too, and was satisfied with the answers I received.

I was now hearing it taught that when St. Paul uses the expression 'be filled with the Spirit',[2] the Greek verb means 'go on being filled.' I then began to see that it is necessary to move away from doing things in our *own* strength; that we must learn and submit to *his* will; and, above all, that we really seek that baptism of the Holy Spirit—inviting him to come into us and fill us—receiving him; then go on being filled with the Spirit. In later years, I heard a speaker express it in a nutshell: "I need to keep being filled with the Holy Spirit, because I leak!" Others do indeed emphasise the importance of a second event after conversion, pointing to the encounter of Paul and some believers at Ephesus who had not even heard of the Holy Spirit.

> There he found some disciples and asked them, "Did you receive the Holy Spirit when you believed?"
> They answered, "No, we have not even heard that there is a Holy Spirit."
> So Paul asked, "Then what baptism did you receive?"
> "John's baptism," they replied.
> Paul said, "John's baptism was a baptism of repentance. He told the people to believe in the one coming after him, that is, in Jesus."
> On hearing this, they were baptized into the name of the Lord Jesus. When Paul placed his hands on them, the Holy Spirit came on them, and they spoke in tongues and prophesied....[3]

There is a rock solid biblical basis for the reality of baptism in the Holy Spirit, which large parts of the church had ignored, neglected or denied. If this seems too simplistic to the reader, then do consult a theologian who will no doubt make it complicated! What the church needs is people who experience more of the releasing and deepening power of the Holy Spirit, however we understand the biblical terms used for his power, or the status of outward liturgical rites of initiation.

In due course the meeting came to an official end, and in came the coffee and refreshments. Everyone circulated and talked. Many questions were still being asked. People were eager for more. Perhaps, just like the onlookers on the day of Pentecost, they were thinking, "What must I do?" "How do I get in on this?" Ron Treasure had recognised that there was unfinished business and suggested we carry on. We all sat down again. This time I found myself seated next to Ron, who explained that he was going to pray for the Holy Spirit to come upon us. As he prayed, I found myself identifying with what he was saying, and he seemed to describe my spiritual condition and my need of a renewed life in the Spirit. Whatever this baptism of the Spirit was, I was convinced that I wanted it, and I needed it. So far as I remember, there was no formal invitation to have the laying on of hands to receive blessing or anointing, as is the usual practice, after the New Testament pattern. However, as we were praying, I was intensely aware of what I can only describe as the presence of Christ. I felt a physical, warm sensation in my whole body, and I was certain that I was being given that for which I was asking. Quite involuntarily, as this was happening, I reached out and grabbed Ron Treasure's arm —he looked a bit surprised, but that spontaneous gesture was like a sealing confirmation that something significant had happened to me. It was not a momentary psychological reaction to the events of the evening; there had been nothing forced, sensational or emotional about it.

From that event, the course of my life and ministry radically changed. Many others, too, were blessed significantly that evening. One thing I remembered Ron saying, when people voiced fears that they may be asked to become like raving enthusiasts (the abusive term 'happy-clappies' had not yet been coined by liberal opponents): "God is very gracious. He treats us like Anglicans." This understanding that the Holy Spirit meets us within our spiritual culture, whatever that may be, was an understanding that helped in my future teaching ministry.

It was now quite late, and as I drove home there was a

sprinkling of snow on the ground. I was in a daze, and in my mind I tried to come to terms with this liberating and uplifting experience. What did it mean? I remembered that John Wesley had spoken of a 'strange warming within' when describing his experience of the infilling of the Holy Spirit, but I could not see myself as another John Wesley! When I arrived home, Margaret was waiting up for me, sitting by the dying log fire. As I came through the door, my first words were, "Do I look any different?" I think she said no, but I certainly felt different! —and I told her what had happened to me at the meeting.

I slept little that night, and the feeling of euphoria persisted until the following morning when, in my study, I prayed and thought about the previous evening. I came down to earth suddenly, when I was convicted of the sinfulness and wrong motives behind all that I was seeking to do with Lamplugh House. It is part of the work of the Holy Spirit in our lives to do this.

> When he [the Holy Spirit] comes, he will convict the world of guilt in regard to sin and righteousness and judgement....[4]

I was shown, there and then, that all my motives were wrong. I was building something that would glorify me and justify my ministry with an edifice of my own devising, not without a measure of vanity and arrogance. The Spirit of God moved me to repentance. With tears and deep sorrow, I asked for forgiveness and renounced the selfish concerns that had motivated my actions. I asked to be shown what I must do; I was prepared to give it all up, if that was what God wanted to happen. I realised what a fool I would look if I now backtracked after we had moved so far with it. But I did not care about that possibility; all I wanted to do was to be used by God as he wished, whatever that might be.

In the following days, I began to understand that it was God who had given us the idea for Lamplugh House, and I linked it with the strange sense that I had been given on entering Thwing church over twelve months earlier. This scheme was God's purpose and he had needed to move me to relinquish my personal ambitions and be led forward by his guidance and in the enabling power of the Holy Spirit — and not in my human spirit. Almost immediately, positive things happened which encouraged me that we had to go on. Some of the current difficulties and problems were resolved as we got the different permissions for this or that, and the Diocesan Board of Finance, because they were unable to give a direct grant, offered to give us an interest-free loan of £500 for two years, to help things along. There were obviously people in York who were sympathetic towards the project. More covenants and donations came in, and soon we realised that we would be able to cover the extra cost incurred in complying with the new fire regulations. I had a new confidence and assurance that God was leading us, and consequently a vision of his purposes began to be revealed.

By the end of November we had received our first booking: it was for a youth house-party from Bridlington Priory church, and they wanted a few days from the following Easter Monday. I accepted the booking, though no work had yet commenced, but the booking gave us a deadline to work towards. Meanwhile, I was now attending the Wolds Fellowship every Thursday night. It was a means of sharing together, over denominational boundaries, a common heritage of life in the Spirit. The members encouraged us with the growing vision for Lamplugh House, and saw it as an indication that God intended to do great things among us. Sadly, Margaret could only be involved when we held the meeting at our house, as the children were not old enough to be left.

Early in January 1972, the way was clear for work to begin. Paul Sutton, the joiner and builder from Wold Newton, set his workmen on to the task, so that soon we were able to see all the structural plans take shape. Most winters on the Wolds can be quite severe, and 1972 was no exception, but this did not stop the work proceeding. However, at the same time, an elderly couple living in a tiny cottage in the village were having extensions built on to their house. They had moved out and were living in a small caravan in their garden. When the snow and frost came, we realised how miserable and difficult they were finding this arrangement and we took pity on them, offering a room at the rectory. They were very thankful to leave the caravan and they occupied one of our bedrooms for several weeks, as a temporary bed-sitter. As this was the room we had earmarked as our own sitting room following the alterations, it was not going to be disturbed by the work that was going on. A spin off from this arrangement was that Margaret could come to the Thursday Fellowship meetings as we had someone in the house.

During this time, we were busy listing all the furnishings and equipment that we would need by Easter. It was a long list, and I estimated the cost of all the items. I sent a copy to the people with whom we were in contact, suggesting that individuals might select an item as their personal gift. There was an encouraging response, not least when someone (who wished to remain anonymous) came to the door and handed me an envelope containing a large sum of money in five-pound notes! Several useful items from the list were also given, including bedding and cooking utensils.

As soon as each divided room was completed and the plaster was dry, we set to work with our helpers from the village, to emulsion the walls and paint the woodwork. The oil-fired central heating only served the downstairs rooms and the main landing of the first floor, so we installed night storage heaters in the two second floor dormitories. I recall that we installed a few electric wall heaters, which served until the following year, when we were able to install a secondary central heating system to serve other bedrooms.

There was a problem over the provision of beds: we bought several single divan beds, and we had also been given one or two. However, the main need was for substantial smaller (and cheaper) camp style beds that would be adequate for young people. At this stage we were still thinking that we would be dealing with youth and children's groups. We looked at several catalogues until we found something that seemed suitable and ordered a quantity of low metal beds with wire bases and thin foam mattresses. It was now early March and the deadline for the first group was growing close, but the suppliers assured us that the beds would be delivered during the week before Easter. The workmen were still there, finishing off various tasks, and we made up bedrooms as we could with the available beds. Margaret planned the meals for the group of twenty-plus people who were coming, and we went to a 'cash and carry' at Scarborough and bought in food supplies. She ordered bread and milk from our normal supplier, who delivered to the door, and meat from our excellent local butcher in the nearby village of Burton Fleming. We took delivery of comfortable chairs for the meeting room, and tables and chairs for the dining room. By this time it had become necessary for us to sell a good deal of our own furniture, but we retained some easy chairs and a three piece suite that was part of the furniture we had been given when we left Bradford. This was used in my former study to make a lounge. One of the large bedrooms had been made into one double and two single rooms, which we allocated for our own family use; together with the bedroom we had reserved for our living room, this now comprised the whole of our private quarters. We used the communal dining room or the kitchen for our own family purposes.

By Wednesday of Holy Week we began to get worried. The beds had not arrived, though the suppliers told us they had been despatched —but that they might be held up because of the Easter holiday. People in the Wolds Fellowship were praying that all would go smoothly, and we shared with them our concern that the beds might not arrive in time for Easter Monday. Leslie Barningham, another farmer and Local Preacher from the fellowship, telephoned to tell us not to worry as he was getting some beds on loan for us. He had contacted other members of the Fellowship and collected from them a variety of beds, camp beds, bed-settees, on loan. On Good Friday morning, after driving to several villages to pick them up in a large lorry, he delivered them to us, so we were able to provide adequate beds for the group. This was an example of the ready and willing help that was often given us by farmers and local people in the years that followed. The beds we had ordered did arrive, but not until the Tuesday afternoon, when our guests were already installed.

The workmen left. They were to return after the holiday and finish off one or two outstanding items. We awaited Easter Monday with excitement and a little trepidation. We had employed no staff except for a lady from the parish who was to come in and do the cleaning several times a week. Margaret decided that she could manage with the help of our two girls, now aged eleven and thirteen, who were on holiday from school. The first group was such a shattering experience that we began to wonder why we were doing all this! A major problem was that neither the leader of the group nor his student assistant seemed to have much control over these boisterous teenagers. (We were still living in the days when it was reasonable to assert a measure of authority and to expect disciplined behaviour.) There was no organised programme for the afternoon periods, when sports, walks or games can provide useful diversions. Consequently, the youngsters ran wild around the house and grounds.

All our domestic arrangements went well, and there were no other problems; the visitors had to make their own beds, and we organised small groups to wash up after meals. On the Tuesday when the beds arrived, we decided to get them in place. Each bed was packaged in corrugated brown cardboard, and we got some of the young people to help us unpack them, which they did with enthusiasm. As teatime approached, the leader returned from Bridlington, to where he had dashed after lunch, and it was discovered that his helper was missing. Looks of innocence on the faces of some of his flock suggested that they knew something about this strange disappearance. We searched around; his was a single room and we went to it. There he was: lying on his bed, bound and tied up in some of the corrugated cardboard from the beds sellotaped around him, with the face of an Egyptian mummy painted on it!

We had a black Scottish terrier, Andy, who was always mindful of his territory where other dogs were concerned, though he usually welcomed humans. He was to develop a burning hatred for bicycles and cyclists that week. We had fresh loose gravel laid on the turning circle by the front door, and some of the boys started a game of racing round this circle on their bicycles, causing the gravel to fly up as they did so and spraying it on to Andy, who was barking wildly and chasing them round. After that, he would go mad whenever he saw a cyclist and we had to be alert and control him whenever one came into his view.

The general verdict was that the four days had been worthwhile and successful from the leader's point of view, and it had been a positive, if eventful, first experience for us. On Thursday, their last evening, the group planned an entertainment and we invited the members of the small management committee to join us for the evening meal and see the house in operation. We were exhausted, and relieved, when they all left the next day.

We had to wait until July for the next booking. It was a group of university students described as 'Hull and East Riding Students Vacation Fellowship' who came for the weekend. On 27th July we organised our first Teaching Day, 'The Fullness of the Spirit'. This was attended by many people from the Wolds area, and was led by Ron Treasure. Renewal Days became very popular, sometimes attracting sixty or more people, and they became a regular feature of the teaching programme. There was nothing then until early September, when a group of sixth-formers, led by several Christian teachers from Knaresborough and Harrogate, had a successful weekend. The leaders came again and again in different capacities, and gave us much support during the next year or so. Eventually, at least three of them were ordained. Bookings began to trickle in for later in 1972 and the following winter, but it was at least a year before we were operating on a regular basis.

We needed to publicise our existence, and, as well as advertising in church newspapers, I wrote to the editors of the news leaflets of the surrounding dioceses, including Lincoln, Durham, Ripon, Wakefield, Bradford and York. All of them placed an advertisement with the exception of our diocese, York. The Diocesan Secretary would not accept it as he said Lamplugh House was a threat to Wydale Hall, the York diocesan conference house. It never did prove a threat; this refusal was to be a great blessing in disguise. When Stanley Linsley, our friend the Archdeacon of Cleveland, heard of it he complained to the Archbishop on our behalf. It seems that Donald Coggan himself was not very pleased either. At very short notice he showed his support by offering to come and officially dedicate and open the new centre! He was due to preach at a Harvest Thanksgiving on the evening of the 5th October at Hornsea, and was prepared to come for an afternoon ceremony at 4.30 p.m. We were jubilant and, with the management committee and the parish, began preparations for the great day. This supportive action by the Archbishop took the wind out of the sails of most of the opposition, and it is surprising that several now thought perhaps it was a good idea after all!

We only had a few weeks to get organised, but it proved to be one of those occasions when almost the whole parish became involved. We arranged to have a marquee on the lawn for the refreshments, as we expected many more people than could get into the house. Parishioners provided all the food and refreshments and it was an excellent spread. We had sent out invitations (and appeal leaflets) over a wide area; over two hundred people turned up, and there was ample food to feed them all! The weather was good, it was a warm, sunny day, and we erected a platform outside the front of the building. I devised a simple dedication service and made sure that the Archdeacon of the East Riding was invited to pray for the future of the Centre. The Archbishop gave an encouraging address, congratulating the parishioners for the way they had supported the venture. He said the church needed many such centres in other parts of the country to enable people 'to learn Christ', and to equip themselves to serve Christ. He described people who would use the centre as 'commandos' who could leave Lamplugh House and 'go into battle'. The concept of Lamplugh House as a 'Christian Commando Training Centre' immediately focussed the vision for the future that had been formulating since that spiritual experience at the Wolds Fellowship, eleven months earlier, when God began to reveal his plans. The official dedication had the effect of putting us well and truly on the map, and we saw the work and ministry take off from then on.

Never satisfied with the status quo, I was dreaming and visualising how things might need to develop. My mind was often occupied on how we would eventually be able to enlarge the house for larger numbers, and enhance it for adult use, not solely for young people. I already had thoughts on using it for renewal conferences and teaching weekends relating to the renewal movement, to seek to help the many people who as individuals had received a renewing experience of the Holy Spirit, perhaps at a Fountain Trust conference, but did not know how to equate their new experience with the life of their local church. I felt these people needed help and encouragement, and many such brought their friends, hoping they, too, might receive this blessing, and several people did. We also arranged special days for clergy, who came to hear people like David Watson and Colin Urquhart. Financial resources apart, we were limited in that we could not make any extensions whilst it remained the parsonage house. My ultimate hope was that the authorities might release the house to us as a Charitable Trust that we hoped to establish, but four years went by before this could happen. One good financial advantage however, was that I was paid my stipend by the church whilst I remained incumbent of the benefice, so that a warden's salary did not have to be found from income. In fact, Margaret worked for nothing and our daughters, helping at weekends, together with Joyce Vincent, a school friend whose parents ran the village shop, were happy to be involved, and were each paid £2 pocket money for their weekend work! Thus we were able to keep overheads low whilst the use of the house developed. Joyce actually worked full time after she left school, and was the mainstay of the catering and domestic arrangements for fifteen years. When no groups were in the house she would prepare food in advance and it would be kept deep frozen ready for use. Margaret's burden was relieved, though she was still kept busy with the household management. We provided nylon sheets not needing to be ironed, and all the washing was done on the premises. Between them, Margaret and Joyce worked out a good system. Mrs Marion Gilson looked after the main cleaning chores very efficiently; she too worked with us for many years for the whole period of our involvement there.

By the Summer of 1972 the bank loan and the first flush of donations had been used up, though a steady income came from the original covenants, and new ones which we were getting all the time. As church property, we qualified automatically as a charity, and were therefore able to recover a considerable amount of money periodically from the covenanted giving. It all involved much administrative work, which I was able to cope with due to my previous experience. I enjoyed all this, together with keeping the accounts and making financial projections so that we kept charges down as low as possible. St. Paul refers to administrators as gifted by the Spirit for the work of the Body of Christ.[5] I never cease to be amazed how many clergy there are who seem to regard administration as something below their dignity; as being somehow in opposition to 'spiritual' activities! We found this, too, with some of the 'super-spirituals' who from time to time were involved with us. They could be so heavenly-minded as to be of no earthly use. There are times for praying together and there are times for 'fellowship' and there are also times for some hard graft! Such folk never seemed to stay for very long: it seemed that the Lord had once more got their case in hand and was moving them on to pastures new! Many people thought we were not spiritual enough. What they were really saying was that we were not pious enough—there is a deal of difference between the two, and we do not need to speak the 'language of Zion' to prove anything at all. Our 'spirituality' has always seemed to work out in practical ways. A favourite prayer we often used was that of St. Ignatius:

> Teach us, good Lord, to serve thee as thou deservest,
> To give and not to count the cost,
> To fight and not to heed the wounds,
> To toil and not to seek for rest,
> To labour and not to ask for any reward
> Save that of knowing we do thy will.

Within the disposition of that prayer comes the reality of the phrase in the Prayer Book collect, '...Whose service is perfect freedom.' We found fulfilment and satisfaction through the total commitment of our lives and possessions, to what we believed God had called us to do.

Back in the summer of 1972, we had set up a small management committee of nine people, including Margaret and myself, the two Thwing Churchwardens, Joan Burgess for Wold Newton, and several others appointed by the PCC, with Arthur Conner as chairman. The committee met regularly to monitor the income and expenditure. The initial bank loan of £3000 had been spent, together with the other gifts and donations we had received. But we were up and going, despite the struggle we had experienced. I was convinced now that the project to which we had set ourselves was indeed of God's leading, and we could confidently step out in faith.

One particular instance of how we learned that God does indeed honour such steps, that are undertaken in obedience and faith, was the need for the proper surfacing of the long drive leading up to the house from the bottom lane. It was, in fact, no more than a foot deep trench in the earth, having been worn down over the years to the chalk rock beneath. It came steeply up the hill for two-thirds of the way, then curved to connect with the gateway to the house. In winter, it seemed it was the first part of the Wolds to become snowed up, and this made vehicular access difficult, sometimes impossible. With all the anticipated extra traffic it was obvious that something needed to be done. The estimated cost of filling it in and giving it a tarmac surface was £300, equal to several thousands today! There was no ready money to pay for it, and some of the committee were uneasy about spending such a sum and adding to the debt. After some discussion, it was decided that the church funds could provide the cost as a loan until it could be paid back. The church treasurer, the wardens and several other PCC people were there, so there was no problem with the proposal.

As soon as possible, we got the contractors in and they did the work, making a tremendous improvement. Before we received the bill from the contractor, however, we received an anonymous gift of £300! The donor was not aware that we urgently needed such a large sum; to me this was nothing short of miraculous, and I could not accept it as being just a coincidence. Prayer and faith were answered. Some of our committee were not at that stage ready to recognise an act of God —they put it down to my perceived talent for attracting financial support! We were encouraged with several such incidents. I believe that they came to build our faith and to encourage us, especially at the beginning. When other provisions for our needs seemed to be met in a similar manner, the sceptics then were prepared to say that I must have "influence with 'Someone' up there!"

Through such incidents we were learning that if the Holy Spirit was prompting an action, we had to say, "Yes" and get on with it. The resources or the resolution always came in the end. God's resources provided for God's work. Some aspects of the vision for the future were gradually being revealed. It was to be many years before they were all seen to be fulfilled. Some of them did not come until over twenty years later, under different leadership. God has his purposes and he always works according to his own timing and plan.

We first met Pam Oldfield about the time we had the first group. She was a widow, living at South Cave, near Hull, and had come into an experience of renewal in the area where she lived. She also had links with Bridlington Priory church, through her elderly father who lived in Bridlington. She became a great supporter and several years later, in 1980, she moved to a cottage in Thwing so that she could be actively involved with us in the running of Lamplugh House. Pam's father, who was a deeply committed Christian, was to die later that year, but he had shown great interest in what we were doing at Thwing and gave a generous gift to help the project on. Pam also had an uncle in Bridlington, her father's brother, Trevor Field. He was a bachelor, old, wealthy and very ill. He did not share the Christian faith of his brother and his niece, and Pam was very concerned for him. She took me to meet him at his flat on Bridlington sea front, where he lived and was looked after by a housekeeper. Pam had told him about Lamplugh House and he was interested to hear that the young people from Bridlington had been the first group. A few days later he sent a substantial gift, which was very helpful at that stage. The following year he also died, in hospital, but not before having become a Christian through the ministry of the hospital chaplain, a curate at the Priory Church, and through the prayers of Pam and others. He was to enter the story again later, in a dramatic and amusing way.

During all this period we were learning more about spiritual renewal, and I was sure that this was God's plan for the institutional church, to give it new life and vitality. St. Cuthbert's Church in York was a wonderful example of what can happen when the Holy Spirit brings revival and renewal. David Watson's ministry was attracting people from all over the country, to see what was happening and to seek the same for themselves and their churches. In a few years the small congregation of five people had grown so that the church building was inadequate to accommodate the several hundreds who were now attached. How they all moved into St. Michael-le-Belfry in the shadow of York Minster, in January 1973, is one of the remarkable stories of the early days of renewal in the Church of England. Often, on Sunday evenings, Margaret and I would go to York after the house group had left, and attend the evening service. The worship was so alive and joyful, but it followed the pattern of Evening Prayer, and the sermon would be long and in-depth biblical teaching, through which we were very much encouraged and inspired. When possible we would also attend the Thursday night Bible study and fellowship meeting. We made many friends in York, and St. Michael's began to use Lamplugh House often for teaching weekends and other purposes that were a big help to us.

We became aware that this movement of the Holy Spirit was raising several centres and communities around the country, with the purpose of encouraging renewal in the church. Notable among these were the Barnabas Fellowship at Whatcombe House in Dorset, the vision of Reg and Lucia East and John Gunstone; also the Post Green Community, near Poole, where Sir Thomas and Lady Faith Lees had opened their home for a similar purpose. There was nothing similar in the North of England, and by now I was sure that Lamplugh House was destined to serve a similar role here.

In the first year we had initiated 'Renewal Days', and soon began holding residential weekends or mid-week conferences, to which people would come from all over Yorkshire and beyond for teaching and ministry led by people who were acknowledged leaders in renewal: Michael Harper and others who were, or had been, connected to the Fountain Trust, such as Cecil Cousen, who was leading a renewal group in Scarborough; David Smith, by then with David Watson at York; Tom Smail and John Richards; Harry Cooke from Burley, Leeds, who had a great testimony to renewal in an inner-city parish —and people flocked to hear them. Richard Hare was a great attraction, being the only English bishop who at the time encouraged and embraced the renewal. Often, we held meetings in the parish church to accommodate others not resident for the conference.

It was to be a long while before I felt confident to assume a teaching role myself, but that was to come in God's timing. Lots of books and testimonies of the Holy Spirit's working in people's lives and churches were being published, and I read many of them. I would go to meetings and conferences on the subject whenever possible, including Fountain Trust, the foremost agency then propagating this new perception. In the course of all this, I became increasingly aware of my own spiritual problems and inadequacies, particularly in the area of personal relationships. I did not yet understand that this is an inevitable process when the Holy Spirit seeks to cleanse and equip us for active service.

Notes

[1] There are several New Testament references to this experience, notably Luke 3:16. In post Apostolic times this was theologically linked in sacramental terms with Christian initiation. The dynamic result of the experience has usually been considered 'Dispensational', thus conveniently giving a rational explanation for the absence of apostolic dynamic in the life of the Church.

[2] Ephesians 5:18.

[3] Ephesians 19:1b–6.

[4] John 16:8.

[5] See 1 Corinthians 12:28.

Six

"Onward, Christian Commandos!"

The official opening of Lamplugh House by the Archbishop of York was widely publicised in the local press and the national religious papers and had the effect of putting us firmly on the map. Bookings for the future began to flow in and we found ourselves catering for adult as well as youth groups. These were mainly for weekends, thus allowing the mid-week break for us to recover and prepare for the next group the following weekend. However, at holiday periods, there would be whole week bookings which meant a continuous operation, allowing less than six hours to be ready for the next invasion. Margaret coped very well with all this, but by now we had a succession of resident helpers from time to time, and our daughters did their bit as their school commitments allowed. Joyce Vincent's having become a permanent member of staff when she left school lightened Margaret's workload considerably.

We had a problem accommodating some of the groups, depending upon their make up. The small camp beds that we had purchased for the opening were quite inadequate. It was here that our builder, Paul Sutton, helped us considerably. He made us a gift of ten sturdy wooden bunk beds, constructed by his joiner, that we used mainly in the two second floor dormitories. We purchased interior sprung mattresses for these and sold the smaller camp beds, the proceeds of which went towards the cost of the mattresses. We often gave up our own family bedrooms, thus releasing four more beds for guests. We had been given an old touring caravan that we had placed near to the house, and the four of us and Andy, our Scottie, would sleep in that for the weekend. It was all part of the fun of pioneering the new enterprise. We knew that at some stage we needed adequate housing provision for ourselves and we envisaged utilising the dilapidated stable-block to make a house. Any work in that area was out of the question however, until such time as we had a trustee body owning the whole property and thus releasing it from the restrictions imposed by parsonage regulations. There was no money for this anyway, and we still had the outstanding loan at the bank, which was due to be paid off by the end of 1973.

We would encourage visiting groups to join in the Parish Communion at Thwing Church on Sunday mornings; many did so, and were warmly welcomed by the local congregation. Later that year, as we were developing our own Renewal conferences, we would incorporate a music group and introduce some of the new hymns and spiritual songs that were becoming popular —many of these were very good, but some were rubbish and not suitable for use in public worship. New and joyful songs and hymns of praise have always marked movements of the Holy Spirit in the church—such as that experienced by the Wesleys—and the charismatic renewal of the twentieth century has been no exception. It is ironic that some parts of the church which reject and abhor the charismatic renewal nevertheless seem to be ignorant of the fact that many of the new hymns they sing came out of the renewal which took place between the 1960s and the 1980s. The form of the Eucharist we were using at the parish church was the 'Series 3' experimental form, which was authorised for use before the eventual introduction of the *Alternative Service Book* in 1980. One of the novel features of this service was the 'sharing of the peace' during which, in the more lively congregations, people would move and 'offer a sign of peace' to one another. This would usually be a handshake, but sometimes a hug or an embrace! Some of the livelier groups would cause consternation at this point, for as well as greeting each other they would proceed around the regular congregation, bestowing their peace in the most demonstrative fashion. Imagine the reaction of some of the stolid, East Yorkshire farmers when they were fallen upon and hugged by these enthusiastic young people! One could almost read their minds: 'You can pat my dog, but keep your hands off me!' It was taken in good part on the whole, though at a meeting of the Parochial Church Council someone brought it up: "What do folk think of this walkabout stuff in the service?" However, as these groups brought large offerings that helped church funds, perhaps their loss of dignity was a small price to pay! The sharing of the peace in this manner is now the practice in many churches. At the time, Richard Hare, the charismatic Bishop of Pontefract, termed it 'Close Encounters of a Series Three kind.'

The summer holiday period was very busy, with a whole succession of parish holiday weeks and our own holiday teaching conferences. By the end of them we were totally exhausted and ready for a holiday ourselves. I cannot remember where we went or how long we were away. However, I shall always remember the day we returned. There was a huge pile of mail waiting to be opened, and the first was an unpleasant letter from the new manager of our bank in Bridlington. He had replaced the previous one who had been so helpful to us when we were starting up. The letter summoned me to go and see him as soon as possible, reminding us that we still owed two thousand pounds, and that it must be paid off by Christmas. He also said that he had heard we were planning more expenditure, and that we still had outstanding accounts with the builder, who incidentally also banked at the same branch. The fact that we still owed the bank two thousand pounds was quite true, but it was adequately covered by the covenanted income and tax refunds being applied to the loan as they came in; the rest was total rubbish. I later discovered how this had all come about. Incorrect information had been provided by another party, and the bank had gained the impression that I wanted to convert the stable-block into a house —but of course there were no immediate plans for that, and nor could there have been, for the reasons already stated. Needless to say, that letter was thoroughly depressing and disheartening. I continued to open the mail, finding enquiries for bookings, one or two bills, advertising—the usual stuff—until I got to the very last letter, which bore the name of a firm of solicitors. I opened it, and there was a letter and a cheque. The letter stated that we had been left a bequest from the will of the late Mr Trevor Field, Pam's uncle. The cheque was for exactly two thousand pounds! Whoever said God has no favourites?

I made the appointment to see the bank manager. I went into his office, waved the cheque at him, and wished him a merry Christmas, though it was still September! I then closed our accounts—those of Lamplugh House and our personal account—and transferred them to the Market Weighton branch, where our old friend Guy Manson was now manager.

That incident I regarded as another miracle. If miracles are intended to show God's power and to raise faith, that is certainly what it did! God's timing is perfect. We believed we were under God's protection in what we were doing, which we were confident was in accordance with his purpose and his leading. We were protected not only from evil spiritual influences, but also from the pettiness of officials, including some who exercised power within the church.

At around the time of this incident, I was invited to take part in a Post Green leadership training course. This teaching community in Dorset was pioneering a course of training they had evolved, in order to equip leaders in renewal to become more informed and effective in their ministry. About twenty five people in Yorkshire enrolled, including Ron and Eliza Treasure from Malton, Mark Simons from Swanland, near Hull, another parish moving into renewal, Kenneth

Nelson, Rector of Crayke and his wife Jean, and Ray Smith, Vicar of Normanton, as well as several other people whom we knew. It was a study course with a major subject for each month, followed by a Saturday together with all the other participants, Tom and Faith Lees and others of the Post Green community, who had prepared all the course material. We met at Normanton for the monthly meetings. The course lasted for several months and was very comprehensive, particularly in the areas of the gifts of the Spirit in ministry and service, counselling, inner healing, the reality of spiritual evil and how it bound peoples lives; and how to use the weapons of spiritual warfare. The ministry of healing was covered in a balanced and comprehensive way. As it progressed, the course had the effect of bringing physical and inner healing, release and a freedom in the Spirit to many of the participants.

Finally, a residential weekend was held in Harrogate. There was an amusing incident that weekend. Jean Darnell, a popular American charismatic preacher, was part of the team who conducted the monthly seminar at Normanton. Like many of her compatriots, she loved a lord or a title and, together with Elmer, her husband, had become associated with Sir Tom and Lady Lees at their home in Dorset. One thing I remember of her when she attended the monthly meetings was her enthusiasm for an American Christian musical *Come Together*. She was involved in preparation for its UK tour. Over this and other things she seemed to be constantly in touch with the Lord, who apparently was in close dialogue with her and constantly guided and advised her as was necessary. On the Saturday of the weekend in question, Jean was due to speak in the afternoon session, but there was no sign of her. When eventually she turned up, later that evening, it transpired that she had made her way to Halifax instead of Harrogate! I was reminded that we are all fallible and do not always hear correctly—and map reading is normally still needed, even for those who usually hear clearly from God! I remained somewhat sceptical about many of the alleged 'words from the Lord' so often proclaimed by many charismatics. Such words really do need to be tested and weighed. In fact, on an occasion when I spoke at Kingdom Faith's Roffey Place weekly open fellowship meeting, many years later, an alleged statement I made was picked up and repeated as a *bon mot*—"I envy these people who constantly get neat words from the Lord; all he ever says to me is, 'Repent!'"

After that first leadership course was successfully completed, the Post Green people suggested that we might form a local team from the participants and take upon ourselves the responsibility for arranging the course the following year for more people. We agreed to this and so Ron & Eliza Treasure, Kenneth and Jean Nelson, Mark Simons, Ray Smith and myself conducted a course in the autumn at Crayke, following a briefing session for our team at Post Green. This time we had the residential weekend at Lamplugh House, and Tom & Faith Lees with some of their community conducted this. It went well, and many people taking part were helped by it. A final course was held the following year, this time based at Thwing. It had been a time consuming exercise for the leaders, but proved very valuable to most of the participants.

I suppose the effects of the course came out gradually in people's ministry. It revealed to me the difficulties I had in relationships, emanating from childhood. A major tenet of renewed faith is the fatherhood of God; it is a theological fact, but in the experience of many people it remains simply a 'poetic' concept, and is not reflected in their day to day awareness. It is surprising how many people there are who have had such a negative, possibly destructive, experience of fatherhood that it is very difficult for them truly to perceive and relate to God as a loving Father. St. Paul tells us:

> ...but you received the Spirit of sonship. And by him we cry, "*Abba*, Father!" The Spirit himself testifies with our spirit that we are God's children.[1]

The Aramaic word 'abba' literally means the affectionate

term 'daddy'. When those whose experience of human fatherhood is that of brutal authority, or cruelty, it is going to take a good deal of inner healing before a true relationship with the heavenly Father can be realised.

It may be hard to believe, but I grew up with an acute sense of my own inadequacy, low self-esteem and an irrational fear of, or deference to, authority figures; this latter weakness however, had gone by the time I was an authority figure in my own right, when I became a vicar. I have already mentioned that I found relating to authority figures in the church was usually a totally different experience than with many in the secular world. I now discovered that the low esteem factor was shared by many of my fellow Christians, and was in itself a major obstacle to the progress of the gospel and the spreading of God's kingdom. We need to learn that God gives necessary power and his authority to minister in his name. It is the authority of his 'children' and 'heirs'.[2]

Although I was quite happy preaching sermons, six feet above criticism and with my hand firmly on my notes, I always found speaking publicly in any other context the most frightening and nerve-racking prospect. It was stupid, it was irrational, but it was very real! I am sure that this was an entirely psychological handicap, but the causes of it had to be resolved by the ministry of the Holy Spirit. Until it was dealt with I would never do more than lead the worship at Lamplugh House meetings or conferences, and introduce the speakers. I felt quite at ease within that role, and I was free and self-confident. At that stage, however, I could never have taken on the teaching and speaking role that was to come later. In my dreams for the future, I thought of the possibility that some person gifted in teaching might at some stage come and work with us for this purpose.

Several clergy conferences and one-day meetings for clergy and wives were arranged, in order to introduce them to renewal. Already, several local incumbents from surrounding villages were themselves into this experience of the Holy Spirit, but it must be something to do with the rural mind in small communities, that it seemed close to impossible to reach many lay people in their congregations. It was a constant source of disappointment to me that the local people seemed indifferent to it all. One could preach and talk about it, they could listen to famous visiting preachers, but it seemed as though they thought it did not relate to them personally, but was probably a good thing for all the visitors! We did have some good, quiet, thoughtful Christians, but there was that typical Anglican complacency with the status quo, so that they did not want any more than what they had already acquired. It was sad to me, because I loved these people who were in my pastoral care, and I knew how much they were missing. So many Anglicans seem as though they aspire to little, and expect little, of their faith. One night I had a vivid dream; in it was a picture of Thwing church filled to capacity, with people singing and praising God, their hands raised in a joyful act of worship. Next morning, the picture remained, and I was elated to think that God might indeed pour out his Spirit on this community.

One characteristic of the renewal movement at this time was the growth of committed communities into which people believed God had called them, so that, on the New Testament pattern, they could have all in common and be free to serve as the Holy Spirit would lead. One such team, which had come to England from America, was 'The Fisherfolk'. They were part of a community led by Graham Pulkingham, a priest of the Episcopal (Anglican) Church of the U.S.A. They were being used effectively in conferences and meetings throughout the country, and their ministry in spiritual song and worship was backing up the preaching about the power of the Holy Spirit in a very remarkable way. We had good friends in a charismatic group attached to a Baptist Church in Moortown, Leeds. Dr. Michael Flowers and June, his wife, with their large family, used their home for a weekly fellowship meeting. They had managed to secure the Fisherfolk to lead a weekend for their group at Lamplugh House. We had tents and caravans, and local people opened their homes to provide bedrooms for the large number of people who came. We also arranged that the group would be at the 11 a.m. service in the parish church, with the Fisherfolk leading the worship, and this came as the climax to a fruitful weekend. We had made it known around the area and invited all and sundry to attend. It was a marvellous service and the worship was uplifting and exciting. As well as their own songs, many of which are now in standard new hymnbooks, there was singing in the Spirit. Although the service lasted twice as long as usual, this was scarcely noticeable. At the end, during a tremendous hymn of praise, I stood and faced the congregation to give the final blessing. When I faced them, I saw the picture I had seen in my dream —the church packed to capacity, with people singing and praising God, many with their hands raised! It was a wonderful sight, though the blessing of the Spirit was not for my parish, as I had mistakenly interpreted, but for the visitors from Leeds!

In March 1974, Bishop Kenneth Lamplugh, another descendant of the famous Thomas, approached us. He had been suffragan Bishop of Southampton, having retired two years earlier. In his family's possession was an oil painting of Thomas Lamplugh. He could not give it to us, but he wanted to make a presentation of a framed photograph of the picture, for display at Lamplugh House. We made a small ceremony of this, and invited Archdeacon Stanley Linsley, as another of Lamplugh stock, and Arthur Conner, as chairman of the management committee, to receive this gift officially. We made sure that we had the press there, and the resultant publicity helped to keep us on the map.

Earlier, I related that Stanley Linsley had been appointed to Thwing after a breakdown, following overwork in his previous appointment. He was extremely active and always on the move, full of nervous energy. He reached the age of seventy and retired from his post as Archdeacon of Cleveland just a few months afterwards. By the end of the year, he died in tragic circumstances. Apparently unable to contend with the enforced inactivity of retirement, his depressive illness returned, and in the mental turmoil he took his own life. It was a great shock to all who knew him. In January 1975 there was a memorial service for him at Northallerton Parish Church, to which Dr. Donald Coggan, who had recently become Archbishop of Canterbury, came to preach. We missed his cheerful help and encouragement. Several months later, at the request of his family, Stanley's ashes were scattered in the grounds of Lamplugh House.

During the oil crisis in the 1970s, there was galloping inflation and prices of essential foodstuffs and most other things were rising almost weekly. This was a problem for us as we were reluctant to be constantly raising our charges. We overcame it partially through buying in large stocks of foodstuffs that could be dry-stored or deep-frozen. We would go on forays to the cash and carry warehouse and load the car to capacity. The continuing economic crisis, with its attendant unemployment and inflation, led to a reduction in numbers of private church and student groups. However, we still went on developing the teaching conferences, to which people came as individuals from different churches. When we managed to get well-known speakers, they would flock to hear them. Over the next few years we had people of the calibre of Colin Urquhart, Tom Smail, John Richards, Cecil Cousen, David Smith (later with St. Michael-le-Belfrey), Michael Harper, Richard Hare —something of a novelty, as he was the only bishop in those days to have nailed his colours to the charismatic mast. Some people wondered if that was the reason for him not to have become a diocesan bishop. With my fully developed scepticism about institutional Anglicanism, I would not be surprised! We were able to bring in Roman Catholic charismatic speakers, notably Ian Petit OSB and Father Michael Simpson SJ.

We had Methodists and United Reformed, Pentecostalists, Baptists, and practically the whole spectrum of Christian denominations, attending. What was proved through all this was that Christians who had received the filling of the Holy Spirit had far more in common than could be contained within denominational definitions. Cecil Cousen, being based locally at Scarborough, came frequently and was a tremendous help to us. Along with the residential conferences at Lamplugh House, if we had a well-known speaker we would sometimes arrange a 'rally' type of meeting in a church or hall, so as to attract as many new people as we could, to help them discover the blessing of the Holy Spirit.

In those early days we were very conscious of the fact that, where renewal teaching ministry was concerned, we were wearing large 'L' plates, though we ourselves learned much from the visiting speakers, and this helped build up our faith and confidence. We had had no previous contact with Whatcombe House or any other similar establishments, but I had heard that the Whatcombe leaders, together with those from Lee Abbey, Devon and Scargill House in the Yorkshire Dales, and others, would meet together on a regular basis for fellowship, prayer and mutual support for their ministries. I thought that it might be helpful if we could join them. So I wrote to Reg East, Warden of the Barnabas Fellowship at Whatcombe, and asked if we could be involved. The reply I received was like a bucket of cold water! A short note explained that my request was not possible because 'it would break the close fellowship' which they had! We recognised from this apparent rebuff that we were out on a limb and were obviously the poor relations on this scene. Out on a limb or not, we knew that God was with us and he had guided us thus far, and we believed that he would continue to do so, as long as we sought his will and were obedient. Ironically, by 1986 Whatcombe House had closed down while Lamplugh House is still going from strength to strength at the start of the twenty first century —under new management, but still under the Holy Spirit, for the vision that was first given to us, being similar to their own, was taken up and pursued by Kingdom Faith Ministries.

A few years later, after they had retired from the Barnabas Fellowship, we met Reg and Lucia East and they became good friends. Knowing Reg East as I now know him, I cannot for one moment think that his letter to me was intended to be a 'brush-off'; it may have been carelessly written, but it was not his purpose to reject us or be hurtful. In the early 1980s, following their retirement from Whatcombe, Reg and Lucia had a very successful travelling ministry and came several times to lead holiday teaching weeks at Thwing. I enjoyed many chats with Reg, and found him a man after my own heart.

A particularly unhappy tendency in those days was to take and to over-emphasise an aspect of renewal, or gift of the Spirit, beyond its function within a balanced and wholesome spiritual ministry. Paperbacks fuelling this tendency regularly appeared and were avidly read, especially when written by charismatic icons of the day, whether home grown or imported from the United States. Subjects like the ministry of healing, deliverance ministry, prophecy and some of the more spectacular gifts of the Spirit seemed to encourage some immature and unqualified people to seek the exercise of such gifts under the wrong circumstances, sometimes with regrettable, if not tragic, results. Many breakaway factions arose, leading to a proliferation of independent 'house churches', which were usually led by strong characters unable or unwilling to accept authorised leadership, or who saw themselves as amongst the Lord's specially anointed. Many appeared to be non-Anglicans who, attracted by the manifestation of new spiritual life, had attached themselves to an Anglican church, but never understood or complied with the required order and discipline. Such a group separated itself from St. Michael-le-Belfrey. It eventually dawned on me that, just as much as the institutional church needs the fullness of God's Spirit, so those 'filled with the Spirit' need the discipline, order and constraint of the institution. The institution without the Spirit is dead. The activities of some charismatic Christians without appropriate, orthodox biblical oversight can be dangerous.

In 1974, following the fashion, we sought to get committed people to join us, so that we might be able to operate as a community. What we did not know was that it was not simply a matter of inviting people to come along and join the party, but that relationships needed much in the way of healing and preparing by the Holy Spirit, before they could be concerned with much more than the personal problems of individual members. Apart from the fact that 'communities' tended to attract a few folk who were quite inadequate for the demands such a lifestyle made upon them, there were inevitably problems of leadership. The leaders were usually socially and financially stable, and by the nature of things were asking from others, less secure, a degree of submission that they themselves did not have to make. Many so-called 'charismatic' communities were short-lived, or constantly needed to change their emphasis and role; there was much coming and going, especially when individuals thought their particular 'up-front' gifts were not being used. One of the most successful and effective communities was Post Green, although doubtless they had their problems too. A member, Jeanne Hinton, who had fine leadership and journalistic aptitudes, related how she had problems in the beginning and that it took her a while to accept that setting out the chairs for a meeting was an important service in itself, the point being that the leader must be as one who serves. During my theological student days I was part of a small group that was sent on an exchange visit to the anglo-catholic College of the Resurrection at Mirfield. On the Sunday, after High Mass in the Community church, we were all invited to lunch with the Mirfield Fathers. One of our number, trying to make conversation, asked one of them if he liked living in community. The old boy replied, "The community is fine, it's the people I can't stand!" I remember, too, on an occasion when I was part of a large, mainly Roman Catholic, conference, having sisters share with me the problems they had relating to each other within their community. If the professionals find it difficult, let amateurs beware!

Our attempt at 'community' was short lived. It could not work—in George Orwell's 'Animal Farm' fashion, 'All pigs are equal, but some are more equal than others!' —and, through it, we came to the conclusion that it was quite impractical for a situation like ours. We were joined, first, by Rosemary Humphries, a member of the Post Green community, who

119

wanted a change of scene, before going overseas. She had already been through the community mill and was very mature and resilient when problems arose. She was a great help to us, and was happy to share in the chores of running a conference centre. Her previous experience apparently helped her to tolerate my/our idiosyncrasies more easily and, as she was not with us on a permanent basis, I think she welcomed the free and easy style of Lamplugh, in between the hectic periods of serving the visitors. There was no doubt that her experience helped us through other difficulties that were to arise later. She was with us for almost a year before going to work in Israel at a conference centre on Mount Carmel.

Mark and Frances Simons, with their small son Joseph, joined us in October of that year, overlapping with Rosemary's time at Lamplugh. Mark was a gifted biblical expositor and teacher, who had led members of his parish, where he was priest-in-charge, into the renewal experience, and it seemed that there was a leading for them to come to Lamplugh. Because Mark was a licensed clergyman we had to negotiate with the York diocesan authorities once more, and they agreed to the arrangement, provided that Mark was paid and housed on the same basis as any other diocesan clergyman. This meant that we had to pay a stipend at the diocesan scale, and provide living accommodation rent-free. It seemed right at the time to go forward on this basis. Like so many other ventures, we believed that if it were of God, the means would be provided. I was aware of the drain on the finances represented by the stipend, especially during the winter, when bookings were lighter than the rest of the year. Morris Maddocks, the Bishop of Selby, another suffragan of the huge diocese of York, was himself involved in the healing ministry, and sympathetic towards what we were doing at Lamplugh. He helpfully suggested that Mark become priest-in-charge of Sherburn, about seven miles away, on a part time basis, whilst still remaining involved with Lamplugh House. There was a house available of course, and the financial obligation on our part was considerably reduced. In March, Mark and Frances moved to Sherburn. The new arrangement worked well for a while, until increasing calls from Lamplugh clashed with Mark's developing parochial commitment. Eventually, Mark's parochial appointment became full-time, and a few years later he became Vicar of Driffield.

Margaret and I had our own substantial roles already fully set out; indeed, we had grown into them from the beginning and they were clear and obvious. I was occupied with the administrative and financial side, for which I had an aptitude, and Margaret was involved in the domestic side of running the centre. Our efficiency in these areas had come through necessity and hard work. Some of the others who came along to help at different times seemed to find it a threat that we seemed to 'have it all together', and were frustrated if we rejected some suggestions they made as to how we should do things. The fact was we had already tried them, or we knew the reason why they were totally impractical!

In charismatic circles, when things go pear-shaped it is often the practice to suggest that the Lord has set it all up in order that we may learn from the experience, rather than admit to human error! That is a form of spiritual conceit which we were to meet again and again over the following years. We made mistakes, and discovered that not every decision we made was really of the Holy Spirit, but that some came from our own human aspirations, as well as a few wrong ideas we had picked up on certain courses. If we do not learn from our mistakes, then we are indeed foolish. I believe God is gracious, and when we admit our errors he forgives us, changes situations and changes us. We may be filled with the Spirit and open to his leading, but we still remain human, and the 'flesh' is still at work in us. The fleshly way forward may sometimes seem harmless, but it is not the way to do the work of God's kingdom.

An illustration of doing the 'fleshly' thing is found in Genesis chapter eleven, where we read the account of the building of the Tower of Babel: what a wonderful example of building and developing a sense of community and creativity

—it all appears so human and understandable. However, in that passage there is no word from the Lord. All that popular activity was not what the Lord told them to do. What had happened? They built something out of accord with God's purpose. The end result was confusion, and they were scattered abroad. In the story of the Tower of Babel can be identified much of our contemporary church life and activity, whatever 'brand name' we carry. So much is of man's devising and does not, in the doing of, it establish the kingdom of God, because it is not in his will and purpose. It gets no blessing because it is not engaged in God's business, and it is not what the Lord tells us to do. It may be fun, but it is a waste of time.

In the summer of 1974 a young couple with a 'Youth With a Mission' background, Robin and Sue Kitchen, joined us. At the time they came we were lent a decent sized mobile home that was placed close to the house, and they were able to live in it. We enjoyed their help and fellowship, until the following year when they left, as their first child was on the way and it was no longer realistic for them to stay.

Many good things were happening during this period. More and more people attended our renewal teaching days and conferences; not only were many people as individuals being blessed and encouraged, small groups from churches were strengthened and encouraged for their role in their parishes. We saw many instances of how the Holy Spirit can change lives and lift burdens from people. Some were healed of sickness, through prayer ministry and laying on of hands. Several medical practitioners—doctors and nurses—attended our conferences, sometimes themselves receiving ministry. There were a few spectacular cases of apparently instant healing. Most were in the area of the psychosomatic, where the release or healing of deep-seated inner needs was met through spiritual counselling and ministry.

We learned, too, of the reality of evil, and at times had to minister to individuals perceived to be dominated by evil spirits. After an instance of a young woman suddenly going into a convulsive state during a quiet time of worship one morning, and mouthing obscenities and strange noises, apparently beyond her control, we were thrown in at the deep end. Having heard the theory of it from experts, we were suddenly faced with the need to exercise a deliverance ministry. Without going into detail, it was an alarming and salutary experience, but eventually the spirit—whatever it was—was bound or quietened. I discovered that the person in question was under sustained ministry in her own church, but was obviously still troubled. It is not a ministry for amateurs to undertake, and enthusiasm is not enough, but this experience helped us. From it, we learned a valuable lesson: that, through simple prayer and command, we had the power, through the invocation of the Holy Spirit, to 'bind' such manifestations from taking place, in accordance with Scripture. It may sound very simplistic, but, believe me, it works. After this experience, prayer for cleansing and protection from evil was as important a part of the routine as cooking the meals and preparing the rooms.

We discovered that Lamplugh House was a special place in God's scheme of things, and guests recognised an atmosphere of peace and God's presence there. Over the years we were given many prophecies (inspired words from God through an individual). Margaret produced the following from the pages of her Bible, that had been given to her, years ago, by a guest:

I love this house, I have placed my Spirit over it, and many shall be blessed. I have chosen this place, and my Spirit is upon it. It shall be used in might and power, to my glory. I love it and have anointed it for my Father's glory.

It might be said that such productions are not necessarily words from God but are simply benevolent fantasy, but let cynics, sceptics and liberal unbelievers dismiss such words as they may, it proved to be the reality of what God was doing in those days. After over thirty years of growth and development, a powerful, Spirit-filled ministry, is still happening there today. The emphasis now placed by the current leadership at Lamplugh House is on revival as well as renewal, and I have no problem with that. There is so much of a corpse-like quality in contemporary church life. The term 'revival' suggests bringing new life out of death —and Jesus said, "I have come that they may have life, and have it to the full.[3] Do we not long to see that new life released in more and more people? It is not possible to achieve it in our own *human* strength, but Jesus Christ can do it. He is indeed bringing life —where people are set free of the bondage of 'churchianity' —the easygoing, undemanding substitute for the real thing—that so widely passes for Christianity today.

Notes
[1] Romans 8:15b.
[2] See Romans 8:17 and Galatians 4:1–9.
[3] John 10:10b.

Seven

'Who Dares Wins!'

The problem of our own personal housing still remained, and was becoming increasingly difficult for us, not least for the restrictions it placed on our daughters. Susan was seventeen and Jane fifteen, and now into important exams, and they were quite fed up with not having rooms to call their own, as they often had to vacate them to accommodate guests. They had been very good about it, and entered fully into what we were doing. They also enjoyed taking part in the youth weekends we arranged, and would encourage their school friends to come to them. I still had the idea that one day the stable block could be converted into living accommodation. Though we were now free of debt on all the initial structural work and equipping of the centre, it would be an expensive item, and whilst the house remained as the legal parsonage house we would be unwise to attempt it. My growing vision of what Lamplugh might become was very strong, and I was confident that it would eventually be realised. However, at that time my vision was tied to the parish of Thwing and the local church. In the end it was not to be so restricted, but God's plan worked out slowly over several years.

People who have visited Thwing may remember the white house by the church at the end of the footpath from Lamplugh House. Laburnum Cottage had recently been enlarged and had four bedrooms and all the requirements for a parsonage house. When it came up for sale, I approached the York Parsonage Board and asked that it might be bought for a new rectory for Thwing. I suggested they sell the old rectory, i.e. Lamplugh House, to a trustee body that we would set up, so that there would be no financial burden on the diocese. I also suggested that if part of my stipend was provided by Lamplugh House this might fulfil the financial needs which justified the hoped for pastoral re-organisation of the surrounding parishes. On the surface it seemed to be an ideal solution to the future of the parish, of Lamplugh House, and the role of a resident parish priest. It was an exciting possibility. The archdeacon examined Laburnum Cottage and could not fault it in any way. The vendors had already had an offer for the house but gave us first refusal for a limited time, so I asked if the Board would treat it urgently. (In the 1960s I had served on a diocesan parsonage board, and I knew that there could always be flexibility, and the officials, where necessary, could anticipate decisions). We waited for a reply, and time went on until the vendor's time limit expired and the house was sold. When I look back now in the light of what eventually followed, I realise that the fact that we were not helped at that point set the scene for the eventual change of the basis and direction of Lamplugh House ministry from being Anglican to broadly non-denominational. Perhaps it was God's will —he proves again and again that he will not allow the purposes of the Holy Spirit to be obstructed, and he will bypass the institutional church when it fails to move in his will. I believed that this latest obstruction was in fact due to spiritual opposition. It is fact that when the Holy Spirit is seen to be active, spirits of an unholy nature are stirred into activity, and seek to thwart God's purposes. I am not speaking of any human individual here. As Paul teaches us, our battle is not against flesh and blood.

In 1975, among the growing numbers affected by the renewal now spreading across all denominations, and especially in the Church of England, there was tremendous optimism, and the hope that through this we were going to see revival over the whole nation in our time! Alas, it was a forlorn hope. True to its historical nature and practice in the past, where Holy Spirit led movements have taken place the church as an institution failed to respond. Consequently, apart from a few notable parishes throughout the country, the renewal, if not rejected completely, has been nudged into limited prayer groups in some parishes, but is not allowed to affect the way the church operates. Now the main activity of renewed and flourishing Christian faith is to be found mainly in the House Church movement and other independent churches. It is a bitter disappointment to thousands who have grown up in, been loyal to, and loved the Anglican ethos. We accept that, in time, the work of the kingdom of God will go forward, whilst leaving pretentious but apostate religious organisations by the wayside.

My immediate (and spiritually suspect) reaction to the failure to get the house was of anger and resentment, and I determined that I would hang on to the freehold of the parish forever and let them pastorally re-organise the world around us, but they would get Thwing only over my dead body! However, it was not such a disaster as at first thought. The people who had bought Laburnum Cottage had been temporarily renting Pear Tree Farm, two or three hundred yards away, facing the other side of the church. The Burdass family had recently purchased the farm, on the death of the previous owner, but the farmhouse itself was surplus to their needs for the time being. They nobly came to our rescue and offered to rent it to us. It was an attractive, Georgian house, with three bedrooms and a long, low living/dining room, carpeted, curtained and partly furnished. In fact, it was so furnished that, with the addition of what was left of our own original furniture, it was completely adequate for our needs as a family —further confirmation that God provides all our needs when we commit ourselves to him.

I had to get permission for us to live there. I forget whom I approached in York in the first instance, but I pointed out the inadequacy of our living facilities, and that they did not comply with the diocesan standards. I was using the small print of the rules and regulations that had often been used against us in previous dealings. This was quite a cheek on my part, of course, as I was the one who had initiated the changes in the first place. However, what is sauce for the goose is sauce for the gander! But we did have friends around the various committees and, to my amazement and delight, not only did they give permission for us to live at Pear Tree Farm, but also they would pay the rent, in view of the fact that they had agreed to the changes in the official parsonage house that had restricted our living facilities!

We moved in to the farmhouse in late January 1975. It was wonderful; we were no longer living 'over the shop', and no more did we need to vacate our own beds for guests. The girls each had a nice big room to themselves, able to contain their own things together, and we were able to have a normal family life, which had been curtailed for three years. We spent an enjoyable three years in Pear Tree Farm: it was without doubt God's provision, and we were very grateful to the Burdass family for making it available to us. Over this period we had a succession of resident helpers who had a room at Lamplugh, so there was always a responsible person there when the house was full of guests.

By this time I was being invited to go and speak on renewal, in parishes, meetings and clergy chapters. My irrational fear of public speaking had been cured in a remarkable way in 1974. In August of that year, the annual Methodist 'Wesley Day' was to be held in Driffield; the theme was renewal. I was invited to speak on 'Renewal in Rural Areas'. There were two other speakers, one of whom was David Watson, who was to follow me and speak about 'Renewal in Urban Areas'. I was aghast at the thought of sharing a platform with David Watson of all people, the most outstanding leader in renewal in the whole country, with the evidence of his own parish to illustrate it! Apart from my firmly established feeling of inadequacy, what could I say? There had been no renewal evident in my two churches, though of course I knew what it was all about in theory. I worried and prayed for weeks about this dreaded assignment. I prepared notes, giving a personal testimony of how it had become real to me, and how we had been led by the Holy Spirit to set up Lamplugh House as a centre to encourage renewal, and how people were coming and receiving blessing from the ministry there.

When my turn came to speak, I nervously clutched my notes, wishing the ground would swallow me up! I started off, haltingly, and then I physically felt the Spirit come upon me and I spoke without my notes and far exceeded the time allocated to me. Most of what I said was unplanned, but it was well received. I realised afterwards that I had experienced for the first time an 'anointing' of the Holy Spirit for that particular task. From that moment I was freed from my irrational fear, and I became confident to go out to speak and teach, and expect that God would reach people's hearts and minds —not by human ability or cleverness, nor by manipulation, for it is:

'Not by might, nor by power, but by my Spirit,' says the LORD Almighty.[1]

It was the beginning of a teaching ministry that came to its fullness during the 1980s. It was not by my devising; it was by God's calling and enabling that it happened. There is a boldness which is one of the gifts of the Spirit —gifts that are given for ministry in God's power, not in our own strength.

Another immediate benefit of our moving to Pear Tree Farm was that we were able to convert our former upstairs living room into two more bedrooms, thus accommodating four more beds. However, at times we were still in the position of not having enough beds, when we had to improvise. In September, Susan had gone to Lancaster University, and soon Jane went to a commercial college in York, so that during term time we were able to put guests in their bedrooms at Pear Tree. Although we had been adequately re-housed for the time being, I still had to plan for the future, and everything depended upon our doing a deal with the church authorities to purchase the property —and still we were faced with opposition. Donald Coggan, who had been so favourably disposed towards us, had now moved on to Canterbury, and in 1975 Stuart Blanch was made Archbishop of York. It was a case of there arising a pharaoh who knew not Joseph! and I could not decently approach the Archbishop about the problem until he had settled in and had become familiar with his new responsibilities, so I left it until 1976.

I devised a change of tactics, and instead of directly approaching the Archbishop, over the heads of the people in between, I decided to approach the patron of the living. It was a Crown living, administered by the Lord Chancellor, who had previously given permission in 1971 for us to utilise the rectory for its new purpose. I wrote to Colonel Salmon, the Crown Appointments Secretary, at 10 Downing Street, briefly explaining our dilemma. Consequently, I was invited to go to London and see him personally. Off I went by train, thinking to myself "the places I get to!" I felt very important walking along Downing Street, being greeted by the policeman outside the famous door. With no apparent signal, the door opened. The porter greeted me by name and I was taken inside— through the hall familiar from television pictures, where important people are photographed in front of the fireplace (not me, I must add!) and on, past the staircase with all the pictures of prime ministers on the wall, to a lift. There, at the very top of the building, in a small attic room with a sloping roof, I met Colonel Salmon, seated at his large desk!

He was very friendly, and showed a great interest in my story of how things had developed since 1971. He indicated immediately that he thought it was a great idea to make use of the rectory in such a way, and complimented me on the initiatives that had been taken. He indicated also that he was not too keen on all the modern developments, whereby dioceses were whittling down patronage with their re-organisation measures. I explained that we needed to expand but were limited by the legal restrictions on the property. I told him that if I should leave or die, or whatever, all the money and effort would have been wasted and the diocese would simply dispose of the house. He recognised our need for freedom in this respect, and said that he would write to both the Archdeacon of the East Riding and the new Archbishop of York, recommending that we be allowed to buy the property. At the same time he advised me to make a formal request to the Archbishop. He led me back down to the front door, saying that as yet he had seen nothing of James Callaghan, the recently installed incumbent of No. 10. I went back home feeling that my trip had been very worthwhile.

The following week, that particular (some would say peculiar) Anglican event, the Archdeacon's Visitation took place. All beneficed and licensed clergy and churchwardens in the deanery are summoned to attend. If, for some reason, anyone could not attend in their own deanery meeting, they must inform the archdeacon and arrange to attend another nearby. Unable to attend as directed, I duly wrote to the arch-deacon, who in his reply said that he had received a letter from Colonel Salmon about the rectory, indicating 'his concern that my pastoral responsibilities might be suffering as a result of my involvement with Lamplugh House'. From my talk with Colonel Salmon I knew that we had discussed my pastoral work in a positive manner, and I had explained that at present I was able to cope. However, I assured him that as soon as I was unable to deal with it satisfactorily, then other arrangements would need to be made (which in fact they were, in due course.) I was so disturbed at this inter-pretation that I wrote to the archdeacon, pointing out that he had the opportunity at his Visitation to question my churchwardens, and I offered to resign if he found that my pastoral responsibilities were suffering due to my involve-ment with Lamplugh. I felt that the widespread spiritual in-fluence through our ministry, and the support of my parish-ioners, fully justified my dual role. Nothing more was said of the matter. Colonel Salmon's letters elicited a positive response from the Archbishop, who advised the board to be sympathetic to our request, and that was quickly followed by official approval. We were directed to get an independent valuation of the property. On the recommendation of John Burdass we invited a Driffield auctioneer and estate agent to make a valuation. We were well known in Driffield and the surrounding area, where all the farmers, their relatives and friends formed a very efficient information network, which would put the modern internet into the shade! Many were aware of the struggles we had experienced and we had much support and recognition, if only as a venture seeking to preserve something of their traditional way of life. The valuation was very much in our favour: £6000 for the rectory, and I think £3000 or £4000 for the ten acres of land. The bank immediately promised us a mortgage, with the deeds as security.

The original debt had gone, and we were still getting income from the original covenants and new ones, together with a steady flow of gifts and donations, so that the mortgage loan was being constantly reduced. We were able to use the facility again later, as we began to engage upon various developments and extensions over the next five years. First, we added two further twin bedrooms over a one-storey adjunct to the kitchen and pantry area. This was not too expensive and the rooms were of a high standard. This addition was finished early in 1977. Then we started on the long desired conversion of the stable block into a warden's house, work on which commenced in the summer.

Another important event in 1977 was the appointment of a new Bishop of Hull, Geoffrey Paul, who came to his new job straight from Lee Abbey, North Devon, where he had been warden. He was immediately interested in Lamplugh House; he came to see us and look round, and was very positive and helpful. He had also had contact through Lee Abbey with the renewal movement. The previous Bishop, Hubert Higgs, had shown no interest in Lamplugh House and had left everything to the archdeacon.

After the years of struggle, by the grace of God, we had won. Our efforts were justified by the spiritual effect which was emerging through our conference ministry. It worked — the original vision we had for Lamplugh House was being realised and further developed. There was abundant evidence that, through it, the Holy Spirit was bringing new life, new hope and new encouragement, not only to Anglicans, but also to Christians of many denominations all over the country. I still held the freehold of the living, so that my stipend as the incumbent was paid by the church, thus indirectly helping the finances, and I was determined to leave it that way for as long as possible. The co-operative attitude of our new area bishop put a positive emphasis on our relations with the authorities. Geoffrey Paul, with his experience of running a spiritual teaching centre, gave us good and useful advice as we sought to make further progress, now that we were free to do so.

The decision to proceed with the stable block conversion was not before time, since the Burdass family indicated that they could do with having Pear Tree Farm back in early 1978 as their shepherd was to be married and they needed a house for him. How favourably everything was now working out for us, though seven years had provided—again and again— instances of 'over the circumstances!' We praised God for the way that he led us and overruled 'principalities and powers'.

Kenneth Nelson, Rector of Crayke, and his wife Jean, with whom I had been involved with the Post Green leadership training courses, was due to retire at the end of 1977, and approached us with a view to moving to our area, so that they might be involved with us in the ministry. Eventually they were able to buy a house in nearby Wold Newton, and moved into it about the same time that we moved into the newly completed warden's cottage. I was finding it a burden now, looking after two parishes, and the Archbishop of York agreed that Kenneth could be licensed as non-stipendary priest-in-charge, to look after Wold Newton on my behalf. This was a great boon all the way round. The parishioners were happy to have a resident clergyman and wife in their midst, and it worked extremely well for the three years they were there. For the first year or so, Jean helped Margaret and Joyce in the running of the domestic affairs, and she and Kenneth became involved in ministry to guests from time to time. Jean was very artistic and made lots of ornamental bits and pieces to sell on the bookstall to help funds. However, her great work of art was two large collages, 'I will make you Fishers of Men' and, 'Go into all the World' —they were very fine in detail and imagination, the latter incorporating well-known buildings and world structures from Yorkshire to the ends of the world, including the new Humber Bridge. They were framed, and eventually hung in the new chapel we built in 1982. I am glad to say they are still on display at Lamplugh House under its current regime.

The novelty, if not the enthusiasm, of renewal was now wearing thin. There had been many horror stories and caricatures of 'charismatics' in the tabloid press and on television programmes, usually anchoring on some extreme statements and actions by individuals, or on division caused in congregations between those who found comfort in the traditional, easy-going, non-challenging Anglicanism in which they had invested their hopes, and the newly renewed enthusiasts who wanted to see their churches revived with apostolic zeal and efficacy. Aspects of renewal caused alarm in some areas, particularly the gift of tongues; though clearly scriptural, it did not appeal to all rational Anglican minds. It is, above all, a new language for prayer, and at the same time demonstrates how God transcends the limits set by purely human abilities and rationality. Traditional anglo-catholics attempted to dismiss renewal as an aberration of the evangelicals, and traditional evangelicals would write it off as 'second blessing' error. This reaction was not new to the Church of England. In the eighteenth century, 'enthusiasm' was the great bugbear, and even though we remember that by enthusiasm they meant what we would now call fanaticism, it is significant. Bishop Joseph Butler is reported to have said to John Wesley that what he termed 'pretending to extraordinary revelation and gifts of the Holy Ghost' was 'a horrid thing, a very horrid thing'.

Renewal was taking place in denominations across the world, and notably in the Roman Catholic Church. It is significant that before the convening of the Second Vatican Council, Pope John XXIII prayed, 'Lord, renew your wonders in this our day and give us a new Pentecost.' John Gunstone quotes from a sermon given by the Pope in 1975 in St. Peter's during the 1975 Holy Year, mainly to Catholics involved in spiritual renewal, in which the Pope invites hearers to reflect on the terms 'spiritual' and 'renewal', saying: "Where the *Spirit* is concerned we are immediately alert, immediately happy to welcome the coming of the Holy Spirit. More than that, we invite him, we pray to him, we desire nothing more than that Christians, believing people, should experience an awareness, a worship, a greater joy through the Spirit of God among us. Have we forgotten the Holy Spirit? Certainly not! We want him, we honour him, and we love him, and invoke him. And you, with your devotion and fervour, you wish to live in this Spirit. This should be where your second name comes in —*renewal*. It ought to rejuvenate the world, give it back a spirituality, a soul, and religious thought. It ought to open closed lips to prayer and open its closed mouth to song, to joy, to hymns, and to witnessing. It will be very fortuitous for our times, for our brothers, that there should be a generation, a generation of young people, who shout out to the world the glory and the greatness of the God of Pentecost!"[2]

How far such a welcome was from the disparaging term 'happy clappies' that was beginning to be used by some. There was no similar encouragement forthcoming from the higher echelons of the Church of England at that time, and the renewal was neither acknowledged nor even mentioned in the General Synod until three years later!

Our experience over five years, through the many conferences, churches and groups with which we had been in contact, helped me to try to ascertain the reasons for the apparent rejection of the message of renewal, despite its acceptance in a growing number of parishes around the country. So far as I could see there was nothing unscriptural in renewal teaching; much of its teaching now made sense of the extraordinary dynamic which the church can show when it allows the Holy Spirit to lead. I could find nothing in Anglican formularies which denied that we must seek the Spirit's power and guidance. We are a church founded on Scripture as the word of God. We affirm at every Eucharist that we believe in, 'the Holy Spirit, the Lord and giver of life'; we say we believe in 'One, Holy, Catholic and Apostolic Church' — and the concept of being 'apostolic' is determinative of the whole of that statement. Many Anglicans love to argue that apostolic succession preserves the true character of the church, simply by the laying-on-of-hands by certain bishops on certain heads over the generations. This is not so. It matters not who lays hands on whom. If the apostolic faith is not there, if the apostolic life and witness is not present, you do not have an apostolic church. It is so strange that Anglicans have *talked* for centuries about apostolic order, and our apostolic faith, and we fancy that we have that (and we *do* in the creeds); and that this is an objective truth which we *say* we believe. We have talked so much about Apostolic Succession, but so little of apostolic success! —the reason being that, for the most part, we have so little of apostolic experience.

It was now clear to me that the renewal movement was bringing apostolic *experience* not only to individuals in their personal lives, but also to the corporate life of churches at local level, with amazing results. Renewed Anglicans were experiencing the power and love of God existentially, not just in theory, and this new dimension of awareness of the Holy Spirit's power was reviving and invigorating Christian life and witness. The love of God was not only breaking down barriers in relationships within congregations but was drawing new people to Christ and to the church because of its reality and attraction, and with it came a new joy in worship and praise. Many traditionally stuffy Anglicans whose religion was a private matter would dismiss the joy of this worship and praise as 'emotionalism'. I think it was Cuthbert Bardsley, a former Bishop of Coventry, who sardonically remarked, "Delirious emotionalism is not the besetting fault of the Church of England." Display of emotion was disapproved of, being considered neither English nor Anglican, especially within the context of worship. Curiously, however, it seems to be acceptable at football matches or other sporting events!

Over the centuries, Anglicanism has instilled more stoicism than essential Christianity into the British character, with its stiff upper lip sense of teeth-gritting duty and service by human effort. The major problem, without doubt, was the *culture* of renewal. This dimension of experience had inevitably been influenced by the Pentecostalists, who were the first in recent times to respond to this revelation of Christian truth. It was inevitable, therefore, that people of other traditions initially associated themselves with a similar cultural pattern. At the same time I was aware that many people were put off renewal by the overzealous behaviour of some, whose new experience, not properly received or understood, caused them to try to convert their fellow church members in an arrogant and overbearing manner. They had zeal to 'change' people, rather than to love them. I would often say that God is telling us to love people and he will change them! The biggest obstacle to the spread of renewal in the Church of England was indeed the cultural one. The demonstrative worship, raising or clapping hands, to say nothing of liturgical dance at rallies and sometimes in the more 'turned on' churches, though scriptural, was perceived as being 'not Anglican!' Sadly, the feeling of some people was 'let the Pentecostals and the Caribbean Christians do as they wish, but our idea of God is English!' Even if dignity is thought to be close to godliness, like cleanliness, it is no substitute!

Other major denominations, the Roman Catholics, the Methodists and the United Reformed Church, each had established 'renewal service' committees for their respective churches, in order to relate this new dimension to their own culture and perspective. I was now fully convinced that we needed something similar in the Church of England. It was essential for renewal teaching to be directed within Anglican parameters if we were to avoid misunderstandings, indiscipline and division in the church. We were not to be narrowly denominational, for in fact renewal was revealing a deep basic unity between all Spirit-filled Christians, quite unknown before. I was convinced that what we were learning and experiencing was for all Christians; that it was truly biblical, and not contrary to what we were supposed to believe anyway. As Anglicans, it was for us to seek to re-discover our own heritage.

The Fountain Trust, a non-denominational body, was the leading agency in the United Kingdom for the furtherance of renewal, which it did to great effect, through conferences, meetings, books and teaching materials. Pioneered by Michael Harper in the 1960s, it was now directed by Tom Smail, a gifted theologian and a minister of the Church of Scotland. It was doing excellent work, inspiring people of all denominations, but by the nature of things, mostly Anglicans. I could not imagine an independent Anglican service committee, and I wondered if now was the time for the Fountain Trust to widen its scope and tackle this cultural problem that I perceived existed. I approached Tom Smail and put my thoughts to him. Tom was not keen on the idea and I accepted his reasoning. The vision for Fountain Trust had always been for the whole church, and it witnessed to the essential unity in Christ that was manifested when the Holy Spirit fell upon dry and needy members of all denominations. The huge and popular national and international conferences witnessed to this, and a real unity of purpose was being seen at local level in many places entirely due to the ministry of the Fountain Trust. Big rallies would sometimes be held in cathedrals, sometimes rather grudgingly, if the Dean and officials did not like the renewal movement and would not themselves be seen to be involved in any way. Recently, I was reminded by Tom Smail of an amusing incident when the Fountain Trust had a three-day happening in York. It commenced with a large rally in the Minster. At the start of the proceedings, the Canon-on-duty that evening, gave an impromptu and apparently slightly embarrassed welcome, saying, "We all welcome and recognise that Fountain Trust has added colour and light to the work of the Holy Spirit!" —and made a hasty retreat.

Despite Tom's reservations about my suggestion, the problem still remained, and the encouragement of renewal was being rejected in many areas because of ignorance and prejudice. The development of my concern on this issue now influenced the content of our teaching at Lamplugh House conferences and meetings, and I was determined to try and encourage people, especially fellow Anglicans, to work prayerfully, carefully and lovingly, within their home fellowships and congregations. Many individuals were tempted to leave their own church for another which seemed to have more life and spirit about it, and consequently, they hoped, the going might be less tough. In those days we would say to such people, "God wants you to grow where you are planted", or, "if God has blessed you, that blessing is for others, not least for your local church." Many renewed people who were in dry and unresponsive churches would attach themselves to inter-denominational prayer groups for fellowship and encouragement, whilst maintaining a quiet role in their own church.

I had much sympathy for many clergy who had come into the fullness of the Holy Spirit and now had difficulty facing the flak from the opposition when they tried to apply the consequences of their experience in their pastoral role. Hidebound traditionalists can be very difficult indeed. Some took the less problematic way of compromise, trying to cater for all requirements, one way or another. Some churches developed into two or even three separate congregations, each following their own spirituality, whether Book of Common Prayer, Series Three or less formal charismatic style. The stronger characters, however, persisted with a single mind and were to lead their people forward, so there emerged many parishes throughout the land which became totally committed to the principles of renewal and remain, to this day, examples of what the Church of England might still become. Usually they are the strongest and most dynamic in the diocese and have little difficulty paying their financial dues —in itself most impressive to the powers-that-be!

Most of 1978 was a very busy year. We were now confident that Lamplugh House was really on the scene, and we were being used by all kinds of people for their own private conferences alongside our own teaching programme. The ecumenical nature of these visits was extremely wide. Ampleforth College, the Roman Catholic public school near York, held an annual retreat for about twenty pupils, conducted by a member of staff. We received Methodists, Baptists, and groups of mixed denomination. A Lutheran Church from Hamburg spent two weeks with us in the summer. (Later another came from Dortmund.) Our previous experience with Anglo-German youth exchanges proved to be invaluable for this occasion. Several student groups from various colleges and universities came. St. Michael-le-Belfrey helped keep us busy, but that church had grown to the extent that Lamplugh House was not big enough for them, other than for smaller groups within their fellowship.

The fact that we were now decently housed in the new warden's cottage, and we had excellent help from Kenneth and Jean Nelson, both in the house and in the parishes, together with other helpers, gave us the feeling that the main struggles were over and that events had justified this huge venture of faith. Almost full use of the house ensured a regular income, so that the finances were in good shape and we were fast reducing the mortgage with which the property had been purchased. We had established the Lamplugh House Trust on lines approved by the Charity Commissioners for England, and the property was now independent of the church authorities. The Charity Commissioners, instead of diocesan officials or committees, would approve future developments.

Following the concentrated hard work of the summer holiday period, we were exhausted and needed a holiday ourselves. We had made no plans for a holiday but, as there was now a break in the bookings during September, we found an opportunity. Looking for peace and quiet and relaxation, we answered an advert that had appeared in *Renewal* magazine. It was for a self-catering holiday cottage in Aberdeenshire, especially for people involved in Christian ministry. Because we had seen it in *Renewal* we knew it came from people sympathetic to the renewal movement, and so we booked. We were able to go on Saturday 9th September, as the last summer group was leaving that morning. We drove the long journey to Netherdale House, between Huntly and Turriff. It was a large country house with an extensive estate on which the cottage was situated, in beautiful countryside bordering the River Devoran. There we met for the first time Colin and Anne Oliphant and their two small children, Jane and Hamish. This meeting was to be of great significance to our future work at Lamplugh House. It was, indeed, arranged by the Lord. The Oliphants had come into the renewal through the ministry of Jean Darnell, whom I had met during the Post Green leadership courses in the early 1970s. They were attached to the Scottish Churches Renewal Fellowship for the North Eastern area, and were actively involved in their nearest Scottish Episcopal church in Huntly. In the course of their spiritual pilgrimage, they had committed themselves and their resources to the service of God. That year, they had been led to make this cottage on the estate available for such as we were at the time: worn out Christian workers in need of rest and relaxation.

Oliphant is a Scottish name, but Colin hailed from Liverpool, where his late father, a director of Tate & Lyle, had in fact been a member of the Council of my old theological college, St. Aidan's, Birkenhead, when Colin himself was a young boy! Another link was Bishop Eric Treacy, a family friend, whom we had known in earlier years as Archdeacon of Halifax. The latter had been a frequent visitor to Netherdale, and had baptised both their children. Colin had trained in the legal profession, and was a partner in a firm of solicitors in Huntly, though he shortly gave that up and worked very hard on the estate, presumably as his own manager.

It seems that we were only the second people to use the cottage in its new role. The occupants the week before, there on honeymoon, had been one of the daughters of our Bishop of Hull (Geoffrey Paul) and her new husband. We enjoyed the two bottles of wine they had left in the fridge! We had an excellent holiday and enjoyed the fellowship and company of Anne and Colin. They took us to their church in Huntly, and we heard from them the familiar tale of woe: of how people were so set in their ways and resistant to any attempt to liven the services or to seek a deeper experience of God. However, as all over the rest of the country, there were lights of new life flickering here and there, even in the far north of Scotland, and their area Renewal Fellowship arranged meetings and conferences similar to those south of the border. It was the beginning of a long friendship and association with our ministry at Lamplugh House, which developed from that visit.

We met the Oliphants again seven months later, in April 1979. The Scottish Churches Renewal Fellowship, North Eastern group, to which they belonged, was arranging a renewal weekend at Kilvarock Castle near Nairn, overlooking the Moray Firth. It was to have been lead by David Smith, an Aberdonian who had lived in England for many years, whose teaching ministry was based at York, where he was an elder at St. Michael-le-Belfrey. Sadly, David became ill close to the date of the weekend and was unable to attend. Colin Oliphant phoned me and asked if I could suggest a replacement speaker. I suggested some names, but Colin soon phoned back to say that none of them was available and they were becoming desperate. Seeing that our Lamplugh diary was clear that particular weekend, I offered to do it myself if they were happy to scrape the bottom of the barrel. In fact, I had now done several such weekends in different places, talking about the basics to people who were searching, consequently I knew the form for such events. He went and consulted the other organisers, and shortly came back to say they would be relieved to have me!

Margaret went with me, and in due course we made the long journey, first back to Netherdale House, and then the next day, following Colin and Anne, to Kilvarock (pronounced Kilrock). It is a small castle, part of it quite old, belonging to the Rose family (of lime juice fame). The current occupant, Miss Elizabeth Rose, ran it as a Christian conference centre, and several buildings had been erected in the grounds to provide conference facilities. A few people were actually accommodated in the castle itself, including Margaret and myself. We found ourselves in an ancient, stone walled room in the tower, complete with slit-windows and a winding stone staircase to the loo. Sparsely furnished, it contained four beds, one in each corner. It was quite an experience for us, rather cold and draughty, and we could see why Mary, Queen of Scots, had only stayed there for one night! The weekend seemed to go off well and the people were appreciative of my efforts; if they were disappointed not to have David Smith, they did not show it. We both enjoyed the weekend very much, especially seeing the Oliphants again and meeting many new people engaged in the renewal in Scotland. Most of the people taking part in the conference were members of the Church of Scotland; the rest were Anglicans, of the Scottish Episcopal Church. We drove back home from there and stayed the night in Dunkeld, and enjoyed the wonderful scenery on our journey back to East Yorkshire.

Colin and Anne paid a visit to Lamplugh House in October of that year to take part in a teaching conference; they came several times over the next year or so, as there was no similar teaching centre nearer to their home. On that first visit, seeing the place and realising its potential and the progress we had made since its inception, Colin felt moved to associate himself with the ministry, and immediately helped with the removal of outstanding debt. He helped with practical plans to further enlarge the facilities, so that with improved accommodation we could become financially more viable. He became a trustee and was very committed to Lamplugh and its ministry. It seemed clear that God had brought the Oliphants into association with us as part of the grand plan. It was not simply the material help they gave, welcome as that was, but the fact that we were on the same spiritual wavelength, and were enabled to share the same vision of what God was doing. Colin and Anne became a great help with spiritual concerns and major decision-making. It was wonderful to have support like this, so we no longer felt 'out on a limb', dependent upon our own interpretation of God's leading. Their participation ensured we made fewer mistakes where major issues were concerned. Colin was a regular visitor for occasional meetings of the Trustees, so that we now had a confident, wise, articulate and practically minded supporter and close associate in the next stages of the Lamplugh story.

In order to raise money for future developments, we had applied to the Charity Commissioners for permission to sell off most of the ten acres of grassland we had been obliged to purchase with the house and garden. They agreed to this and it was put on the market in two lots at a minimum sale price approved by the Commissioners. We had no problem selling one plot that lay in front of the house, which was more compact and could easily be fenced-off and remain clear of our comings and goings. The larger lot, however, was awkwardly shaped, and nobody was prepared to pay the reserve price for it. Seeing that this particular piece of land might be useful in future years, should other buildings be needed for Lamplugh House, Colin offered to buy it from us, with the provision that the Trust could buy it back from him at any time. Meanwhile, we could use the land, a good part of which was used for car parking. (He did, in fact *give* back the land to the Trust, several years later.) This practicality was typical of Colin; he had become a good friend and I valued his advice and wisdom.

Following the sale of the land, we could now proceed with a long desired improvement. We needed to replace the roof over the part of the second floor that was only loft space. We were able to install five new twin bedrooms with dormer windows, a great improvement, and one of the existing larger second floor rooms, which had served for a short time as a temporary chapel, made a small, enclosed suite of twin bedroom and bathroom, where we would often place speakers, and they could enjoy privacy for preparation. Generally speaking, all the improvements we had made resulted in a high standard of accommodation and facilities, a far cry from the spartan beginnings of 1972. The final development of the property in our time there would take place to mark the tenth anniversary of the opening and dedication of Lamplugh House, in 1982.

Notes
[1] Zechariah 4:6b.
[2] *Pentecostal Anglicans* Hodder & Stoughton 1982, p. 16
© John Gunstone, Used by permission

Eight

Another Canterbury Tale

An event in 1978 was to prove instrumental in the establishment of Anglican Renewal Ministries three years later. It was the international Anglican Renewal Leaders Conference at Canterbury, inspired by the 1975 conference in Rome, and designed to take place immediately before the 1978 Lambeth Conference. This ten-yearly event brings together most of the bishops of the Anglican Communion from all over the world. About thirty overseas bishops came early so that they could participate in this charismatic pre-Lambeth conference scheduled for mid July. I was surprised to receive an invitation to attend. John Gunstone describes the conference thus:

> 360 attended, mostly clergy including 32 bishops; two-thirds of the participants were from overseas. The conference culminated in a lengthy and joyful Eucharist in the choir of Canterbury Cathedral. A memorable moment was caught by the camera as Bill Burnett, then Archbishop of Cape Town, led the bishops in a gentle liturgical dance round the high altar.[1]

Michael Harper wrote an account of the conference

entitled *A New Canterbury Tale*, in which he described the occasion.

> After a Eucharist lasting over three hours, the worshippers walked out of Canterbury Cathedral still praising God. People from nearby public houses came out on to the street to see what was going on. Didn't that also happen at Pentecost? A few bishops were singing just outside the cathedral and were told to be quiet by the gatekeeper. A tourist from the United States was caught up in the service and converted to Christ. Another tourist, like the spectators on the day of Pentecost, amazed at the sound of praise coming from the cathedral, asked the verger what it was about. "It's a Church of England service," the verger replied.
> "It can't be," retorted the tourist, "I'm Church of England. They must be Mormons."
> He could well have said, "They must be drunk."[2]

My invitation to attend the Canterbury conference came as a surprise because it was the first time that such recognition of our ministry had categorised me as 'a leader in renewal'. It did show, however, that our work at Lamplugh House was now becoming widely acknowledged and we were no longer the 'poor relations' in the movement. The dominant renewal activity in Yorkshire was, of course, through David Watson and St. Michael-le-Belfrey, York. That excellent ministry and witness was drawing people from all over the country, indeed other countries too, to see what was going on and what could be learned from it.

The ministry at Lamplugh House was less dramatic and on a lower profile, but was no less the work of God, and part of the renewing wave of the Holy Spirit now touching many lives and churches. I saw this as further evidence of how, by God's grace, we were succeeding 'over the circumstances' of the tenuous struggle we had experienced to see the vision implemented.

The Canterbury conference was a definitive moment for

me because it helped me finally to throw off personal inhibitions about my own inadequacies and to acquire a measure of confidence in my own calling and role within renewal. Nor was I alone in this respect; there were many others there whom the Holy Spirit was using in leadership. Sadly, the Church of England was very short on episcopal representation. Of the thirty two bishops attending, I think there was only one English bishop present, and that was Richard Hare, Bishop of Pontefract. This was a sad reflection on our home team, wary and indecisive as ever, and not wanting to show positive support for a controversial phenomenon still not officially recognised. Despite their reservations, however, most would beam graciously on renewal happenings in their diocese, as long as no one appeared to be 'rocking the boat' too much; but none at that time expressed any real commitment to it. Nevertheless, for the most part, they were able to recognise where the real spiritual life was within their own pastoral areas.

That there was huge spiritual strength and growth in many overseas Anglican circles was abundantly evident, particularly in Africa and Asia. The Anglican Church in South America appeared also to be experiencing new growth, renewal and evangelistic activity; at the same time, many parts of that continent were experiencing rapid growth in the Pentecostal churches, at the expense of the Roman Catholic Church.

Predictably, the Americans had a huge contingent, and the former dominions and colonies were also well represented. There were several outstanding speakers, and what they said was inspiring and encouraging. I was impressed most of all by Charles Irish, the Rector of St. Luke's, Bath, near Akron, Ohio, and the Director of Episcopal Renewal Ministries, which served the whole of the United States. He had a great testimony of how he had come into the fullness of the Holy Spirit through some members of his church youth group, who had themselves received this blessing. Through this, the whole basis and direction of his parochial ministry changed from conventional 'churchianity' to a Spirit-filled, apostolic dynamic. During this transformation, St. Luke's had over-come many problems and difficulties, so that now a huge congregation of Spirit-filled people was moving out in posi-tive ministry and evangelistic activity. Episcopal Renewal Ministries was based at St. Luke's, and members of the church were actively involved in the running of it. Charles "Chuck" Irish and his team conducted conferences and teaching events throughout the United States, to great effect.

Listening to Charles Irish had the effect of reviving my ideas about the need for a similar renewal agency in the Church of England. I was intrigued by the fact that his wider renewal teaching came out of his personal parochial experience. It was at this conference that I first met John Gunstone, and I shared with him my thoughts on this subject. He shared my views and so did several other leaders. It was certainly not intended as a potential threat to Fountain Trust. We all thought that an Anglican renewal service agency might be somehow included within the role of the latter. However, there it rested for a while and we all went home at the end of the conference.

It became evident that Fountain Trust saw any move for an Anglican agency as a threat, particularly as most of its ministry was in fact to Anglicans anyway, though not in terms of the specific role—of relating to the structures—which eventually emerged. Unbeknown to most of us, a change in the Fountain Trust leadership was imminent. Michael Barling replaced Tom Smail as director. Tom became an Anglican and, soon after his reception into the ministry of the Church of England, became vice-principal of St. John's College, Nottingham. John Richards was assistant director from 1977, and overlapped with the new director. All three had admirably led the work of the Trust, and it was evidently flourishing. No one expected that within three years it would close down. As there was no hint of this whatsoever during the Canterbury conference, I suspect there may have been some well-concealed tensions in Fountain Trust at the time.

The Lambeth Conference took place during the following weeks of August, and in due course the official report, no doubt influenced by the bishops who had attended the previous conference, declared:

> We praise God and thank Him for the influence of the renewal movements in the life of the Church today. In recent years we have seen increased instances of parish life being renewed; of individual ministries becoming effective agencies of God's power to heal and to reconcile; of witness to the Christian faith, and of the proclamation of the Gospel with converting power over individuals, communities and institutions. We rejoice at the abundant evidence from many parts of the world that new forms of the Holy Spirit's gifts and fruit are being bestowed to cleanse, sustain, empower, reconcile and build up the body of Christ.[3]

Later in 1978, the General Synod, awoke to the realisation that a movement of the Holy Spirit was occurring in the Church of England, and could no longer be ignored. Consequently, it commissioned a report on renewal in the Church of England. John Gunstone pointed out that it was the first time the Synod had been given an opportunity to air the topic, *sixteen years* after the appearance of the pentecostal movement in the parishes in this country!

Richard Hare, the Bishop of Pontefract, who was first bishop in the Church of England to testify to the blessings of the renewal in his own ministry, said during the debate: "I believe that what we are seeing is the renewal of the Church in the power of the Holy Spirit, and I believe that we are seeing the Lord in our day coming upon the Church in power to restore it, to renew it and, praise his name, unite it.[4]

Heady days! This was considered a breakthrough, and the top leadership could no longer ignore what was happening. Most Anglicans are very conservative, and loyal to the system. The backing of the bishop of the diocese often went a long way to helping ordinary mortals in the pews to accept change, even reluctantly. Despite my own earlier endeavour to heed the psalmist and put not my 'trust in princes', etc., I shared in the general excitement in renewal circles at the way things were progressing. At last, the church seemed to be taking notice.

There had been many people at Canterbury who shared my view that we needed a specifically Anglican renewal agency, but there was no-one who made a concrete suggestion as to how it might be achieved. For several months I constantly thought and prayed over this single issue. As often happens with prayer, sometimes we are called upon to *be* the answer, so I decided to take a lead myself. I wrote to Charles Irish and asked if I might visit him and see something of the work of Episcopal Renewal Ministries in the United States.

In March 1979 I went on a three week visit and headed first to Lexington, Kentucky, where ERM was running a weekend conference for parishes in that area, on the theme of renewal, emphasising that basically it meant re-discovering our heritage as Anglicans (or Episcopalians.) This impressed me very much, and I could immediately see how an adaptation of this programme for English participants could be very productive at home. Notably, Terry Fulham, Rector of St. Paul's Episcopal Church, Darien, Connecticut, where remarkable renewal had happened under his leadership, gave several addresses. Charles Irish also spoke, as well as others on related themes, leading people to baptism in the Holy Spirit. The conference ended with a Eucharist with renewed worship and presided over by the local bishop. These conferences were the main feature of the ministry of ERM and were being held all over the United States to great effect. I attended another one, two weeks later, at the Episcopal Cathedral in Atlanta, Georgia. This followed more or less the same pattern, and I was confirmed in my opinion that we needed something like this in England.

Following the first conference at Lexington, I went back with Charles Irish to his parish of St Luke's, Bath, Ohio, where I stayed for several days, experiencing the life and worship of a parish that really was renewed in the Holy Spirit, with its whole direction and purpose geared to that fact. It was an inspiring, encouraging and informative experience. Before the Atlanta weekend, which brought to an end my visit, I went along with Charles Irish to the national conference of Roman Catholic priests who were associated with renewal in their church. There were at least a thousand of them present at the University of Steubenville, Ohio. Charles had been invited to speak, and also to minister to about forty non-Romans who were also present. The latter included a female Episcopal priest, who stuck out rather in that assembly! In 1979 this was quite a novelty for me, as the issue of women's ordination was still only a distant rumble in the Church of England. There were several bishops present, including the Apostolic Delegate to the United States.

There were several other speakers with Charles Irish, including Fr. John Bertollucci, a fine speaker and preacher, dubbed the 'catholic Billy Graham'. I was very impressed by this conference. As an annual event, many priests obviously found it a great inspiration and it was eagerly anticipated. A particular aspect I noted was the way the people were formed into groups of twelve, each of which would meet once or twice a day, to share informally their members' personal needs and problems. I saw what a benefit it was, for not only did it ensure that no single person need feel lonely or isolated (which can happen even in small conferences) but also many individuals were ministered to in a personal way, sometimes for healing, counselling and specific prayer, some receiving the baptism of the Holy Spirit if they sought it.

For the duration of the conference I was billeted, with three priests, in the home of a lady of Polish origin, whose views on non-Catholics seemed very much in line with those of Irish origin I had known in my younger days in Bradford! One priest had an Irish name and one was Hispanic American, whilst the other could have been of Polish extraction. In the nightly conversations back at our 'digs' I was very clearly the odd man out, and was subjected to their rather simplistic versions of ecclesiastical history. They knew a lot about Henry VIII, nothing of 'Bloody Mary', nor that England had become Catholic again before Elizabeth I came to the throne. They all believed that the protestants had stolen England's beautiful cathedrals and ancient parish churches from the catholics!

That, however, was by the way. My overall impression of this conference and its effect convinced me that I was there for a purpose. In fact, the whole three-week visit was to give me firm indications of how we should seek to relate renewal insights and teaching to the ethos of the Church of England. My thoughts were constantly occupied with the purpose of my visit, though I had no inkling that the eventual implementation of these ideas would become my responsibility.

That whole conference was inspiring, but one part above all was momentous. John Bertollucci spoke to the meeting one evening at great length, and his theme was an apostolic view of ministry. Though he was primarily addressing Roman Catholic priests within their own pastoral situations, every word applied equally to Anglicans. Apostolic ministry has to be Spirit-filled and Spirit-led, and he took us on a tour of the New Testament, relating the teaching to practical modern day ministry. It was inspiring and challenging, and all the time centred on Jesus Christ as living Lord, present now by his Spirit. The long address ended with a call for repentance, re-dedication and commitment to Jesus as personal Saviour. I could see why they called Bertollucci the catholic Billy Graham! During this period of prayer everyone was standing; I was very moved indeed, and just wanted to respond completely to this challenge and invitation. At the same time I had a sense that my hope for the Church of England was going to involve me in a different aspect of ministry and responsibility: what it was, I did not know, but I said, "Yes" to the Lord. Suddenly, I felt a reassuring hand grip my shoulder. I looked round, and there was nobody there! Nobody, that is, near enough to have made that gesture. I was sure that moment was a confirmation that my willingness to be used, in whatever way, was accepted by the Lord. It was another of those determinative moments of which I had now had several over the years. It was not my imagination or wishful thinking and, like the other similar experiences at certain times, it needed future events to prove the reality of that moment.

After the conference I flew from Pittsburgh with Charles Irish straight to Atlanta, Georgia, for the second ERM weekend already mentioned. I saw the value of the teaching pattern of these conferences that seemed to cover the basic essentials of relating renewal to the local church, and I now appreciated the importance of having parochial clergy who were themselves into renewal and leading their congregations into this new dimension. Their personal testimony was most important if doubters and enquirers were to be convinced. After Atlanta I returned home, my mind full of ideas of what could be done in the Church of England. Briefly, I was resolved on these points:

(1) We needed to have area conferences for Anglicans, in deanery or local areas.

(2) There should be an annual conference for clergy (and wives), to give mutual encouragement, as well as get inspiring teaching.

(3) We needed opportunity for small group ministry and sharing, as well as experience of renewed worship and music. But who would put this into effect? —that was the question.

At that time I was not quite sure what Michael Harper was doing, following his departure from Fountain Trust, apart from speaking at meetings and writing books. He seemed to me to be possibly the most likely person to take up this issue of Anglican renewal. I had again spoken to John Gunstone and several other people and eventually contacted Michael, who was in agreement that what I was suggesting could be a way forward. He was not able himself to be actively involved in such a project, as he was now setting up Sharing Of Ministries Abroad (*SOMA*), a charismatic agency to help create international links mainly with Christians in the developing countries. Nevertheless, he was sufficiently keen about it to set-up a 'consensus' type meeting of renewal 'leaders' (that word again!) —to see if general agreement could be found for putting the idea into practice.

A few weeks later, the first of two one-day meetings was held at the Calvorcoressi's house in Green Street, off Park Lane in London. Most of the people invited ought not to have been there. There were very few parish clergy present — the *real* renewal leaders, leading where it was all supposed to happen, in the parish! Their needs and requirements were not considered. There were several 'leaders' whose ministry was 'on the road', going around addressing large meetings and rallies, and they were largely independent of local church attachment. At the time, some American-style 'big name' activities were exploiting the renewal, and some personality-centred, 'big rally' ministries were emerging. I was forming the opinion then that some ministries were in danger of focussing only on the more sensational gifts: casting out any number of demons, lengthening, (or shortening) legs. I believe that the gifts of the Spirit, which include healing, deliverance ministry, prophecy, are to be exercised appropriately within the life of the body of Christ, and there are some good, genuine public ministries using these gifts. So maybe the impression I was gaining at that time was something of a caricature. The important thing is always to be discerning, with the discernment that comes from the Holy Spirit. All the glory must be given to God. The fruit of the Spirit is vitally important, as are the gifts of the Spirit, and all true ministries have to be marked by genuine Christian love and pastoral care. Our understanding of these things needs to be as mature as that of St. Paul, expressed in his first Epistle to the Corinthians. He tells us clearly that all the gifts and abilities count as nothing in God's eyes if love is missing.[5] Like Parson Haslam of Cornwall, there is sometimes need for us to be converted by our own sermons! The spiritual gifts are to be used, but always in Christian love, not for personal gain, and not for self-centred reasons. The best of the 'platform ministries' can be wholesome and encouraging—some are truly anointed by God—and media-based ministry can sometimes reach with the gospel people who would not be reached in any other way, but the centre for ministry is ideally the local church.

There were also being established 'communities' to support some independent ministries, and these were represented at the meeting. It is wholly understandable that a new Anglican organisation could be seen as competition for the same constituency. This first meeting ended with no conclusions, and a date was set for a further meeting in six months. I went back to Yorkshire feeling very disappointed. There had been no sense of the Holy Spirit leading, or even being present! I could see that I had been rather naïve. I became aware of rivalry, jealousy and suspicion among some of the 'leaders', who went around the country and appeared to be such experts, and whose activities were given undue weight in the minds of some simple folk, who consequently sought out such events in place of properly exercising their role in their own local church. This is understandable, given that so many churches were failing to offer sound teaching and the fullness of life in the Spirit.

I was not happy at all with the constituency of that initial meeting, but dutifully I went to the next one six months later. This meeting was a replica of the first; we got nowhere, and too many individuals seemed to be addressing their own agenda. Naturally, fears were expressed that an Anglican set-up would be a threat to Fountain Trust; but the Trust was already making special arrangements with a Roman Catholic service committee, so what some of us wanted was not all that revolutionary. But the Fountain Trust representative remained silent. It seemed to me that some of those present felt we were not there so much to seek God's will for future happenings, but to protect the status quo —a typical Anglican reaction!

When the meeting ended inconclusively, John Gunstone and I left in disgust. On the short walk to Marble Arch Underground station, from where John was off to Euston for his Manchester train, and I to King's Cross for the one to York, we agreed on an idea which John came up with: in effect, 'Let's ignore this lot and try something up north, where people were used to a bit of straight talk, rather than the unproductive waffle which had characterised these two meetings.' Consequently, as John recorded in *Pentecostal Anglicans*:

> Lawrence and I decided to organise, at Scargill, a conference on the renewal for clergy of the province of York. We thought this would be a means of testing quietly to see if there was need for an Anglican service committee—far enough north not to be noticed by the leaders of the renewal who lived in the south of England![6]

I took this idea on board with enthusiasm, and offered to do all the administrative work through our facilities and staff at Lamplugh House. Initially I sent notices to all the clergy in the northern province whom we knew to be interested in renewal. At the same time, I thought it wise to put a small advertisement in *Renewal* magazine about it. This was the only publicity we issued. Such was the interest shown by the real renewal leaders, the concerned parochial clergy, that within a very short time we had so many applications that we had no further room available at Scargill. We gave priority to the northern clergy. On the strength of the national interest being shown, I booked The Hayes Conference Centre at Swanwick, Derbyshire, which could take several hundred people, as opposed to around eighty at Scargill. Before the Scargill conference actually took place in July 1980, the first National Conference in September 1981 was almost fully booked. Such was the expressed need for help and encouragement for the local church and its leaders. The pundits were wrong, and so was Fountain Trust; it seemed clear to us the Holy Spirit was leading us in this particular direction.

The Bishop of Pontefract, Richard Hare, presided over the three day Scargill conference, and it ended with a 'long-playing' and joyful Eucharist, directed by Richard in his unique and gifted style. In this final act of worship a member of the Scargill community was confirmed and baptised in the Holy Spirit at the same time. The result of the conference clearly indicated that the parochial clergy in renewal would welcome the kind of help that we were proposing. There was a reluctance to undermine the Fountain Trust, which I shared, as did Richard Hare. I was still hoping that they would take on board my concerns about the direction of renewal in the Church of England. No immediate decisions were made following the Scargill Conference, other than to wait until the National Conference that was arranged for September of the following year, 1981.

While all this had been going on there had been several months when we had been anxious about the future of Lamplugh. This began after the burst of development around the time we bought the rectory and established the trustee body. We not only became uncertain about the future of Lamplugh, but, more directly, about our continuing involvement with it. There were increasing problems of reconciling my local parish responsibilities with the full time administrative work, and we were constantly aware of the need for more permanent staff to help.

We had a succession of resident helpers who stayed with us for a while. One of them was David Abbot, who had been with Colin Urquhart when the latter left his parish of St. Hugh's, Lewsey, Luton, to begin a travelling ministry, David had been his helper, co-driver and assistant. David was very practical and helped us a good deal, not only with looking after the visitors, but by doing repairs and improvements around the place.

There had been an economic slump and the number of visitors seemed to decline. Putting it simply, we needed a bigger income if we were to have more staff, and if I gave up the parish my stipend would have to be found from income. The growing number of 'live' churches now meant there was a need for centres with a much larger capacity than ours, in order to accommodate their weekends and residential training courses. In human terms it was 'getting us down'. But the vision for Lamplugh remained. During this rather negative and depressing period, I was drawn to the book of the prophet Habbakuk, where he declares:

"...THE VISION STILL HAS ITS TIME, IT PRESSES ON TO ITS FULFILLMENT, AND WILL NOT DISAPPOINT [will not lie, will not faint], IF IT DELAYS, WAIT FOR IT, IT WILL SURELY COME, IT WILL NOT BE LATE."[7]

"...IF IT [the vision] DELAYS, WAIT FOR IT, IT WILL SURELY COME...." I was sure that this word of scripture was for our immediate situation. The light began to break from a most unlikely source —a little cottage prayer meeting at Keith, North East Scotland. Colin and Anne Oliphant had sensed that we needed to come away from Lamplugh for a few days, away from the pressures, and they invited us to their home in Aberdeenshire, so that together we might share and pray and discuss around the whole situation.

Part of Colin and Anne's role in the area renewal fellowship was occasionally to lead this house meeting, particularly for the benefit of elderly people unable to travel the long distances to other meetings in that part of Scotland. Also at this meeting was a lady from farther north, whom we had met during a previous visit to Scotland and who had no idea that we would be present, nor for what purpose we were there. During the meeting she was given a prophecy, and prefaced this word from the Lord with the remark that she did not understand it or know for whom it was intended, but she felt very strongly that she must speak it. The four of us knew for whom it was given! It was for us; it was about Lamplugh House and the future, and about immediate decisions we should make. Unless they are written down immediately, the exact words of a prophecy are not always easy to remember, but the gist of it certainly was. As Colin paraphrased it afterwards that evening, when we were praying together, the Lord was saying, "THIS IS MY PLACE, MY WORK, I HAVE ESTABLISHED IT AND I WILL DEVELOP IT —AND YOU HAVE JUST GOT TO HANG IN THERE!"

We were convinced that we were being told to stay on at Lamplugh and await the further development of the vision "...AS IT PRESSES ON TO FULFILLMENT."

We gladly said "Yes" to the Lord. Colin and Anne's sense

of our need, and our visit to Netherdale House, had been God's way of getting us back on track. During the rest of that year began a series of developments, whereby God honoured his word "…. IT (the vision) WILL NOT BE LATE." On the financial side of things, following a drop of income and fewer guests in 1980/81, the first half of the financial year 1981/82 showed a 30% increase, and we found advance bookings for groups and individuals coming to our teaching events at the highest level ever! It seemed we had been allowed to reach that low state previously, in order to concentrate our minds and to renew the vision we had received. It seemed that God was confirming that there was a future for Lamplugh House. So strongly did we believe this that we began planning for the extensions that would mark our tenth anniversary in 1982.

It was during this period that Pam Oldfield decided to sell her house in South Cave and move to Thwing so that she could be fully involved with us. In no time she found a buyer for her house without having to advertise it, and a cottage in Thwing also was to be sold. It belonged to Mr & Mrs Edgar, who had camped out in the rectory in the winter of 1971. They were moving to live nearer to their family. We told Pam of this cottage and she came immediately to see it. It was ideal for her, and she arranged there and then to buy it. From then on, Pam was a great blessing, and we often had to restrain her because of the great amount of work she did and was prepared to do. She had independent means and would take no payment for her work.

Then came the conference at Swanwick that had been arranged the previous year for the overflow from the Scargill conference that had been such a success. This had been fully booked for several months, and there was a long waiting list. We had hundreds of clergy, and some wives, and there was tremendous blessing through this first nationwide event. There seemed to be unanimous agreement, by the end of it, that we should somehow go ahead and set up an Anglican organisation to minister specifically to Anglicans at a local church level. The great surprise, however, was the news that

Fountain Trust was to close down. People were quite shocked to hear it, as it was totally unexpected. The council had determined that its work was done, and it seemed that God was now moving us to a consolidation of renewal at the level of the local congregation. The way was now clear to make our decision. How things had worked out clearly confirmed in my mind that I should offer myself as co-ordinator of a new agency. After the name of our sister American organisation, I suggested we should call it Anglican Renewal Ministries, and that we should operate it under the aegis of the Lamplugh House Trust. It seemed foolish to set up a new trust, buy buildings and look for a leader. Lamplugh Trust had the precise aims of what we proposed to do through ARM. I had arranged the two conferences, gained a vision for its work through my visit to America, and really felt that I was being called to this role. The framework was already in existence; certainly there was no queue of people wanting to take on the job. There was general agreement that I should do it, so I became what was then called Co-ordinator of Anglican Renewal Ministries, and I was sure that being based at Thwing indicated that it was another example that, "the vision . . . . presses on to fulfilment." The Swanwick conference ended with a joyful Eucharist, and from that gathering of not very well-off clergy came an offertory of over £3000, to help set things up.

A small Advisory committee was established, consisting of John Gunstone, Michael Harper, John Finney, Trevor Marzetti, and Harry Cooke. Peter Peterken (representing anglo-catholic renewal) and Ian Savile. All except Trevor Marzetti were ordained. Of these, apart from John Gunstone and Michael Harper, all had parish ministries and had seen their parishes brought to new life in varying degrees. John Finney, together with Felicity Lawson, had produced a teaching course entitled *Saints Alive!*, which had been pioneered in his former parish, St. Margaret's, Nottingham. (He had now become Advisor for Evangelism in the Diocese of Southwell.) One of the first things we did when ARM was established was to publish this course. Several more teaching courses were to follow, but *Saints Alive!* was an outstanding success and instrumental in the deepening of renewal at local church level. For several years, Trevor Marzetti had produced a news-sheet entitled *Anglicans for Renewal*, and we quickly incorporated it as the quarterly magazine of ARM.

Following the great send-off and commissioning we had received at the close of the Swanwick conference, it was now time to end my role as Rector of Thwing. I was still technically Vicar of Wold Newton, even though Kenneth Nelson was licensed as Priest-in-Charge. In any case, the Nelsons were now looking for a permanent retirement home and were to move to Harrogate by the end of the year. I went to see the Archbishop of York, Dr Stuart Blanch, and explained to him what was happening and that we wanted to base Anglican Renewal Ministries at Lamplugh House. He was very interested to learn that our aim was to try and overcome the 'charismatic' culture barrier, and that we sought to serve the Church of England and encourage renewal in the church structures. He was very positive about it and agreed that the best thing was for me to resign my living so as to devote my time fully to the enlarged responsibilities. He would arrange for me to be licensed as honorary Curate at Driffield Parish Church, where Mark Simons was now the Vicar, so that I would still have an official title within the diocese. This was a device often used for helping non-parochial clergy who were still working within the church, to safeguard their pension rights. It did not necessarily mean that one would do much work in the selected parish, apart perhaps from preaching occasionally. I resigned at the end of October after giving the statutory one-month notice. I was sad about it, and it was quite a wrench to finally cut myself off from parochial ministry. It was a small parish with a small congregation, all the members of which we considered friends. Thwing had managed to keep its independence for the eleven years since my induction in 1970. By now everyone realised, not least because of the increasingly higher contributions that had to be paid to diocesan funds, that widespread pastoral re-organisation was a sensible necessity. My last service as Rector ended, and after I had pronounced the blessing, John Burdass, the churchwarden, came up to the front with a parcel. He said that, though they all realised I would still be around in the parish, and indeed I would occasionally still conduct the service, they wanted to give me something, and that they wanted to be sure it was something they knew I would use. So I opened it, and there was a very fine, cut-glass whisky decanter!

We still kept the link with the parish church, and sometimes groups from the house would all attend the Sunday morning Eucharist in the lovely old Norman Church. I shall always have good memories of the parishioners, especially those who first supported the Lamplugh venture and thus made it possible. That church still has a very special place in our affections.

The parish of Thwing eventually became part of a new benefice that included three more villages, and the Incumbent was based in a new parsonage house at Langtoft, the largest of the four. Wold Newton became part of another similar benefice, consisting of villages along the Wolds valley, with the incumbent based at Burton Fleming, where there was already a parsonage house.

Something else of significance happened in 1981. Geoffrey Paul, Bishop of Hull, was translated to Bradford, where he became the diocesan. Our former archdeacon, Donald Snelgrove, then became Bishop of Hull. By now, old difficulties were 'water under the bridge', and all we had struggled for was achieved. He was now bishop over that area and, good Anglican that I am, I was determined that I would be subject to him 'in all things lawful and honest', as one is required to be! My resigning from the benefice would mean the diocese could now proceed with the long planned pastoral re-organisation. It had been a long struggle; in the end we both achieved what we felt to be right. He had simply done his job as he saw it within his terms of reference, and I sought to do mine, as I believe God was leading me.

Notes
[1] Op. cit. P*entecostal Anglicans*, Hodder & Stoughton 1982.
[2] Grove Books, 1978.
[3] Extract from *The Lambeth Conference 1978* (Church Information Office, 1979) is copyright © The Secretary General of the Anglican Consultative Council.) Quoted by John Gunstone. Ibid.
[4] *Pentecostal Anglicans* p. 25. ibid.
[5] 1 Corinthians 13.
[6] Op. cit. p. 26.
[7] Habbakuk 2:3. [Not *NIV*]

Nine

To be Real it Must be Local

Following the successful Scargill conference there was a small negative reaction from individuals who had attended the two useless London meetings —not officially or directly, but it came down the grapevine. I think they thought they had been upstaged by our northern initiative, and they were right. However, our efforts had the effect of discerning the way the Holy Spirit was leading. To my mind, those people seemed to be mainly representative of independent ministries and were, in fact, really addressing their own agendas rather than the declared need for an Anglican renewal agency. On the other hand, we were seeking the opinion and approval of interested parochial clergy within the Church of England— those whom we held to be the truly authentic 'leaders in renewal'—and without doubt their approval and support for the idea was overwhelming. John Gunstone's proposal for the Scargill conference proved to be inspired.

The establishment of Anglican Renewal Ministries was eventually confirmed by the response to the first National Conference at Swanwick in September of 1981. As an organisation, however, it had been embryonic since the idea to have the initial exploratory event at Scargill House. We were engaged at Lamplugh with all the organisational and administrative work relevant to the two decisive conferences, and it was anticipated by our steering committee that it would be welcomed and approved. The enthusiasm shown, not only by the people who had attended Scargill, but also by many more clergy after they had read or heard about it, indicated what the final decision would be. However, as we had only 'tested' the idea first in the north, we were obliged to seek national acceptance.

The report of the General Synod on 'Renewal in the Church of England' was published in the summer of 1981 and coincided with the Swanwick Conference, where we sold large numbers. It was held to be encouraging, and raised hopes as to the future spread of renewal on the Anglican scene. Together with that, the news of the imminent closure of Fountain Trust had removed the strongest objection to a separate organisation, and we were free to go forward. However, I must re-state that my original hope had been that Fountain Trust might be able to accommodate an Anglican service committee in the same way as it had done for Roman Catholics, though I had no personal ambition to lead it. Eventually, through the fast moving events and the circumstances of my involvement, I soon became convinced in my heart that I was in fact being called or prepared to give the lead in the new development. It seemed the logical outcome of my previous concerns, and the inspiration for Anglican Renewal Ministries had come in part through my visit to America. Though I was thus inwardly convinced, for my own assurance I wanted confirmation from the constituency we aimed to serve: the grass roots clergy, whom I have always held are the real renewal leaders. I did not need it from the self-appointed generals without armies, of whom there were now a growing number around the renewal scene.

When that confirmation came, I regarded the decision to base the work at Lamplugh House as fully consistent with the vision for Lamplugh and its role, which we had been given and which had been gradually revealing itself. We never forgot the words of Dr. Donald Coggan at the dedication of the Centre in 1972, that it should be a 'Christian Commando Training Centre'. Another thought which constantly emerged, was the New Testament picture that, like a 'city set on a hill', the whole region around it would be influenced. The collage by Jean Nelson *Into all the World* reflected our desire not to become an inward looking, cosy, 'Holy Spirit Club', several of which were now evident on the renewal scene. We never lost sight of the fundamental belief that renewal by the Holy Spirit was primarily for the local church. If what it gave to people as individuals was not worked out corporately to build up the body of Christ, it could lead to an unbalanced, individualistic spirituality, at the same time in danger of becoming dismissive of necessary order and discipline.

The aim of Anglican Renewal Ministries was to serve the church—the clergy and people in the parishes—not to become less Anglican, but rather truly Anglican in the way that I believe our formularies prescribe! We were not a bunch of experts telling them how to do it, but were to encourage faith and trust in the power of God, who would enable them in their own situation. I liked to describe ARM as 'the oily rag' on the engine.

Trevor Marzetti, who was editing *Anglicans for Renewal*, came and joined us at Thwing in the autumn of 1981. The idea was that he would find a suitable house in the area and then bring his family to live there. His immediate concern was with the upgrading of the magazine, and he was involved mostly with that. Previously, he had done it from his home in London, having behind him the security of his employment, and also that of his wife, Jean. I was uneasy about this arrangement, though not from any concern that he would not be a useful colleague —he was committed, efficient, and enthusiastic about the role that ARM might play, and was keen to be part of it. We got on reasonably together, though I know that he found me rather moody at times —but, as Margaret might say, 'who didn't?' At this early stage I was uneasy about him, his wife and two school-age sons, suburban Londoners, uprooting themselves, buying a property in remote, rural East Yorkshire, and settling there. At the same time we would be committed to finding another full time salary at a time when the new development was not yet stabilised. It seemed easier for such a move if it was only one person, but with a whole family involved, it was a different scenario. Also, there seemed to be great difficulty finding a suitable house in the area. For several weeks, Trevor commuted to London and back most weekends. Clearly it was unsatisfactory and we were unsure what we should do. We invited John Gunstone, chairman of the advisory committee, to help find a solution. He met with Margaret and me, and Trevor and Jean separately, as well as all of us together, and finally advised that it would not be feasible to proceed with the idea. Had it been two years later, when ARM was firmly on course and the combined work of Lamplugh House increasing, I think it could have been an ideal arrangement. Trevor returned to London but retained an active role as a member of the advisory committee and helped with many of our conferences around the country. He soon wanted to be rid of the magazine after his years of pioneering work on it, so it was officially purchased from him and edited and published by Anglican Renewal Ministries as its 'in-house' magazine.

We had now finalised the plans for the tenth anniversary extensions. They included two offices, which would accommodate the increased staff and administration needed for the enlarged operations. A very pleasant surprise came when we were given £10,000 from the proceeds of the sale of Fountain Trust property and equipment. We were able to allocate this towards the cost of the new offices and for office equipment. A later gift of several thousand pounds purchased a computer, at that time becoming an office necessity. Following a newsletter sent out on both the Lamplugh and ARM mailing lists, we received more in donations and interest-free loans. The total cost of the offices, the enlarged dining and conference rooms and a small chapel cost about £30,000, but did not prove a burden and was paid for in a short time.

The extensions were finally completed, and on 4th September we had a special service at Lamplugh House to mark its tenth anniversary and to dedicate the new chapel and extensions. Of course I invited Donald Snelgrove, now Bishop of Hull, to perform the dedication; he had been at the original official opening in 1972. We still had the same Rural Dean, John Badger, and I invited him, too. Over the years he had accepted Lamplugh House as part of the local scene. It was a great affair; in a way it was a triumph, for Lamplugh's facilities were now equal to the best of similar centres in the country, and it was also the base for a positive new role in the church at large. The chapel, though small, had a dividing screen, so that it could be opened up to incorporate the dining room extension when we accommodated large groups. With it thus opened up we were able to accommodate all the guests who came to celebrate with us this significant milestone on our journey. Many local people attended, together with others from farther afield, including some who had worked with us over the years but had now moved on. The extensions had given us large picture windows in the enlarged dining and conference rooms opening on to the lawn, where, at the original dedication in 1972, we had held an open-air service. Now everyone was able to crowd inside for the proceedings. I had devised a suitable service for the occasion, which included lively worship and praise, with several other people having a part. Brian Thomas, a leading local Methodist businessman, who had been a supporter for many years and was now a trustee, said a few words. He knew the struggles we had experienced in the early days, and he spoke of how we had faith to go on, and overcame all the difficulties placed in our way by the church authorities. In fact we had also received a good deal of help from them, as I have recorded. However, most people there were aware of what had gone on. It was all part of our testimony, anyway, as to how we felt that God had led us forward. (Each new group of visitors was given a short account of the history, and many enrolled as prayer and financial supporters). However, at Brian's words, all eyes turned to the Bishop to catch his reaction! He was reasonably pleasant towards us these days, and if not exactly won round to our particular theology and practice, could not fail to be impressed at how things had developed at the former rectory, now the base of a national ministry. When he delivered his address, he had the grace to admit that he had had reservations at the beginning, but events had proved him to be mistaken. That was the gist of what he said; I can no longer remember his exact words, but the people present were quite astounded by his admission. What he said finally disposed of unhappy memories that had persisted for a long time.

Our daughter Jane, who had been a receptionist at several large hotels over the past few years, including the Royal Hotel in Scarborough and the Pitlochry Hydro in Scotland, had an operation for a knee injury. It was not very successful, and she suffered with it for many years. As she could not continue in this type of work at the time, she came to work with us at Thwing. As well as acting as my secretary she was a very efficient help with the escalating administrative work: recording bookings, planning conference details, room lists, despatching mail orders for books and teaching courses and many other jobs. It was not long before we needed more help, and we employed full-time a young man, Chris Mesley, a graduate who was a committed Christian and both reliable and efficient. Together with Chris and Jane working mainly in the office, we had a part-time office helper, Sandra Westerway. Sandra's husband Steven had lost a leg, after an injury had led to cancer. He was now clear of the disease, and with commendable courage was overcoming the limitations with which he was faced. It had been a traumatic experience for this young Christian couple who had been the subject of the prayers of many people around the area. Steven was a surveyor for the local county council (Humberside as it had been grotesquely named in 1974, but now happily returned to East Yorkshire!) Both he and Sandra were great helpers and supporters of Lamplugh House in many ways. A gifted pianist, Steven often led the worship at our meetings and conferences, sometimes with a small group consisting of Sandra, Chris and anyone else who might be around at the time. Leading worship on such occasions is more than 'have guitar will strum' —it needs spiritual awareness and sensitivity if it is to be an offering to God rather than a display of talent. Steven had those qualities which were needed.

As a useful ARM promotion, we had incorporated into the Lamplugh programme *Music in Worship* weekends. Andrew Maries, the musical director of St. Michael-le-Belfrey, York, conducted these. They proved to be extremely popular, and people from all over the country were attending them. So popular and apparently worthwhile did they become that it was not long before other centres were copying the idea. In these teaching weekends Andrew was not concerned simply with the new renewal music and songs, but with church music in general, classical and modern. A good part of these weekends often required a measure of personal ministry to participants seeking deeper commitment and understanding of their role as singers or musicians leading worship. Over the weekend the participants would form an orchestra and choir, which sometimes would lead the worship in Thwing Parish Church on the Sunday with a special musical setting of the Holy Communion, and with prepared anthems and solos. These quite remarkable occasions were much appreciated by the regular congregation. Our church organist, Lorna Coates, surprised us on one of these occasions by identifying one of the participants as a member of *The King's Singers*, a popular television singing group! *Music in Worship* weekends were so effective and popular that we held three or four a year for many years and thereby, I believe, helped to raise music standards in many churches.

We were now including in the ARM programme a pattern of activities strongly influenced by the ideas I had collected in America. The annual conference, mainly for clergy, had been fixed several years ahead for the third weekend in September; it was very popular, and always full to capacity. Though many clergy and wives would come year after year, a good 25% each time would be new. Some of these were persuaded to come to experience what renewal was about; others were paid for by hopeful parishioners, praying that their clergy might be 'renewed in the Spirit!' As a result, many individuals found great blessing so that their lives, and subsequently their ministries, were transformed as a result. Others found they needed this annual boost to keep them on track in their parish situation where often they met with hostility from parishioners over-satisfied with the status quo.

The music direction at these conferences was of a very high standard; John Marsh, Vicar of Christ Church, Ossett, West Yorkshire, a fine pianist, would lead the music, together with several talented instrumentalists, assembled from several parishes that were into renewal and a more lively style of worship. Many of the best of the renewal hymns and songs were used, some of which were new ones being aired publicly for the first time.

A different theme was used for each annual conference and several good speakers took part, including sometimes speakers from the United States, such as Charles Irish, the Director of Episcopal Renewal Ministries, through whom had come much of our initial inspiration for the work of ARM, and Terry Fulham, Rector of St. Paul's, Darren, Connecticut, which was into renewal in a big way, who was a magnificent teacher and also pianist! Another was John Howe from Fairfax, Virginia, who was pioneering an excellent lay leadership scheme in his parish. It was also usually a good idea to have at least one 'big name' speaker, as well as our home-grown, well known 'charismatic stars', who were thick on the firmament in those days. Interesting and gifted speakers they were indeed, but not necessarily addressing the basic problems that their hearers and admirers faced in parish ministry. However, they helped provide a rounded conference, for many participants were much in need of personal help and ministry, as well as inspiration for their work. Often the latter was dependent upon the former having taken place. I also tried regularly to include unknown parochial clergy speakers who were seeing things happen on their local patch. These ordinary parish clergy were often of more encouragement to the troops. I was always on the lookout for clergy who were making great headway in their own situation, so that their subject matter stemmed from their experience and not simply theory. One of those who were not all that well known in the early eighties was to become a very well known speaker! At the second National Conference, in September 1982, George Carey, who that year became Principal of Trinity College, Bristol, following a notable renewal ministry at St. Nicholas, Durham, gave the three evening teaching addresses to great effect. He remained a warm supporter and encourager of Anglican Renewal Ministries throughout the years, as Principal of Trinity College, Bristol, and Bishop of Bath and Wells, until he was placed in the hot seat at Canterbury.

At these conferences we used to great effect the system of small groups, for personal sharing and ministry, which I had first encountered at the huge Roman Catholic conference at the University of Steubenville, Ohio, back in 1979, and with which I was so impressed. A feature of most of our conferences, this proved extremely valuable for ministry to individuals. We would divide the participants into small groups, being careful to separate husbands and wives or vicars and their parishioners or curates! Each group would be led by a person whom I had previously selected for their listening and ministering gifts. The groups met twice a day for about an hour, and much good work was done in them. Many people were healed not only of psychological hang-ups, usually from broken relationships or from childhood problems, but helped to see themselves properly as children of the God who is a loving Father, though not only children, but heirs of Abba, and learn to live in an assurance of their standing and their calling and all the resources they needed to serve him. Basically, it was the removal of poor self-image and inadequacy, which seems to be so common in the lives of many Christians, not least clergy and leaders.

The final morning of the three-day conference would be devoted to the closing Eucharist: a joyous affair, presided over by Bishop Richard Hare and always a great experience.

It would follow the pattern of the (then) Series Three Holy Communion rite, but included periods of informality when there would be singing in the Spirit, prophecies and many manifestations of gifts of the Spirit. After lunch, people left for home rejoicing, many having already booked for the following year's conference, some reserving places for parishioners whom they hoped to bring along. There is no doubt that these annual affairs were a great blessing and encouragement throughout the land. This fact was attested by some of the many letters we received when, in 1989, I retired from the directorship of Anglican Renewal Ministries after the first gruelling but rewarding eight years.

For the considerable financial support needed, we looked mainly to the involved clergy and their parishes, and they responded magnificently. There was always a large offering at the end of the annual clergy conference, on which we relied to help cover not only the expenses of the conference but the considerable overheads incurred in running a national agency. Although ARM was initially subsidised materially by the Lamplugh House Trust, the growing work and staff needs called for more financial support, and that support came in generous measure.

In the early days we had the management committee to advise on the running of ARM, which included John Finney and Michael Harper. I was disconcerted by the apparent assumption by some that the income of ARM was somehow being used to develop Lamplugh House, not least because we had the tenth anniversary extension programme in hand. This was simply not the case, for all that was given specifically to finance ARM did indeed do so. In later years, when ARM became a separate trust and owned property, it was a great deal more expensive to finance and maintain. Lamplugh House had become a widely recognised centre for teaching, training and renewal, and considering the circumstances it was right to use it as the base for Anglican Renewal Ministries. It seemed that God blessed the arrangement, and clearly it was integral with the vision and purpose for which Lamplugh had been established. When eventually we did separate the two ministries I was never sure that we had done the right thing.

In the autumn of 1982, I started to arrange an English equivalent of the local area renewal conferences, which had impressed me so much in America. I saw these as a means of reaching to the grass roots at parish level, thus hopefully, influencing many Anglicans —clergy, lay leaders and ordinary members of the church, many of whom would not go away to conferences or big rallies. The first three were held in the autumn of 1982; the first of these at St. Chad's, Lichfield. Prebendary John Widdas gallantly allowed us to use his church and there was good support from local parishes. Richard Hare, John Gunstone and Trevor Marzetti were there with me. From that initial event we shaped the general pattern for these area conferences, not replicating precisely the American ones, but suitably adapting to the ethos of the Church of England. Shortly afterwards, we did one at Hayward's Heath, arranged by Michael Harper, who lived there, and the third one, that autumn, more locally at Driffield Parish Church, where we had links with Mark Simons, now Vicar, and where I was licensed as Honorary Curate.

In 1983 these area renewal conferences really took off, and we held about twenty four such events during the following years, in all parts of the country. They were hard work, and much preparation and organisation went into them. Clergy would be encouraged to host a conference in their deanery or area; I would first go there and meet the interested local clergy, and explain the aim of the conference and their role in it. I soon discovered that local preparation was the key to a good and productive conference. Where there was prayer and commitment from the participating churches, together with good publicity leading to the event, it was always well attended and fruitful. If there was not much local effort beforehand, then it was less effective, though very few came into that category. These weekends, Friday evening to late Saturday afternoon, all followed the same pattern, though we had different speakers most times, but I would myself give two of the main addresses, and sometimes preached at the concluding service. I found soon that I needed to be prepared to deal with most of the subjects covered in the conferences, so as to fit in with the subjects of the invited speakers; or to act as stand-in, should one fail to appear at the last minute! However, it was not a one-man band: we went as a team, and often would provide the musicians if they were not available locally. We always suggested that local organisers invite their bishop to come, especially to preside at the closing Eucharist. These were Anglican conferences after all, and there is nothing more reassuring to parishioners than to have episcopal respectability grace such an event. Some bishops welcomed the opportunity to take part, and gave much encouragement, whilst others did their duty!

A further aspect of our work was the sale of Christian books and other literature, along with the several teaching courses that ARM had published. We had registered as booksellers, and so received full trade discount rather than only 10% on a sale or return basis —a good source of income, though it could be hard work, and we had to keep up to date with the prodigious turn-out of charismatic biography and testimony, which was in huge demand. Some of it left much to be desired, but we had no time to read them and vet all new publications! This was another area where my business and administrative skills had been put to full use. We carted the supplies to all the conferences and meetings now happening all over the country. It was worth this effort because we made enough profit to cover at least my salary for the year. Though I was no longer employed as a parochial clergyman, I never paid myself more than the going rate for a clerical stipend. Soon we had nine staff to run the combined work and ministry of Lamplugh and Anglican Renewal Ministries. Two of those, Margaret and Pam, worked for no remuneration; five others, including a gardener/maintenance man, were full-time; and two were part-time, including a cleaner. We were to realise later that it had been a mistake not to make pension provision for Margaret over the many years she worked. Nevertheless, we felt amply rewarded by the fulfilment of our hopes, prayers and endeavours over the years, and the apparent indication that we were working in accordance with the vision we were given.

How different it was now, following all those earlier years when we performed our stint with seemingly little success in one parish after another. In this experience, however, I was far from being alone. I discovered that it was also the experience of many parochial clergy, at least those concerned with the success and usefulness of their ministry, rather than career people who sought to climb the greasy-pole of preferment or to seek recognition and advancement within the structures of the church. I often remembered the technique for preferment favoured by my first vicar, at All Souls', Halifax, whose advice I never sought to follow. What had become manifestly clear to me was that the cause of this difference is the reality of the Holy Spirit at work in our ministries and personal spiritual experience. He brings into existence that apostolic dimension to which the New Testament so eloquently witnesses, which every church needs.

The charismatic renewal was not without its problem areas, but one could say that now we were dealing with the problems of life rather than the problems of death. There were many parishes with testimonies of how new life and love in the congregation, new joy in worship, together with new vision and purpose in evangelistic activity, had come as a result of this openness and desire for the blessings of the Holy Spirit. Some of these experiences, doubtless, flowed from the area conferences on local church renewal; others from the inspired leadership of clergy who had attended the special meetings and conferences arranged first by Fountain Trust and later by ARM. Many churches were experiencing growth as new people were drawn in by the welcoming love and warmth that they encountered; thus many turned to the Lord Jesus Christ in fresh and deep commitment. Where it happened, it was like the 'new pentecost' for which Pope John XXIII had prayed. ARM's teaching course *Saints Alive!* contributed in no small way to this success story.

On the other hand there were some parishes where, through weak or timid leadership, major problems were caused by the way the renewed people tried to deal with the traditionalist element who apparently wanted none of it. Behind this often quite vehement rejection there lay a fear of the unfamiliar, and the evident question mark placed over their own position in the church was a threat in itself. There was fear of the unknown, so that talk of the Holy Spirit actually doing things in a church notorious for its predictability, seemed to them to be strange. Again, this negative and fearful attitude seemed to me to reflect the rather shallow foundations of so many churchgoers. Even so, some of these objectors would be won over because of the love and care ministered to them by 'Spirit-filled' people when they found themselves beset by personal crisis, bereavement, sickness or whatever. Within the renewal, many congregations were learning, in a refreshing way, 'one anothering', as it has been described —the New Testament instruction for building up and nurturing the Body of Christ. 'One another' seems to ring out from its pages: 'Love one another'; 'forgiving one another'; 'bear one another's burdens', and so on. Chapters four and five of Ephesians provide examples, and there are many more.

There were other problems arising from the insensitivity and clumsiness of some so-called 'Spirit-filled' people who sought hastily and aggressively to change everything and everybody without tact, sympathy or any understanding. They would forget how long it had been before they had been lifted out of the rut, but now wanted quick response from others. We had discerned this fact in the early days of the Lamplugh House renewal days and teaching weekends. I had discovered that it is sometimes useful to admonish with a joke, and I would describe such people thus: "We seem to get lots of people here very anxious to change others. We get some wives wanting to change their husbands, husbands wanting to change their wives, parents wanting to change their children, vicars wanting to change their congregation and congregations wanting to change the vicar! [As I have previously mentioned] What God teaches us is: You *love* them and I will *change* them!" The command to love is surely the most difficult command of all. How in fact do you love the manifestly unlovely? By human effort? By teeth-gritting determination? Humanly speaking, it is impossible, but when we seek to be open to God's Spirit we can become channels for God's 'agape' love, which is a very different picture.

When the Holy Spirit becomes active in a church, other unholy spirits make themselves known. When the local church is being the Body of Christ and gifted for kingdom service by the Holy Spirit, the devil does not like it at all and seeks to undermine it, becoming quite active. This is a new phenomenon, because ordinary congregations that ignore the Holy Spirit, 'having a form of godliness but denying its power',[1] see little of this, because the devil is perfectly happy with them; they are no threat to his domain whilst they are not about God's work in the Holy Spirit's power.

In order to attack, the enemy seeks to use the faults and failings of individuals to stir up trouble. There is no smell of sulphur, no comic figure brandishing a toasting fork —in fact the devil is so presentable as to appear quite attractive to human beings, and they do not know he is around, except when they come within the sphere of the Holy Spirit and are on active service, as it were. There are, of course, some instances of demonisation, but I am talking here of general, subtle enemy activity, which is dangerous and can destroy the work of the kingdom in that place, whilst sometimes leaving behind a *seemingly* flourishing church.

More problems for renewal were sometimes caused when individuals fancied that they had been given some special (usually spectacular) gift of the Spirit and, as a result, assumed there was therefore an especially exalted position for them in God's scheme of things. It was always necessary to try and teach people that gifts of the Spirit are not badges of merit, nor signs to denote that one has acquired 'spiritual 'A' levels', but that they are tools for service, and that the gifts of the Spirit are to enable God's people to do God's work in his power, not in their own human power. Above all, manifestations of prophecy, words from God, pictures, dreams —all need to be tested in the fellowship of believers. It is easy to produce fleshly or sentimental fantasies, or even barely concealed admonition of the leaders or other group members. Amazingly, some such individuals attached to their utterances a higher degree of infallibility than that claimed for any pope.

Hence the need for skilled and gifted leadership, whether over the congregation as a whole or particular charismatic groups or fellowships; and, correspondingly, a submission to and recognition of the authority of the leader(s) within that context. Much gentle and wise guidance, sometimes admonition, could be required and difficult lessons learned. I hope all this is not too negative, but charismatic renewal was not, and is not, all triumphalistic. There is always the need to discern what is real and what is not genuine (as is true in all aspects of ostensibly Christian life.) There was tremendous need for teaching about renewal and how to relate properly within the local congregation. So as to help clergy in this vital area, we began to arrange conferences entitled *To be Real it must be Local.* I am not sure from whom the slogan was stolen, but it seemed adequate to describe charismatic renewal and some of its manifestations.

These conferences were usually held twice a year at Swanwick, and were specifically designed for parish groups to come with their clergy and PCC members, to learn together and from others how they were adapting to this new way of parochial life. We did not rely on 'big-name' speakers, but invited some articulate younger clergy who were singularly successful in applying the lessons of renewal and seeing lively growth in their churches. We would have good expositors to lead the morning Bible studies, such as John Gunstone, Michael Harper, John Finney and others. These conferences were a great help to many parishes and enabled the development of confidence for team ministry and evangelistic activity.

The late 70s and 80s saw the proliferation of many house-churches and independent charismatic fellowships, and what could best be described as 'Holy Spirit clubs'. As I have described elsewhere, some people, seemingly finding their wings clipped somewhat on the sensible and balanced Anglican scene, and unable to find their fancied qualities recognised, soon hived off into one or other of these organisations. Free now (so they thought) of the gentle discipline of Anglican structures, they were soon to find themselves under very strict authority and discipline indeed. There were also others, people frustrated by opposition and animosity to renewal, who gave up on the institutional church, and I could understand their reasoning. For how long must you seek to take root if you are placed on barren rock? This was the dilemma faced by many deeply committed and sincere people who, though they dearly longed for their church to come alive in the Spirit, reluctantly gave up on it and joined a 'house church'. Among such were our friends Colin and Anne Oliphant, who had dutifully endured hostility and opposition in their local Scottish Episcopal Church, and eventually left it for a house church. From their new base, Colin and Anne were to find an outlet for a fruitful non-denominational ministry, often using their large house and grounds, Netherdale, for meetings and teaching conferences. They maintained their commitment to our ministry at Lamplugh House.

A number of independent ecclesial bodies arose under powerful individual leaders, and sometimes they pursued a particular emphasis in an unbalanced way. Usually they came from the United States, where so many independent ministries flourish. A trademark was often dictatorial leadership, where everything seemed to be designed in order to support the great leader's ministry. There was the so-called 'prosperity gospel' teaching; and there arose a variety of different uses of the prophetic, for which, as has been observed, much careful discernment is necessary. It is sometimes the case that an aspect of scriptural truth which has been neglected in historic denominations is recovered, but then not always held in correct balance with other biblical doctrines, and therein lies a danger.

At the beginning of the twenty first century there is a growing dissatisfaction in some of these independent churches, and members and leaders alike long for the sort of balancing structures of the institutional churches, particularly the Anglican, and in recent years many have returned. Needless to say, the historic denominations remain in constant need of renewal in the Holy Spirit, and must continually be recalled to authentic biblical faith, accepting reform when necessary.

Anglican Renewal Ministries was totally committed to the possibility of spiritual renewal within the structures of the Church of England. How this was perceived as not only a possibility, but seemingly a growing reality, is covered at length in *The Good Wine: Spiritual Renewal in the Church of England* by Josephine Bax, published for the Board for Mission and Unity of the General Synod.[2] It is an extremely thorough and scholarly work, and is still worth reading today all these years on —perhaps by those whose initial enthusiasm for renewal has waned somewhat.

Whenever ARM held an area or deanery conference for groups from local parishes, we sought to demonstrate firmly that there was nothing about spiritual renewal that was contrary to the formularies of the Church of England, and we pointed to the fact that in the creeds and liturgy, every Sunday, we declared our belief in the living Holy Spirit, the 'Lord, and giver of life'. There was a great need for this teaching, to inform Anglicans that, in renewal, God is telling us to believe in what we say we believe, and become what he calls us to be!

When we first became involved in the charismatic movement in 1972, I soon became aware that an obstacle to the spread of renewal in the Church of England was the style or culture within which it was often presented. Many Anglicans, after years of unexciting conformity to the conventional parochial round, suddenly found themselves released into a new ethos of joyful worship and praise, and many assumed that the outward style was an essential part of it all. Thus, when they tried to interest their vicar and fellow churchgoers, which they would attempt with great enthusiasm, they often got a negative response. This was sometimes a reaction to the cultural wrappings that, for some, could make the real message hard to receive. After facing rejection, some of the more radical enthusiasts would doubtless have ditched the entire structure of the parish, throwing out in an undiscriminating way the Prayer Book, liturgy and old hymns —maybe together with the unresponsive churchwardens, church council and vicar, given half a chance! That may be a caricature, but it illustrates that, whilst the church without the presence and leading of the Holy Spirit is moribund, the Spirit-filled Christian needs to discern and value what is scriptural, good and helpful in the life and activities of the denomination, and use such features as a point of contact with other church members. To be filled with the Spirit does not mean that we have to reject what is good in old structures in an undiscriminating way.

Having seen some of the extreme aspects of freelance charismatic activities, I was convinced that the Church of England structures provided an adequate vehicle whereby the lessons we were learning could be put into effect —a view, I must add, that was not universally shared, hence the breakaways. Nonetheless, this was a view given weight by the witness of a growing number of parishes throughout the country which had become more open to the work of the Holy Spirit. A caricature of a church without the power of the Holy Spirit might be a car without fuel to make it perform its function. I would often adapt an illustration I had picked up from Terry Fulham, which made what I felt was a good rhetorical if not theological point: Anglicans could claim to be the sanest church of all —in theory, that is. Our church has a wonderful balance of tradition and authority, freedom, dignity, order, spontaneity, word and sacrament—on paper! It could be said, 'We are the Rolls Royce of churches. The trouble is, for the most part, we seem to stand around admiring it —all gleaming and polished up, though it is without petrol to make it go!' Of course, that image in itself will not really do, since to be able to see church life as God sees it, we need to make a close study of what the New Testament has to say about churches, their problems and shortcomings; and the warnings in Revelation to the seven churches need to be taken on board by all, not just the established and institutional, but house churches and independents also. It was often said, 'There is no such thing as a perfect church, so there is little point in seeking one — even if you find one, don't join it or you would spoil it!'

What are we to say, then, if false teaching comes from leaders in the established church? The thirty nine articles of religion make it abundantly clear that churches do err; some bishops have departed from clear biblical teaching, and some seem to have resisted the work of the Holy Spirit. In such cases, the appeal is to the Bible, which the same articles re-affirm contains all things necessary to salvation.

Other reasons given by those departing the Church of England included issues surrounding worship. It is of course the case that the Spirit-filled Christian has a profound longing to enter into the throne room of the Father in praise and worship. He or she is no longer just singing songs *about* God, but longs to praise him for who he is and tell him how much we love and adore him. Until a churchgoer has been filled with the Holy Spirit and knows God as Father, he can never enter that dimension. So there is a clash of needs which is far more than the familiar clash of outward styles; it goes to the very root of the matter of the relationship made possible in the new creation.

Today, much more is being discovered by Spirit-filled believers in all denominations about what is needed, in terms of hymns (old and new) and praise songs *that are addressed directly to the Lord*, and which are thoroughly biblical in their words, rather than just poetic reflections addressed to each other; and there is a growing recognition that musicians themselves need to be open to the Holy Spirit as they exercise 'worship leading' roles.

This need is being met within many Anglican parish churches today, and times of Spirit-led worship can now be found in a substantial number of parishes. This process illustrates how, sometimes, an appropriate 'cultural change' can take place within the institution, over time.

Notes
[1] 2 Timothy 3:5a.
[2] Church House Publishing, 1986.

Ten

Signs and Blunders

The first ten years, 1972–1982, marked the long stage of struggle and development, and unmistakably the vision for the use of the former rectory had at last been fulfilled; the prophetic scripture from Habbakuk had 'surely come' in 1979. The following ten years, to 1992, were also significant, not only because the successful incorporation of Anglican Renewal Ministries was seen as analogous to that vision, but also there arose the question of the aptness of the decision to separate ARM as an independent trust in 1985. I afterwards had cause to have doubts —but more of that later.

Saints Alive!, published in 1982 as a teaching resource for parish use, became extremely popular and was used to good effect in many parish churches, as well as by other denominations. It was translated (with or without permission!) into several languages, including German. A revised, Roman Catholic edition was produced wherein certain Anglican or protestant expressions were changed in order to make them more palatable for the faithful! By 1985 we had sold over 100,000 participant's workbooks, together with an appropriate number of leader's manuals. The sale of these and subsequent teaching courses was a valuable source of income and, along with proceeds of book sales, helped to keep the show on the road. There was an outlay on publication costs, plus royalties to the authors, but it remained my aim to keep these publications at as low a price as possible so that their use would not be inhibited by cost. After all, we were supposed to be there to serve the church, not to exploit it! The course came with a filmstrip on the passion of Christ, to accompany one of the sessions, so that users needed access to a filmstrip projector—they were not completely out of date at that time—but I found myself resisting pressure to replace it with a video, because of the extra costs involved. My attitude was 'If it ain't broke, don't fix it' —and if it is selling well, don't spoil things by making it too expensive! Some thought I was protective of the finances to the point of obsession, but this was not so. Being one of a rare breed (of clergy who did not think administration was beneath their dignity) I had the ability to project potential income and expenditure and thus keep reasonable control. In later years my successors handed everything over to a larger publisher. Hitherto, we had used a small Christian publisher in Ilkeston, Derbyshire, to whom the loss of the ARM orders was a substantial blow. Whether the action was of particular benefit to the finances I do not know.

A further spin-off from this direct sales activity was that we were able to keep closer contact with the troops in the trenches whom we were primarily there to help. By monitoring sales, not only were we able to observe which churches were using the course and how frequently, but also to ascertain where renewal was happening and growing. Teaching weekends were arranged at Lamplugh House and in the Midlands, specifically to help clergy and lay leaders get the best from the *Saints Alive!* course. John Finney and Felicity Lawson, the co-authors, conducted these weekends. This particular course achieved phenomenal success where it was used properly. Regrettably, however, there were some clergy who 'cheated' by watering down the session dealing with teaching on (and the ministry for) the baptism in the Holy Spirit. Consequently, they omitted the crucial aspect that would make doing the course worthwhile by radically changing lives and, possibly, the course of their ministry. Similar treatment is accorded by some to the popular *Alpha* course produced by Holy Trinity Brompton, which has been experienced by millions all over the world. More recent, but not unlike *Saints Alive!* in many ways, its use and efficacy, like that of its predecessor, depends on how the teaching on the Holy Spirit is given and received. Sadly, there are still a number of clergy and pastors who remain 'the cork in the bottle' and have power to suppress spiritual renewal and revival in a local church.

We first met Michael Harper in 1974, through Cecil Cousen, who was associated with Fountain Trust in its early days. Cecil encouraged us to invite Michael to Lamplugh House, to head a clergy conference on renewal. On one of the days, we arranged a big rally service at St. Martin's Church in Scarborough, to which people came from a wide area. Cecil had started a Scarborough renewal fellowship, meeting first in his own home and, later, in a church building, initially to nurture people in the area who had come into renewal through Fountain Trust conferences at Cober Hill, Scarborough and elsewhere. Cecil himself had been involved in renewal in Canada and was a great biblical speaker and preacher. He was to become closely involved with us at Lamplugh House and became a Trustee and a regular speaker on the programme, especially after his wife Jean was left practically housebound following a stroke. Cecil's participation and fellowship in the ministry was warmly welcomed and appreciated. He died in January 1989, and was greatly missed. An association with Michael Harper continued over many years. Michael was a visionary and a planner, and pursued his objectives enthusiastically. For my part, I appreciated all the help and support he had given to establish ARM. He had welcomed the initiative taken by John Gunstone and myself following the sterile talks in London. After he left Fountain Trust in the mid-seventies, he carried on writing, and remained a member of the original ARM consultative committee before it set up its own trustee body in

1985. It was not long, however, before the giant stirred, and by the late seventies he was instrumental in setting up *Sharing of Ministries Abroad* (SOMA) together with some of his international contacts. I had no objection to the aim of SOMA, to share resources and ministry with poor, developing countries. What I did question was the need for some of the air travel, moving international leaders around the world for meetings. With my cost-conscious mind, I disliked what I felt was extravagant spending by an organization, especially when the funding was voluntarily given to broadly outlined causes, and I was irked concerning the way in which the ARM constituency was being approached for support. However, I was not opposed to the work of *SOMA* and, over the years, substantial sums were given towards its very worthwhile activities, on the authority of the ARM Trustees, when funds allowed.

I was very uneasy with what I then perceived as various 'charismatic fashions' that emerged over those years, for with them was always the danger of over-emphasis of one aspect of teaching or ministry, and a consequent loss of perspective. I was especially concerned at that time by some of the phenomena in the meetings of John Wimber in the early 1980s. The support given by many, including David Watson, Michael Harper, and Bishop David Pytches surprised me. This is not, of course, to deny in any way the supernatural working of the Holy Spirit but, again, I do stress the need for discernment. All who lead meetings where unusual phenomena are manifested need to be very conscious of the biblical teaching on discernment of spirits, and well-versed in the history of revivals. The way Wesley coped with some of the 'disruptive' occurrences in his early meetings makes a useful and relevant study.

What I witnessed at a Wimber event at Wembley, for which Margaret and I had been given tickets, caused me some concern. We saw the reactions of some in the audience: screaming; strange noises; rolling on the floor—one joyful (or was it delirious?) female actually traversed all round the front of the circle area, doing somersaults, and I wondered what was going on. My thought at the time was, 'Well if she falls off, John, you have a great opportunity to demonstrate your skills!' Despite all the backing from charismatic leaders, I was doubtful about what I had seen, though, with hindsight, what matters is whether people hear the word of God preached under the power of the Holy Spirit; how folk react will vary, depending upon what is in their hearts. It is not always easy to handle situations in which strange reactions are occurring! As in the early church, so today, where the Holy Spirit is at work, signs and wonders may occur as people encounter the living God. There is always a need for wisdom from above in such situations as those we were seeing. Sadly, there was adverse press and televison coverage of a kind that tended to have an adverse effect on public perception of the renewal scene as a whole.

The power of the Holy Spirit must be welcomed within the institutional structures, and I agree with Wimber's thesis that the West is disadvantaged by its materialistic world view, compared with the perceptions in Asia, Africa and South America. Put simply, the latter tend to be expectant of supernatural happenings, whilst, for the most part, the former is not.

My reservations about the way in which the phenomena were being handled was not very welcome, and several thought I had lost the plot, including some of the ARM trustees. But I never denied that God heals the sick, casts out evil spirits and works miracles; after all, we had witnessed many such events since 1972, at Lamplugh House and elsewhere. I had my own testimony of the immediate healing of a very painful muscle and joint problem in my left shoulder, following an accident several years earlier. I was at a consultation with Scottish renewal people in Dunblane, when one afternoon I was having considerable pain and discomfort and I asked for prayer for healing. As hands were laid on me with prayer, I felt a tremendous heat in the area of all the pain, and suddenly it was gone —never to return. I believe that St. Luke's account of the return of the seventy two puts the signs and wonders that accompany ministry in the right context, teaching us the Lord's own priorities in these things:

> The seventy-two returned with joy and said, "Lord, even the demons submit to us in your name."
> He replied, "I saw Satan fall like lightning from heaven. I have given you authority to trample on snakes and scorpions, and to overcome all the power of the enemy; nothing will harm you. However, do not rejoice that the spirits submit to you, but rejoice that your names are written in heaven."[1]

This means that disciples, then and now, need to get their priorities right. Personal salvation ('your names are written in heaven') is a far greater cause for rejoicing than the dramatic exercising of delegated authority, however amazing the evident results of the latter! The work of the Holy Spirit is always to point to Jesus as Lord, for only in obedience to him can the church be properly equipped to do the work of the kingdom of God. Signs and wonders are indeed to be expected in the course of true, Spirit-led ministry, but anchored in the context of the whole of scriptural teaching on discipleship and ministry. That there was a hunger for the reality of God's power and presence was evident from the fact that many would travel to the USA, Toronto, and other places around the world where such things seemed to be happening, and I was concerned that people felt they had to travel to certain centres in this way.

In 1984, an idea was emerging of holding a large, international, charismatic event at the NEC, Birmingham. To be held in the summer of 1986, it was to be entitled *Acts 86* (after the Acts of the Apostles 8:6). As Director of ARM, I represented the largest body in the country from which might come the most supporters and attenders, so I was invited to join the consultative committee from the start. Somewhat reluctantly I agreed, with the concurrence of the Trustees, to be drawn in. It was soon evident that this one would be the biggest event of its kind ever held in the UK. It was hoped that the anticipated large audiences of many thousands might cover

the massive expense of the venture. The planning necessitated international meetings over the almost two years —
first in Hamburg, next in Amsterdam, and then Berlin, where
we daily passed through 'checkpoint Charlie' to meet clan-
destinely with some Lutheran pastors who had contacts with
charismatic Christians in parts of Eastern Europe, with the
hope that some of these might get through the Communist
restrictions in order to attend the conference.

A further meeting was held in the less colourful setting of
the NEC itself. This added to my concerns as to the projected
scale of the conference, and I discovered that several others
shared my misgivings, including two German representatives.
I was also uneasy with the manner in which these meetings
were conducted. Obviously, and I suppose inevitably, there
was an inner core, which came up with major suggestions
previously discussed —for the rest of us to ponder and
approve. Enjoyable as these trips were, I doubted the need
for so many to attend. My time was already sufficiently occupied, and the cost of air fares and expenses was a significant call on funds, a sensitive issue to me, as on various trips
to America to see ERM people and parishes I chose always
to pay my own airfares and never charged them to ARM. In
order that developing country representatives were not pre-
vented from attending, there was a move to solicit funds from
parishes so as to pay their costs and provide accommodation. Undoubtedly this was a noble consideration, but I wondered how practical it was, knowing the expenses involved,
and how cash-strapped were many of the constituents. Was
it lack of faith on my part, or the re-emergence of my usual
concern about economy? By this point it was evident that
there might easily be a financial crisis if the thousands of
people expected to attend from home and abroad did not
turn up. The last straw for me was when, out of the blue, it
was announced that John Wimber had been invited as the
star attraction, and that this would draw in the crowds, which
I thought to be an unworthy consideration. Part of Wimber's
renown was that he would rarely be nailed down for an en-
gagement until either the last minute or when eventually he

turned up, so for some time there remained a question mark over this idea. I related my misgivings to the Trustees and they left it to me as to whether I should go along with it or not. I decided to withdraw ARM's official sponsorship. Nevertheless, though I felt unable to be involved any further, I did not want *Acts 86* to be more of a flop than seemed to me likely, and I made no public announcement that we were no longer involved; nor did I seek to influence people as to whether they should support it or not. In the event, it did not attract enough people, and it ended with a considerable financial deficit that had to be made up by appeals to various sponsors and followers. Subsequently, the relationship with Michael that I had found difficult during the Acts 86 episode was fully restored to a friendly basis, and remained so. On reflection, I can now see that my single-minded concern for local church renewal blinded me somewhat to wider issues, so that I now see that I over-reacted when maybe I should have stayed with it.

I have always had a particularly high regard for Michael Harper, who was involved in *Acts 86* from the outset, and he was used in a wonderful way, through both Fountain Trust and his many writings, to encourage the renewal in Britain and beyond. I was very touched when, several years later, in 1994, during my convalescence at our home in Kingsbridge following open-heart surgery, Michael and Jeanne, who were staying for a New Year holiday on Dartmoor, made the twenty five mile journey specially to come and see me. It was kind and thoughtful of them, and showed real care. Michael eventually left the Church of England over the issue of women's ordination, and joined the Antiochan Orthodox Church, the membership of which includes other former Anglicans; and I understand that Michael plays a leading role in that denomination. I hope they are both happy and fulfilled, but it seems sad that, having played such a leading role on the Anglican renewal scene, they should have left over the issue of women's' ordination, for in all probability it will eventually become more or less universal. It will come sooner or later to the Roman Catholic Church, without doubt; the

Orthodox, probably, will be the last to give in —but give in they surely will, in the end.

My concerns about some features of the way certain 'platform ministries' seemed to be working, and my failure to attach ARM to all that was going on, led some clergy and leaders to assume that I had gone off the rails somewhat. But I still held firmly to the vital importance of *local* ministry, on which I had based the role of Anglican Renewal Ministries. This policy meant that issue of unbalanced emphases needed to be addressed, because it really seemed to me that well-known, popular itinerants were attracting the faithful, who flocked in large numbers to their meetings. Some people felt that if they had not been 'slain in the Spirit' (falling down under ministry) then nothing they had received in the way of blessing could possibly be authentic! Nowhere in the Scriptures is such a requirement imposed. It sometimes occurs, and may well be authentic, but people should not gain the impression that anyone who experiences such phenomena is somehow 'more spiritual'. It can indicate a need; it can sometimes accompany a work of healing, or another work of the Holy Spirit; but the person ministering needs to be aware of many pitfalls, and to be careful to exercise a balanced ministry, soundly based on scriptural priorities. The supernatural gifts of the Holy Spirit, like everything in Christian life and ministry, are to be properly used, giving all the glory to Jesus.

I remember an inter-denominational charismatic meeting at All Souls' Church, Halifax—where I had served my first curacy twenty years earlier—when David Smith and I went together to speak and minister. The Vicar, Geoffrey Thomas, warned us that there was a tendency with this group for people to fall down under ministry. He also mentioned that a lady who usually wore a large hat had developed a gracious method of falling down without dislodging it! When it came to the prayer and ministry time, David said, "Now if you all sit down, you won't need to fall down!" David had a powerful, spirit-filled ministry, but his sense of humour helped many to keep their feet firmly on the ground. There was much need for 'down to earth' teaching of this nature, and David was a great help to our ministry in this respect over many years. His practical, unambiguous, layman's approach, was of great appeal. He and his wife Jean were widely used, and together they must have counselled hundreds of people.

In Spring 1988, my candour led me into more controversy. Prophecy is another area of ministry which can be open to misunderstanding and even misuse, and a popular magazine on the subject, edited by Clifford Hill, was widely read and highly respected, especially for its emphasis on the prophetic witness of the church to the world. I was soon to leave for Montevideo, where I had been invited by Bill Godfrey, the newly appointed Bishop in Uruguay, (then in the process of separation from Argentina, to become a separate diocese.) I was busy preparing a periodical newsletter to be despatched before I left, when the latest edition of the magazine arrived. I was profoundly disturbed by one article, which referred to several spectacular accidents and natural disasters in the country, which had hit the headlines in recent years: the Kings Cross Underground fire, the sinking of the ferry 'Spirit of Free Enterprise', the great hurricane that destroyed lives, property and millions of trees in southern England, and a recent substantial fall in the stock market. These happenings, were cited in the article as clear evidence of God's displeasure with the state and conduct of our nation, and it was suggested that the events represented his judgment and punishment. I disagreed with this interpretation of events, and reflected on how this suggestion would be received by all the people hurt and bereaved through what were either natural disasters (which go on all the time in some part of the world or another), or man-made tragedies, behind which lay human error or negligence. Whilst God's anger at injustice and disobedience is a vital biblical theme—and is not in any way contrary to his love, calling people into relationship with himself (and indeed judgement will be a reality for all) —I was unhappy about this particular association of that series of events with divine retribution. So in the newsletter I sounded a cautionary note, giving my own view of the matter. I did not expect much reaction to this, so I was surprised on my return from South America to discover that Margaret had to face telephone calls from the editor and others, who obviously thought I had let the side down and was quite out of order. Calls for my head were made to John Gunstone and other Trustees, but I gathered that most of them supported me. In due course we were inundated with letters and calls of support for having tackled an issue that had worried and upset many people. The support was about 80% in favour, 20% against!

A vital and revealing aspect of renewal was the way it brought Christians of different traditions and denominations into close fellowship. In the fellowship of the Spirit there was true unity that overcame the barriers of traditional, cultural or perceived doctrinal differences. In a conference Eucharist it would have seemed almost blasphemous not to receive Holy Communion when the participants had so much in common, having been released into a shared experience of God's love, by the Holy Spirit. We had regular speakers from different denominations at both Lamplugh House and ARM conferences. A popular guest was Jim Graham, Minister of Gold Hill Baptist Church in Buckinghamshire, who came to give Bible studies at several major conferences at Swanwick. After his first experience of Anglicans offering worship and praise during a joyful three hour Eucharist, which included singing in the spirit, prophecies in tongues and their interpretation, he said he had never thought it possible in the Church of England, and it had changed his pre-conceived ideas about Anglicans! There were several Roman Catholic priests and religious who were regular speakers, including the late Ian Petit OSB, who was released by his Order to conduct a nation-wide renewal ministry that became ecumenical in practice, and Michael Simpson SJ, now a married Anglican clergyman.

Because of our link with Roman Catholic charismatics, I was invited to attend a large conference at the De La Salle College in Southampton, chiefly to preside at a daily Anglican Eucharist for the several non-Catholics who were also attending the conference. There were many priests and religious, and laity —quite a number from Ireland. It was a pleasant experience for me, and great fun into the bargain, and I felt completely at home and welcome. I was invited to give the homily at the closing Mass on the final evening. During coffee after supper that evening, a jolly lady with an Irish accent said to me, "I believe you are giving the homily tonight."

"Yes", I replied, "I hope you are not afraid you will get heresy in the pulpit!"

"No, no," she said with a straight face, "don't be troubled about it, we get it every Sunday!"

On the subject of Christian unity, like most others, I had regarded it as primarily a matter of sorting out doctrinal and cultural differences between denominations. My knowledge of how the Holy Spirit deals with people through the renewal dimension gave me a totally different understanding. We should first be seeking unity at our own communion rails, the unity in divinely given love that overrides differences and which only the Holy Spirit can impart. There is a great deficit in this area in so many churches that seem to host a number of opposing factions, some which rarely or never even meet. Unity had to be local, too!

In addition to regularly arranged conferences and regional day meetings for clergy, under the auspices of Anglican Renewal Ministries, I was often invited to parishes to conduct weekend renewal teaching meetings. Over the years, this took me all over the country and to churches of different churchmanship: urban, suburban, inner city and rural. It was here that my previous experience in different parishes proved a help; for the most part I was able to identify and approach particular aspects of ministry that were distinctive of each kind of setting. It must be said, nevertheless, that the basic personal spiritual needs within each situation were identical. To me, the priority need to be articulated was, first, a personal commitment to Jesus Christ and, second, the baptism in the Holy Spirit (whatever terms are used to describe that wonderful event). As this comes about within a relationship to God as Father, it was a true Trinitarian understanding, better experienced than theologically described.

During two consecutive weekends this fact was graphically demonstrated. The first was at Benwell, a run-down, disadvantaged, inner-city part of Newcastle, with all the associated social problems, particularly crime and wide-spread unemployment. Murray Haigh and Debbie, his wife, were so used to burglaries at their vicarage that they had become routine. The church, however, had come very much alive under their ministry, and many parishioners, despite their problems, had found a rich new element in their lives which had lifted them above the bleakness of their surroundings and given them a mission to their neighbours. It was great to see unemployed young people, who were vibrant with God's new life, witnessing to Christ in their surroundings and using their time in so positive a way. There was an atmosphere of love in the church, and it bore much fruit. The next weekend I spent at West Chiltington in the comfortable and wealthy 'stockbroker belt' of Sussex. There it was obvious that few if any, were lacking in the material comforts of life, but it soon became evident that beneath the wealth and comfort lay a deep longing for spiritual reality. Wealth was not enough and they knew it. Many of the people who received prayer and ministry found a deeper relationship with the Lord who alone gives inner peace, joy and satisfaction. The two contrasting weekends proved to me, beyond all doubt, that whatever their environment or circumstances, Jesus is the basic fulfilment of human need.

A few years later, during the course of ARM's peripatetic wanderings from base to base, and when we had established it in Knaresborough, practically a suburb of Harrogate, I received a letter from the wife of a young vicar in Bradford's inner-city, who was well known for a deep concern for social issues. She deplored our settling in a socially 'privileged' place like Harrogate, and suggested we might instead have purchased a large enough house in Bradford to be based there. She described at length the needs which their parish sought to address —needs not unknown to me, and I did not hesitate to rebut her observation on ARM's location, mentioning that I had been on the Bradford scene probably before she and her husband were born. I told her of my time with the Bradford Cathedral 'visitors', who had sought to minister to people in the back-to-back slums just down the road from their parish. I could have pointed out that the 'deprived' now lived in modern flats and council houses — the modern 'slums' that had replaced the old—and that people's spiritual needs were basically the same in both Bradford and Harrogate.

How Anglican Renewal Ministries eventually moved to Knaresborough is another topic. The few years following the tenth anniversary of the completion of Lamplugh House as a conference centre and office base for ARM saw a huge growth in the activities of both. The work could be hard and time-consuming, but it was fulfilling, and we really believed that this was what God had been preparing and calling us to from the beginning. We had come 'over the circumstances', and were now seeing the fulfilment of the vision that had matured over the first ten years. There was a good spiritual base; we had a small fellowship that worshipped and prayed together daily, and that underscored all our activity. Sunday mornings marked the climax of our weekend teaching conferences, with a long, informal, but no less Anglican Eucharist; we used the informality allowed within the *Alternative Service Book 1980* to allow for prophecies, singing in the Spirit and congregational participation as the Spirit would lead. This service commenced after breakfast and went on until almost lunchtime, with a break for coffee at a suitable place. When private weekend groups were 'doing their own thing' we helped maintain some link with the parish by worshipping at Thwing church. On 'free' weekends, if I were not away, Margaret and I would occasionally manage a few days peace and quiet at our mobile home near Harrogate.

In 1984 the sheer pressure of work was continuing to increase. At Lamplugh House, almost every weekend and often mid-weeks, too, were taken up; and, at the same time, I was having to travel all over the country to the area renewal conferences and other teaching weekends. This situation led us to consider the possibility of appointing a suitable person or couple, with a special remit for the Lamplugh House teaching and conference ministry, thus relieving the growing burden of work. We were aware, nevertheless, that such a solution would bring its own problems, and it would be difficult indeed for a new couple to carry on when we both were still around. The problem was to be resolved in another manner.

I was increasingly uneasy at implied criticism by two members of the advisory committee of ARM, of it being based at Lamplugh House. I was not aware that any of the other members were thinking the same, but I was getting irritated and ill at ease, as it seemed to suggest that there was something doubtful about the existing arrangement which was going so smoothly. This began, as mentioned earlier, with the suggestion that ARM was subsidising Lamplugh House, but now an added complaint was that Thwing was too far away from everywhere —not that they came all that often, as most committee meetings were held at Swanwick, when we were all together for a conference. So far as travelling distance to and from Thwing was concerned, I was the one who happily did it! Whilst they recognised that we had done a lot at Thwing, the vision that we believed we were following did not perhaps enjoy quite the measure of acceptance on the part of our detractors. There may have been issues about control, under the surface of things. Some had been happy to see me take on the burden at the start, when the future was uncertain, but now that things had expanded considerably, perceptions by some of the leadership had altered. When ARM did set up its own legally constituted trustee body, the original committee was largely replaced by people who were more strategically placed near our new base. My feeling was that I had been made the driver of this vehicle, 'over the circumstances', and I intended to remain so until 'HQ' determined otherwise. This was not arrogance on my part, for I strongly believed that I was doing what God required of me, and I endeavoured to follow the agenda I had been given and not allow anything to intrude that appeared to be contrary to it.

None of us is perfect (whatever illusions we might allow ourselves), and we all make mistakes; I am certain that I made more than my share; but I believe we are allowed to make mistakes, and it is better to make them when seeking to obey the will of God than blandly to ooze along, doing little of consequence. The glorious thing is that God can take our blunders and weave them into the pattern of his tapestry. The decision to separate ARM from Lamplugh House was probably within that category. Looking back over the years and considering how things turned out, I remain uneasy about how quickly and thoughtlessly I allowed us to be pushed forward —that episode seems very much 'under the circumstances' rather than 'over' them. It is so easy, in spiritual matters, to get out of the habit of hearing God's fine tuning and falling into the 'that's a good idea' mode —or 'Christianity by committee', the manner in which the church, for the most part, organises itself. The separation of ARM was a decisive point, from which came a distinct change, not so much in the nature of the work and ministry, which continued, but with the sense of protection and assurance that had marked our location at Thwing. At one stage, the idea of moving from Thwing was unthinkable, but under pressure of events we moved, and it happened very quickly.

Things came to a climax in late 1984, when the committee, upon hearing of our dilemma with regard to coping with both major operations, strongly advised taking ARM to another location as an independent establishment. Humanly speaking, there was now enough evidence to justify such a move, and we concurred reluctantly. The logistics of this step were considerable, as not only did we need to find a new warden and wife to run Lamplugh House, but also a suitable base for ARM and adequate living accommodation for Margaret and myself. There was general agreement that we should aim to be based in a lively and sympathetic parish situation, where we might find a supportive fellowship.

Events moved so quickly from this point that superficially one might believe that God was preparing the way and making it possible to proceed. In fact, I was no longer in charge of events, simply being carried along by them. To this day I am still not sure that we did the right thing; this decision and its consequences seemed completely out of character with the way we had seen God working during the previous fifteen years, and the unique spiritual ambience of a very special place that he had set apart and upon which his Spirit rests.

A fresh couple to run Lamplugh were made known to us through the commendation of John Gunstone. Norman Howard was vicar of a parish in Oldham, where there had been a measure of renewal, and where we had based an area conference in 1982. The possibility of Norman and Jenny taking over was placed on the stocks.

The second need, of a parish base for ARM, was quickly satisfied when John Pollard, Vicar of Haddenham, Buckinghamshire, came up with the suggestion that part of the old village school in his parish, now church property, might be used. John had plans to develop this building into a church centre, and it would be possible to incorporate a second floor, to provide spacious office accommodation. Here, again, we had held an area conference, and many of us knew John through other conferences and activities, and had a high regard for him. So there was the possibility of a base for us, and the committee welcomed this as a good idea. The feasibility of this decision was enhanced by the fact that Harry Cooke, a stalwart friend and supporter of ARM, who shared in many of our conferences and teaching activities, was about to leave his parish, St. Matthias, Leeds, for a parish near Oxford, and from there would have a closer relationship with us when we got to Haddenham. It was a terrible shock to learn soon afterwards that Harry had died suddenly of a massive heart attack, still in his early fifties. His death came just one year after the death of David Watson in 1984.

The need for a house for us was also resolved quickly. At an autumn conference for parish groups at Swanwick, the plans and needs for the move were outlined to the conference for their prayers. The probability of going to Haddenham and buying a house on a mortgage arrangement was mentioned, but it never reached that point. At the conference was a couple from Teesside. They were former owners of a small supermarket chain there, which had recently been bought out by a larger company. They had established a charitable trust and offered to invest some of its funds to purchase a house in Haddenham —and we could live in it rent-free. This generous offer was immediately accepted, and John Pollard was detailed to seek out a suitable property for the purpose, which he quickly did when a parishioner was selling a modern, four bedroom house.

With remarkable speed, plans for the separation had taken off, but I remained uneasy and aware that now we were most certainly being carried along with events, without much choice. We were under pressure, with a deadline ahead for January 1985, when Norman Howard was appointed warden for a period of five years. I remained chairman of the Lamplugh Trustees, and kept a watching brief in that role. I had a deep unease about what would happen to Lamplugh, and I had no peace about it until 1991, when Kingdom Faith Ministries took over. Our main concern was that our successors had the right vision. Understandably and properly, that would be to fulfil their own role in the work of God's kingdom.

At that time we had a small flat in Scarborough, in which Jane was living and from where she commuted each day to Thwing. By the end of January, negotiations for the purchase, and the minutiae of the agreement for ARM to use the property, were not yet complete, and we were not sure when we could move to Haddenham. So we had to move our furniture from the warden's cottage and place it in store pending our move south, and went into the flat with Jane for a period. We commuted backwards and forwards, not only to see to the ARM administration, but also to try and work alongside the newcomers, simply to help them find out where everything was and what needed to be done. Just records and equipment relating to ARM remained, along with a few bits and pieces belonging to us.

I will never forget the day when I went over alone, to supervise the removal of the remaining possessions. It was with a great wave of emotion that I realised this was the end of an extraordinary and exciting period of God's working, of which we had been privileged to be part. Had I done wrong? Was I being disobedient to the vision that had so painstakingly materialised? Were these the people of God's choice who were taking over?

I wandered round the grounds and came to a favourite corner of what had been the orchard, from where there is a magnificent view of the rolling Yorkshire Wolds. The pain of leaving it all hit me like a bolt, and I simply broke down and wept. I do not remember how long I remained there, but finally I left. I could not face anyone as I drove slowly away, down the long drive. As I did so, I was conscious of the Lord speaking to me, and the words were, 'Don't look back!' I recognised that this was a word of reassurance, similar in a way to when I had felt the hand of the Lord on my shoulder at that conference in America, and it gave me much comfort. By the time I returned to Scarborough my mood had changed and I was looking to the immediate future with interest, anticipating how God might use us in the next stage of our lives.

Notes
[1] Luke 10:17–20

Eleven

Entirely New Circumstances

Jane did not want to move south, and intended to return to her previous work as a hotel receptionist, this time in Glasgow, but she came down with us to Haddenham to help 'set up the stall' and give us time to get adequate office help. The office area that had been set up for us in the former school building was one large room that had been created in the main hall and screened off by boards and a door, and was unsatisfactory because we were subject to the noise from various daytime activities connected with the church and parish. It was a marked contrast with the exceptional office facilities that we had enjoyed at Thwing, and another disturbing feature that made me question the decision to move away from there. However, we simply had to make the best of the situation. By now I was fully aware that we were operating 'under' not 'over' the circumstances, and I felt that the 'committee men' had triumphed. Events were to prove that this crucial decision (to which I had assented) did, in fact, mark the beginning of the end of my role. Though there were four years to go, I remain convinced that we had voluntarily, if reluctantly, moved out of a special place of God's presence and favour.

On reflection, I can see that, had we not made that separation, Lamplugh House might have fulfilled its ecumenical role whilst remaining an Anglican base for renewal. But that is purely speculative on my part. I must not attribute too much to my own importance in decision making! The Lord's will is what matters.

We quickly found an excellent secretary in Jill Gillan, a member of the church. Margaret, who had always helped with the bookings and running arrangements of the major residential conferences, as well as performing her role as housekeeper/manager of Lamplugh House, being now without the latter, was for a time able to adapt to a home routine. John and Judy Pollard, the vicar and his wife, were very kind and gave us a warm welcome, as did many of the parishioners. From the start, John would be with us regularly for daily prayers and was very caring and concerned for our well being, which we appreciated. We have remained friends with them ever since. The church was into renewal in a large measure, but there were some members who displayed the antipathy that is so common. It was a large congregation, with many London commuters and professional people. One Sunday at the main service, one man looked familiar but I could not immediately place him. He was Hilary Minster, who played the role of General von Klinkerhofen in the popular television series 'Allo, 'Allo, but without his uniform he was not easily recognisable.

We soon identified a major problem with the temporary office accommodation. The plans for redevelopment of the old school were not off the ground, and there was some opposition to the idea in the parish. It appeared that it could only go ahead with the financial help of Anglican Renewal Ministries. I had naturally imagined that we would pay a reasonable rent for any facilities we used, as we did for the temporary office, but when it was suggested that we pay a one-off, large capital amount to cover the major cost of the structural work, we realised we had neither resources nor a remit to do that. I soon recognised that here was the first problem arising from the hasty way we had separated from

Lamplugh House. We could not settle to the idea of the temporary facility becoming permanent, for I had no separate office/study and we were all together, with the whole stock of books and publications, in the one big, noisy room.

The idea of having a parochial base was not the good idea that it had seemed. I found, not only at Haddenham but also later at a church near Harrogate where I was licensed, that one could easily become a point of disruption. Some imagined me to be the great authority on how to run a renewed parish, which I am not, and I would be approached for my opinion on something, usually something with an implied criticism of the way the vicar was doing it. I needed to be careful not to appear to share their views (and thus seem to give support to the elements who would see pushed out of the church all who did not share their brand of fervour for the truth.)

Eventually, we solved the office problem by moving it to the house which had been provided for us. There was already the base for a dining room extension to the living room and newly built kitchen. With the permission of the house owners and the newly-formed ARM Trustees, we had the extension completed in a very short time, there already being planning permission for this work. Immediately, this released the existing small dining room for use as an office, adjoining which was the former kitchen/utility room, and I adapted that as my own office. Meanwhile, we rented a small storeroom at the old school, where we kept the books and publications. It was not ideal, but it was an improvement and it meant we were now independent of the ins and outs of parish politics with which John Pollard had to cope. The necessary funding was soon made available. Despite any blunders we had made, we perceived that God still met our needs.

One of the first tasks was to set up a Deed of Trust, and an appropriate body of trustees. The former was done for us by Ian Anderson, a lawyer in York and a member of St. Michael-le-Belfrey, who had helped us with all our legal needs since the beginnings at Thwing. For the trustees, apart from

John Gunstone, as chairman, I approached none of the former committee, inviting instead a new team, most of whom lived in the area: Teddy Saunders, former Vicar of St. Michael's Chester Square (who had taken on board David and Ann Watson when they left York) who now lived in Oxford; David Bishop, Vicar of St. Clement's, Oxford; John Marsh, Vicar of Christ Church, Ossett, later to become chairman; Don Brewin, a vicar in Aylesbury, who became the director of SOMA after Michael Harper; John Pollard; and James Haigh-Ferguson, a retired businessman involved with Stanton House, a retreat centre in Oxfordshire. As we were still in the age of male chauvinist piggery, there was not even a token woman, though Margaret always came to meetings. Neither of us were trustees, and following my own choice of the group I became legally subject to them. They were a good team and very supportive. Teddy Saunders, in particular, took his role very conscientiously; not only did he give immense help by editing *Anglicans for Renewal* but, together with his wife, Margaret, showed the two of us real pastoral care at a time when we were coming to terms with a new way of life following the move from Thwing.

The work of ARM still proceeded apace, involving much travel to conferences, meetings and parishes. We still kept on our mobile home near Harrogate, mainly because Margaret's father was in a nursing home in that town, so we were able to combine a welcome break from the pressures of work with a visit to him from time to time. It proved a useful base sometimes for ARM ministry in the north. An important family event in July 1985 was the marriage of our eldest daughter, Susan, at Haddenham Parish Church. Though both she and her fiancé were based in Newcastle, they came down with their friends and his family, and were traditionally married from our new home.

Benny Hazlehurst, upon finishing his degree course at Brazenose College, Oxford, spent one of two years 'time out' with us, prior to training for the ministry. We came to know him well, first when we did an area conference based on his father's parish in Bolton, and then when he came and spent summer student vacations helping us at Lamplugh House. He came to Haddenham on a joint arrangement with the parish and ARM. He was involved part-time with a young people's venture that he set up, and which occupied him some evenings and Sundays, for which the parish provided him with accommodation, whilst ARM provided him with a small salary. He came in the summer of 1985 and remained until the following summer before going to Hong Kong, where he served for a time with Jackie Pullinger in the notorious hidden city area.

Benny was a great helper, supporter and general encourager —the ideal person to have joined us at a time when a character like his was a godsend. Very practical and gifted, and with a mature faith and commitment, we found him thoroughly reliable. He helped in the office routine and with the conferences, and accompanied me on several parish weekend engagements. He was able to lead worship and played a guitar. One Friday evening, we arrived to do a weekend at Bideford Parish Church, North Devon, to find that the main speaker had not turned up. I had never met the missing speaker, but he had been recommended for his musical and teaching abilities, and I expected him to have a substantial role in the programme. Frantic telephone calls revealed he had not, in fact, left home. I have difficulty recalling the precise details as to what had gone wrong, or how lines had become crossed, but he promised to turn up the next day. Thankfully, Benny had his guitar and quickly the pair of us set-to hastily to re-arrange the planned programme. Years later, I met up with the Vicar, Prebendary Paul Smith, where he was now based in Exeter, and he referred to that Bideford weekend and remarked what a good thing it had been for the church. The Holy Spirit had blessed the proceedings —one might say, 'over the circumstances', in this case. Meanwhile, Benny made his mark in his own way and provided a valuable contribution to our work and ministry. He was great fun to have around and we grew very fond of him; he was like one of the family. During a visit to several renewed parishes in America, I picked up a youth training course produced by the assistant curate of a church in Nashville, Tennessee, and did a deal with him to produce and distribute it through ARM. It needed adaptation (and a degree of translation) for publication in Britain, and I had no hesitation in handing it over to Benny to undertake the task. He went off to Nashville and worked over it with the author. I was really glad to give Benny that opportunity and experience, for he had been such a great support to us. He made an excellent job of it, as I knew he would, and it was duly published.

Sadly, the time came for Benny to leave, when his year was finished, six months or so before we were to move back up north with ARM. He visited us several times, wherever we were, until we returned to Lamplugh in 1990. We lost touch with him after his ordination and his marriage, neither of which events we had been able to attend as they clashed with the conference activities. He is now in charge of a parish in Brixton, following several years ministry to the bleak social needs of southeast London. Knowing Benny and his commitment, I am convinced that the Lord will bless him in all that he does, and his remarkable gifts and personality will be well used.

It would not be long before we were on the move again. As we produced all the newsletters, annual programmes, circulars, booking forms and so on, we needed extra staff and more office equipment, which included a large, up to date photocopier. We also despatched *Saints Alive!* and other course books. We soon realised we had outgrown the space available. The trustees recognised the need, and allowed us to pursue the possibility of seeking new premises. The trustees of the house declined to be part of any new plan and we realised that, ideally, ARM should now seek to own its own property. Apart from convenience of nation-wide travelling from a better-placed area, we opted for the Harrogate district because of our need to be in touch with Margaret's father, and the nursing home where he resided. Another consideration was that property prices then were still much lower than in the south east. At the same time, I envisaged using the magnificent new conference centre in Harrogate for some of our one-day conferences, and this we did in due course. We found an ideal Edwardian house in nearby Knaresborough. It had five good sized bedrooms, three reception rooms, and a basement area already fitted with shelves and cupboards which could store all the books and publications and be used as a mailing room. In 1987 it cost £72000! The bank arranged a mortgage loan for us and we moved from Haddenham to Knaresborough at the end of January. The owners of the house at Haddenham sold that at a good profit for their trust fund. They later gave a donation to ARM towards the cost of the extension we had made, which had obviously contributed to the sale price. We engaged new staff, and Margaret now took over the mail order and conference bookings full-time. Though the house was ideal for the purpose, Margaret was experiencing increased pain and discomfort from an arthritic hip, and ascents to the first floor office and descents to the basement did nothing to improve matters.

I was also aware of increasing health problems; I was no longer as fit and able, and I realised that all the stress of the last eighteen years was beginning to take its toll. I had now reached the age of sixty, and I began to wonder who might take over from me when I eventually retired. My thoughts centred on the possibility that a suitable person might come along who could work alongside me and then take over as the next director of ARM. In pursuit of this possibility, I approached one or two individuals, none of whom seemed right, except one, Nick de Keyser, vicar of a parish in Grantham. He hailed from a parish in Beckenham, Kent, where Trevor Marzetti had been a lay reader, and was well known to him. I recognised that he was keen, and I was becoming quite desperate and seriously thought he might fill the role for, perhaps, two years, after which I would retire. Naturally, I put the possibility to the trustees, but they insisted that a small group of them, under John Marsh, should examine the situation and make a decision. They turned him down and came up with no other suggestions at that point, and it seemed at the time as if they did not realise my predicament. I was aware, however, that there was now an element among the trustees who might wish to define a new agenda for the future of Anglican Renewal Ministries, which my eventual departure would facilitate. That did not present me with any problem, and I saw there would be a need for change following the unique circumstances that had placed my imprint so firmly on how ARM was run.

My concern for the future was at one stage compounded further by a sudden realisation that we were heading for financial problems. Ever since we had moved ARM away from Thwing we had needed more and more money to keep things going, but there came a period when income and projected income seemed inadequate to cover all the extra cost of salaries, mortgage repayments, office and travel expenses. This worry added to a growing sense of depression and gloom at the dramatic turn-round of all our previous hopes and certainties. Once more I regretted our leaving Lamplugh, whilst at the same time I was aware that we needed to trust God to bring the situation fully within his control. In the next newsletter, more as a request for prayer than the inevitable appeal for more funds, I shared our worry, the concerns, and the burden we were bearing. We were soon completely overwhelmed by the loving response from our supporters 'out there', who obviously empathised with our situation. We were sent money gifts and interest-free loans to ease the financial burden, including one gift of £30,000! I debated whether to use that to substantially reduce the mortgage at one go, or to keep it in an interest bearing account and use the income towards the monthly mortgage repayments. I chose this latter course as we were now back into a safe financial position because of the generous response we had received. That large sum then remained as a capital standby, in case of future emergencies. The £30,000 remained in the bank when Michael Mitton succeeded me, and the mortgage loan was now considerably reduced. The finances were now healthy.

The massive support by phone calls and many letters from

the people whom we were there to serve was heartwarming; it came as a great encouragement and tonic, softening the disappointment wrought upon us by the position taken by the trustees. Their rejection of a desperately needed assistant came as a salutary experience to me, as I had previously made such decisions myself. After all, I thought, I was the one in the hot seat with the full time commitment to ARM; and I felt that, for the most part, they seemed to be unaware of the seriousness of the situation.

There had been the visit to Uruguay, at the invitation of the new Anglican bishop there, Bill Godfrey. We had first met him several years earlier at Lamplugh House, and then David Smith and I conducted a renewal weekend at his parish in Hucknall, near Nottingham. A small inheritance I had received made the trip possible, and Margaret was happy for me to go, as we thought the change of scene and a new experience away from the pressures might be good for me. So it was that, in March 1988, off I went from Manchester via Frankfurt on the long journey to Montevideo. All I knew of it was that it was the resting place of the German Battleship, 'Admiral Graf von Spee', scuttled there in 1939, following the Battle of the River Plate. It was a most interesting and enjoyable two weeks, and I stayed with Bill and his family. It was good to see the growth that was taking place at the Cathedral church in the city, and its social ministry to poor people in the area. I went with Bill, his son, and an assistant minister, on a visit around the country to various Anglican communities, and did my share of preaching at services (usually interpreted into Spanish). A wealthy looking community of prosperous elderly ladies, complete with blue-rinses, at Punta del Este, looked more than vaguely familiar! We arrived at Salto, on the river border with Argentina, in the middle of the Mardi Gras celebrations. There they were busy preparing for a visit from the Pope.

I also went on a two-day visit to Buenos Aires, a two hundred mile flight away, where I stayed at the Bishop's house. It was interesting to see some of the work of the Anglican Cathedral, and to meet descendants of English settlers, fully part of the cosmopolitan variety presented by that attractive city. I could see immediately why it had been described as more like Paris than New York. It was only six years since the Falklands War, but as an Englishman I was warmly welcomed. The only reference to the conflict that I saw was a large notice at the airport declaring, 'The Malvinas are Ours!' My short visit gave me a sympathetic view of the Argentinians and all their suffering under various military dictatorships —today replaced by their current economic problems. Incidentally, I was struck at the time by the quantity of tawdry medallions and souvenirs of Eva Peron that were sold everywhere.

One of the highlights of my trip, to which I have often referred as an example of the need to translate charismatic renewal into familiar culture, came through a charismatic mass at a Roman Catholic church. Bill had been invited to attend, and I went with him. We were placed in two seats of honour in the chancel, from where we were able to observe the congregation. It was a weekday evening and the church was literally packed to the roof, for at the back was a huge ascending balcony and every seat was occupied. It was the noisiest, liveliest and most spontaneous display of charismatic abandon that I have ever witnessed. Though it was strange to me, for these people it was a natural expression of joy and worship, and fitted in with their culture. It was obvious that it was not imposed upon them as a new form, and they were very happy with it.

Upon my return home, and back into the routine, the pressures continued to bear down on me: not yet so much the pressure of work, but the stress of concern for the future, and it became evident, particularly to Margaret, that I seemed to be heading for some sort of breakdown. This pressure was relieved considerably when Jane once again left her hotel receptionist work in order to come and help with the administration, in which she was well versed and efficient. We had also another girl helping at the time, and she and Jane remained until Michael and Julia Mitton had settled in, the following year. This relief was short-lived, for my health problems were deepening. Before long, I found myself scarcely able to concentrate by midday, and often needed to lie down. They were very able to cope with things and thus relieve me considerably. One afternoon I was lying down, pondering what may possibly happen in the future, by now convinced that there was no chance of an assistant director being appointed. I had never thought of giving up or retiring, as I still had a few years to go before qualifying for the full church pension after thirty seven years of service, and at the time I knew nothing of sickness benefits being available. However, just as on other occasions, I felt prompted in my mind, and there came the immediate decision that I must visit a doctor and ask him whether or not it would be right to consider early retirement. This was my first visit to a doctor since moving to Knaresborough, and I did not know him nor did he know me, but he soon identified stress-related problems and advised that if I could economically take early retirement then I certainly should do so. He promptly arranged for me to go to Harrogate Hospital as a day-patient, for a series of examinations and tests, the results of which provided sufficient grounds to retire, and which were accepted by the Church of England Pensions Board. I discovered that the state sickness allowance would keep my income at the level of a clergy stipend that I already received.

So the decision to go was made —four years and two bases on, following the questionable move from Thwing. Margaret was relieved; she had had enough, and by now her hip condition was getting worse. In December 1989, eight months after our departure, she had it replaced with an artificial one. She had shared all the weight of work and ministry from the very start, and without her abilities (not least putting up with me!) none of it would ever have taken place. Although, in the nature of things, I had the 'up-front' role, we were very much a partnership. This was recognised by all and, deservedly, she received many tributes. Tom Lees, in view of my bulk, referred to her, as 'Lawrence's better third'.

The trustees were informed of my decision, and I gave six

months notice, so that there was good time to find a suitable replacement. The eighth National Conference in September was imminent, and there our departure was announced. We knew it was right and we felt it was clearly of the Lord, readily placing the future in his hands. It seemed that we had been prompted and prepared by him for what to us was a momentous decision, and that we had not been forced by the position to take the easy way out. Quite definitely, once again, this was 'over', not 'under', the circumstances. During the next six months I took things easy on the administrative side, but continued with most of the normal undertakings that were in the programme, though there were a few where I had to find people to step in for me. One such occasion was a day of renewal at a London Church, St. George's, Holborn, where Tom Smail had been booked to be the main speaker. However, two days earlier, I was suddenly beset with heart pains (later recognised as the onset of angina) and we felt it would be unwise for me to make the journey. I was very grateful to Tom, who at short notice took on the whole proceedings himself on our behalf.

Now we began to think of who might be a good successor to suggest to the trustees—perhaps it was not for us to do that, but nevertheless one person emerged in my thoughts as eminently suitable. He was Michael Mitton, a young man very keen on Anglican renewal, and vicar of a parish in Kidderminster. I had met him and was impressed by what I saw. He obviously knew what it was all about, and displayed admirable leadership qualities as leader of the Worcester diocesan renewal group. Before ARM moved back up to Yorkshire, Teddy Saunders accompanied me and shared in a diocesan day of renewal, arranged by Michael at the home of the Bishop of Worcester, Hartlebury Castle, so he was known by one of the trustees at least. I approached him and suggested he might fill the role. The trustees were not happy with this, however, and insisted that they would look around for someone. The post was advertised, and they insisted that Michael would need to take his chance with the rest. He had been seen by a few of them and told more or less to go and find a vision —which in due course he did, and he was universally accepted as the next Director. It was with a degree of satisfaction that we saw events confirm that we had been right after all, and the Holy Spirit had indeed pointed us to God's man for the job. But let Michael 's own story tell what happened, as he wrote in the very last issue of *Anglicans for Renewal* in Summer 2002 when, in the wisdom of the then Trustees, ARM and its function came to a full stop.

It was a warm sunny morning in July 1988. I clearly remember the moment in my vicarage office, thinking to myself, 'It feels good to be settled in this job.' Then the phone rang, and a man I had met only once or twice before spoke to me. It was Lawrence Hoyle, who told me that he was retiring as Director of ARM. He had been praying about who should succeed him, and was convinced the Lord was calling me to take on the work. I laughed politely, and then gave him the names of three other people that I felt were far more suitable. He then gave me the Yorkshire version of 'calling a spade a spade', and insisted that I give thought and prayer to his suggestion!

It became clear that I was to offer myself for this post. A week before the interviews, I went to the convent at Malvern with the specific intention of asking the Lord for a vision for the work. Without a vision, I felt I could not proceed to the interview. Towards the end of that retreat, I went out for an evening walk and suddenly felt the Lord saying almost audibly to me, 'Turn left down that road and study the sign that you will see.' I obediently turned left and came upon a signboard with a picture on it. The board was advertising a leisure centre and there was a large picture of a fruit tree on it. I sensed the Lord was saying that ARM was to help the church to bear important fruits. As I walked back to the convent, I saw in my mind's eye each fruit being picked from the tree and presented to me, and I watched as each one was opened to reveal its meaning. The six fruits were: prophecy, spiritual warfare, worship, prayer, great celebrations and God's mighty acts. I related this vision at my interview with the ARM Trustees and found that this accorded very much with the vision in their hearts.

Thus it was that Julia and I and our three children found ourselves travelling up to North Yorkshire to begin a new work.[1]

Margaret and I rejoiced at Michael's appointment, convinced that, as he was a man who listened to God and was prepared to be obedient to his leading, ARM was indeed in safe hands.

We now set about finding a suitable house, having been advised by the Pensions Board of their equity mortgage scheme. Unhappily, this was the time in 1988 when house prices shot up, and we had great difficulty getting one. We would look at something, like it, make an offer, then every day face an increased asking price. We learned the meaning of 'gazumping', and were disappointed many times until we managed to get a small bungalow at Morton-on-Swale, near Northallerton. We had to dispose of much of our furniture and possessions, some of it to our daughters, in order to fit in. We moved in a few weeks before we were due to finish, on 31st March. Jane commuted daily down the A1 to look after the office, but Margaret and I only occasionally made the journey. Now that the right decisions had been made and we were in a new home, the burden of stress quickly lifted and I soon began to resume a normal life, but now with regular medical check ups and medication. Meanwhile, Margaret still suffered much pain from the arthritic hip and had to wait a further eight months before it was dealt with.

Over the months following the announcement of our departure we were inundated with letters of love and appreciation from so many people. We had never quite realised just how deep and widespread the effects of ARM's influence had been during the eight years of its existence.

From the start we had received much personal support and encouragement, and had made many friends during this time. We were very moved that such a large number of people took the time to write to us personally, and it was heart-warming. In a somewhat confused and stressed state at that time, I felt unable to reply to them individually, but I still have them all, and now and again I read them. Eventually, we put a general letter of appreciation in *Anglicans for Renewal* and thanked everyone for the most generous cheque with which we were presented and to which so many people had contributed. Our official 'send-off' from ARM took place at a day event at the Harrogate Conference Centre in June that year, when we were officially thanked and presented with the cheque and a huge bunch of flowers for Margaret. It was a very emotional moment for us. We were leaving many friends whom we loved —and who loved us, too!

There were no regrets at leaving ARM; it was time to go, and in this area at least we had now been honourably discharged. However, there still remained the question of Lamplugh House; we both remained Trustees and I was the chairman and, as such, had been involved periodically during the time since ARM was separated and taken away. The idea for the latter had grown out of the former, and that was a vision for which we were still very much concerned. We had not yet been released from that, and we were determined not to give up on it until we were confident that it was safely operating in accordance with God's purpose as it had originally been revealed to us. The Warden's five-year contract was due to end in January 1990, and we felt it was right that it should. We were not at all anxious to hang on to the responsibility, but we knew that when the right solution came we would know, and we would have peace about it. We had previously looked at the possibility of Lamplugh House being absorbed with a large centre in North Wales which also ran some smaller subsidiary places, but after several months it became clear that this was not the right course and we pulled out from it. Later events with that organisation showed we had been right in the action we had taken (I say 'we' meaning the Lamplugh Trustees, who shared the deliberations and decisions. Nevertheless, I had always made the initiatives and continued to do so.)

I knew that Whatcombe House in Dorset had eventually closed down, following a change of direction after Reg & Lucia East had retired, though I was not aware of any particular reasons. I also knew that care must be taken to see that Lamplugh did not get into the hands of anyone who might be associated with a 'phoney' part of the charismatic scene. Such places could go astray, and we wanted to ensure that Lamplugh would continue on sound, biblical lines under wise, mature leadership. God had declared Lamplugh House to be a 'Christian commando training centre' and we were determined to ensure that it did not become a 'spiritual massage parlour' instead!

During the summer I approached a few people whom I thought might be interested in applying for the post of warden, but to no avail. Next, I advertised the post in the church press and had a few replies, some of which seemed to be clergy bent on escaping from parochial ministry. None were to my knowledge actively involved or qualified to encourage renewal teaching and ministry. Soon, autumn arrived and the date for Margaret's hip replacement was fixed for early December, after which she made a remarkable recovery and entered on a new lease of life. When in January still no replacement warden had been found, I offered, with Margaret's help to keep a watching brief on Lamplugh's activities as a *pro tem* measure. There was no programme prepared for the year ahead, though a few private groups had booked some dates. We lived sixty miles from Thwing and thought we could commute and stay there when necessary, to oversee the few days of any bookings in the pipeline, and this we did from the end of January, when the warden's contract had ended.

Joyce Welburn (nee Vincent), who had been the mainstay of the catering side from the early days, was still there, as was the gardener/maintenance man. The departing couple had informed us that the two voluntary women helpers, including Pam Oldfield, who had been there nearly ten years, would not be staying on. Some people assumed I was sacking the incumbents in order to come back and rule once more. This was not so, but I received several letters more or less accusing me of this, which hurt deeply. Pam was an old and loved friend, and remained so, but she was now over seventy and had done more than her share of hard work over the years, so we did not feel it would be right to impose on her good nature by asking her to remain. There was no criticism at all of any member of staff. Barbara Worrall had moved to Thwing a few years earlier, with the idea of associating with the work and ministry at Lamplugh, and she offered to help with the office work, and Mary Somerville, also from the village, gave much help in the kitchen.

We soon found that it was too inconvenient to travel back and forth, especially when more was happening. We had of necessity compiled a programme of conferences and renewal days, not least because we needed a cash flow to keep things going until new arrangements were made for the future. By April it became necessary to move lock, stock and barrel into the warden's cottage, and though I did not become warden, Margaret became officially the manager/housekeeper. We made this move reluctantly, but sensed it was what God required of us, and thought it would only be for a short period. In fact it was to be over eighteen months before a satisfactory solution was found.

To cut a long story short, it was all resolved in August 1991, when we came to an arrangement with Kingdom Faith Ministries, based at Crawley in Sussex. We had known Colin Urquhart for years, from the early days of his travelling ministry in the 1970s, and he had been several times to speak at Lamplugh before his ministry developed on a much larger scale. Colin heard that we were looking for a new future for Lamplugh House. So it was that Lamplugh became part of a much bigger venture, but each had a complementary vision. The trustees agreed to the plans, and one or two new members from KFM were added to their number. All went smoothly, and Margaret and I were able to pack up and leave for the last time, happy that the Lord had made this possible but had required our obedience to return to Thwing when we did, so that it could happen. It was with different and happier emotions that I drove away down the drive this time as compared with 1985. Because of the impending change we had run down the programme and there was nothing left in the pipeline. We slipped away quietly, without fuss or ceremony. How different it all was from 1971/72, when we had such a struggle to convince others of the feasibility of what we sought to do at Thwing. Now, after more than twenty years, there was official recognition of Lamplugh House in *Seen*, the York diocesan newspaper, which ran the following article from Ron Treasure.

Rectory is transformed into centre with vision
Ronald Treasure gives thanks for a Centre
of Christian Renewal and its founders.

1992 sees the 20th Anniversary of the remarkable institution of Lamplugh House at Thwing on the Yorkshire Wolds. Lawrence Hoyle, together with his wife Margaret, transformed their over-large Victorian Rectory, with great vision and immensely hard work into an ecumenical centre for spiritual renewal

During these twenty years countless Yorkshire folk and many others from further afield—leaders, lay people and enquirers—have come to conferences, retreats, teaching days, seminars, holidays and parish weekends and to learn about charismatic renewal and to be refreshed, strengthened and renewed in the service of Our Lord....

The article then went on to describe how Anglican Renewal Ministries was formed there, with myself as its first director. It was all the work of God, and it was indeed over all material and human circumstances.

Note
[1] *Anglicans for Renewal* Summer 2002.

Twelve

Prayers in the Wilderness

In mid November 1991, following our short spell back at Thwing when, from our point of view at least, the future of Lamplugh House was finally and satisfactorily resolved, we returned to the bungalow at Morton-on-Swale. It had been empty and on the market for eighteen months, and we kept it on sale until, shortly after Christmas, we received an offer, which was acceptable to the Church of England Pensions Board. We had opted to move to Kingsbridge, Devon, during our reluctant, post-retirement sojourn at Lamplugh, so that we could be close to at least one of our daughters. Jane, now married to a submariner in the Royal Navy, was living at Saltash, over the Tamar from Plymouth and twenty five miles from Kingsbridge. Susan, our other daughter, was settled on Tyneside, but we never felt any urge to move there. When we had previously looked at properties in the Kingsbridge area, for the most part the prices were beyond any financing arrangements that might be made with the Pensions Board. Happily, by this time the Pension Board had revised its equity mortgage conditions in order to allow for the vast increase in house prices that had happened since 1988; and we were able to obtain a delightful bungalow situated above the

Kingsbridge/Salcombe estuary. We enjoyed Devon and its natural beauty, rating it second only to Yorkshire for its scenery! Five miles to the east, west and south, we had sea, beaches and cliff walks, whilst Dartmoor, to the north, had the effect of creating a mini-climate in that part of the South Hams. With mild winters, and little in the way of snow and frost, we were able to create a pleasant garden out of what was chiefly grass; we obtained great pleasure from it, together with the novelty and enjoyment of exploring our new surroundings. With the settlement of the future of Lamplugh, we were free at last of the cerebral burdens we had carried from our former responsibilities, happy in the knowledge that God had established new leaders in both ventures, and we felt we had now been properly released to enjoy our retirement.

The church situation in that area left much to be desired, or so we thought, having had our experience of lively worship and energetic faith, and we were not attracted to what we sampled around the area. Much of the scene could best be described as hidebound, traditional and complacent, and renewal was not in evidence. It was not that we were necessarily in search of exuberant worship, but what would have been welcome was more evidence of living faith and real fellowship, rather than the 'socially conventional' religion apparently practised by the elderly imported retired, like ourselves, who formed the majority of each congregation. Eventually, we began attending Modbury Parish Church, ten miles away. We knew the Vicar, John Cole, and his wife, Liz, who came to ARM conferences, and there was a substantial group of believers to whom the Holy Spirit was real. We were welcomed there and soon felt at home. I would occasionally preach or conduct a service, or be involved in teaching courses. Regrettably, we lived too far away to be properly involved in the life of the parish.

From the start we enjoyed being at Kingsbridge, and we were very happily settled, in spite of continuing health problems that had caused my early retirement: from the undefined stress-related problems had developed hypertension, diabetes and angina, and now the latter was becoming very acute, so that it was difficult to walk any distance without medication. Eventually, in December 1994, after several tests and a long wait, I was sent to the Royal London Hospital, Whitechapel, where I underwent quadruple, heart by-pass surgery. All went well, and consequently my health improved dramatically, so that I could walk without chest pains, and found fresh energy and a new lease of life. I was still subject to stress problems, so I needed to take things easy and keep on a level keel. The diabetes and hypertension were kept under control by medication, now a routine part of life. Margaret, meanwhile, still benefiting from her hip replacement of 1989, was very well, and threw herself enthusiastically into gardening, grandmothering and as a member of a local committee that worked for the South West Children's Hospice.

During most of our nine years living in South Devon, we had very little contact with either Anglican Renewal Ministries or Lamplugh House, apart from Michael Mitton during his early days. We had attended a day meeting in Plymouth where he was main speaker, and returning from a visit to our daughter on Tyneside, we responded to an invitation to go and see ARM's new offices and headquarters in Derby. A visit to Lamplugh House whilst on a rare visit to East Yorkshire was a strange experience. The place was thriving under KFM as a Bible college, under the leadership of John MacKay. We had known John and his family years earlier, when he was a lecturer in theology at the University of Hull, but for several years he had been part of the Kingdom Faith organization. He had produced an in-depth teaching course on living in the Spirit, and now Lamplugh House was being used for resident students doing this course. We were thrilled to see how well the house was being used, and how they had improved amenities by utilising the extensive basement area for administration and mailing facilities. The gardens were well kept and attractive and it was obvious that KFM took its stewardship seriously. There were students from many different countries on the course, and on qualification, several teams of young people were being sent to serve in various parts of the world. People totally dedicated and committed to the Lord were truly fulfilling the vision of a worldwide ministry, emanating from a tiny village on the Yorkshire Wolds. Here indeed was a Christian commando training centre! The strange thing, though, was our being once again in this place that had been of such significance to our lives but no longer recognised by the people there; apart of course, from the MacKays themselves. Individuals move on, but God goes on working out his purposes. This visit was further confirmation, if such were needed, that we had been right to return to Lamplugh in 1990 and to wait on the Lord for guidance for its future.

Less than nine months after this visit, the mysterious design of God's purposes provoked shock and surprise once again. John MacKay, we discovered, had contracted a blood disorder and was in hospital for tests. It was a virulent form of leukaemia and he died six months later.

By 2002, Lamplugh House was a branch of Kingdom Faith Church, a new development of KFM's ministry, and now large numbers of people from a wide area converge on Thwing on Sunday mornings to worship there. There was a time when I would have deplored such a development; I am sure there was once a time when Colin Urquhart himself might have deplored it. But no longer —ministry in the power of the Holy Spirit has been offered in and to the institutional churches for a long time, and there has been much rejection. Now he leads people, particularly the young, into a new environment for worship and service in the kingdom. Whatever doctrine of the church one may hold, or has held, the doctrine of the kingdom of God is higher, and of the most importance. Kingdom Faith Church, and others similar to it, should be welcomed for emphasising that the full, Spirit-led, apostolic Christian message allows no compromise to worldly norms and fashions. Thank God for a growing number of Holy Spirit led churches, of whatever description or name. God the Father recognises no one by his or her denomination; I believe that he recognises us only as he sees us in Jesus Christ, in whom believers live according to the Spirit.

By 1999 we had begun attending Ivybridge Parish Church, fifteen miles away from our home, for two reasons: John and Liz Cole were moving to a new group of parishes near York, Alne and Brafferton; and Jane and Ray, now with two young children, had moved to Ivybridge after Ray left the Navy following twenty five years service, so we could all be there as a family. After several months we were getting rather weary of travelling all that distance, and coming away wondering why we had been there in the first place. I suppose being a clergyman does not help. I found the predictability boring, and often came away wondering whether attending a particular service had been worthwhile. I had become disillusioned and bored with the church (not with the church in the biblical sense of all faithful people, under the headship of Jesus Christ, but with many local and denominational manifestations). What we needed was fellowship with like-minded people, and I missed that a great deal. During this 'wilderness' period I never lost my faith, and I felt able to communicate with God without the benefit of the clergy! Increasingly, we found ourselves going nowhere for Sunday worship. I had now given up taking services as a retired pulpit-filler, of whom there are many in South Devon. The main reason was the old stress problem: I would soon become hassled and confused when taking a service and preaching, not least because every church had a different way of doing things. Several had little service books devised by some previous vicar, which bore little resemblance to any known liturgies! I have no particular axe to grind on churchmanship, but I could not stand sterile churchianity, of which there was a large measure.

I am not one of those retired clerics who feel that they 'must have an altar'; I do not believe that presiding over the Eucharist is simply a part of the clergyman's private devotions. I came to believe that the ministerial role is basically a functional one, as the spokesman or woman who leads and presides on behalf of the local people of God, and I am quite at ease being a member of the congregation. As a consequence of my involvement in charismatic renewal, and a developing understanding of every-member ministry, I came to share the outlook of St. Peter, that the highest form of status and ministry in the church is *Ho laos tou Theou* — the people of God—and all other orders are to be dedicated and marked by *service* in the Body. I have come to be wary of the connotation of the term 'priest', and its easy (though incorrect), often-assumed relationship to an Old Testament type of sacrificial priesthood. The word in the New Testament is *presbuteros*, or 'elder', from which we get the more correct word 'presbyter', which denotes a pastoral overseer. I do not hold to the medieval superstition still current in areas of the Church of England that something supernatural happens simply by repeating certain words. Words are important, and there is power in the word of God, but faith, and the anointing of God, are of key importance. I do not seek to diminish in any way the sacredness of the sacrament, nor the symbolic reality that in the form of bread and wine we receive the Body and Blood of Christ, for the sacrament is indeed a divinely commanded ordinance, but I believe that is what the Lord himself makes it, not 'priest' or celebrant. The 'liturgy' is the service, the offering, of the *people* of God; and, in my view, the celebrant represents and speaks for them. To perform this role within the church is an honour and a privilege, though I can see no theological reason why a respected layperson within a local congregation should not be appointed to preside at the Eucharist. It may well soon come to this by sheer necessity as the number of serving clergy diminishes and parishes are grouped into mini-dioceses! In most rural areas, and in many urban ones, ordained clergy are more or less performing like medieval 'mass priests', whose chief role is to travel from place to place 'doing' the Eucharist.

'Every member ministry' is more than a charismatic slogan; it is the formula for the church of tomorrow. Lack of finances and shortage of ordained clergy is forcing the church, even the church still in 'self-management' mode, to radically change its way of going about things. It would be more positive and less painful if we were able to recognise where the Holy Spirit is leading, for in submitting to his guidance and wisdom, we find the apostolic way of Christian growth and ministry. St. Peter's use of the term 'royal priesthood' for the people of God is more than a nice poetic expression; it teaches us that Christian believers can lay claim to the highest, most important role and status anyone can have.

But you are a chosen people, a royal priesthood, a holy nation, a people belonging to God, that you may declare the praises of him who called you out of darkness into his wonderful light. Once you were not a people, but now you are the people of God; once you had not received mercy, but now you have received mercy.[1]

Earlier in that chapter, Peter describes the 'priestly' function of the whole people of God, not individuals specially called out from it.

As you come to him, the living Stone —rejected by men but chosen by God and precious to him—you also, like living stones, are being built into a spiritual house to be a holy priesthood, offering spiritual sacrifices acceptable to God through Jesus Christ.[2]

During my time as director of Anglican Renewal Ministries, I had the privilege of visiting several Episcopalian (Anglican) parishes in the United States, where this apostolic teaching was fully pursued. All had large congregations, and every person in the church was under a lay pastor or elder (*presbuteros*), each one called from within the congregation, and taught and equipped for the role. As the church grew, more such leaders would emerge. The clergyman was in effect an overseer (*episkopos*) over them, whose main function was to train and pastor these leaders. Together, under God and using the gifts of the Spirit, they were engaged upon the apostolic instruction to 'build up the Body of Christ'. Such a local church, functioning under the Holy Spirit, is an evangelising agency in itself, because people are drawn to it. There are a few parishes operating on the same lines in England today, and they are live, growing churches, engaged upon the work of the kingdom.

In April 1999, we had a visitor at our door —Brian Turnbull, who lived just a few hundred yards down the road from us. He and his wife Ann had just returned from an ARM Lent Retreat at Swanwick, and had been given our address by John Gunstone, who had led the retreat. They attended Dodbrooke Church, which was our parish church too, but we had only been there once when we first came to Kingsbridge in 1992. It was so refreshing to meet people who seemed on the same spiritual wavelength, and to learn of a small group at that church who had formed a prayer fellowship and met weekly, not only to pray for the life of the church, but also for spiritual renewal. Consequently, the following Sunday we started going to Dodbrooke and joined in the prayer fellowship, and by doing this we got out of the spiritual doldrums. The organist and his wife, Robin and Mary Brett, were also members of this group. How refreshing to find a church organist eager for renewal —quite often they tend to be vociferously against it! Brian and Ann became close, supportive friends, and the following year, 2000, we went with them to that year's ARM Retreat, this time at High Leigh, Hoddesdon.

It was now ten years since my retirement, and to both of us it was quite an exercise in nostalgia; we met many old friends from past days, who welcomed us with much warmth and love, and reminisced about many times of blessing. It was particularly good to meet up again with Ron and Eliza Treasure, who were involved in leading the retreat with John Gunstone, and the present director of ARM, John Leach, whom we were meeting for the first time. Ron and Eliza, who 'retired' around the same time as we did, were still effectually involved in their quiet ministry of prayer, counselling and spiritual encouragement. Ever since a memorable Fountain Trust conference, at Guildford Cathedral in 1971, they had been used to help many people into the experience of the Holy Spirit's power and presence. In fact, that one-day 'Day with Holy Spirit' conference in Malton Parish Church in November of that year, which had started me off, was one outcome of Guildford. All through our years at Thwing they had been around and were great encouragers. With the rise of ARM, they often helped with personal ministry in the groups at many of its conferences, and many people can testify to great blessing through their ministry.

After all the years of non-involvement, I quickly perceived that things had changed —inevitably, of course. Michael Mitton had followed me as director and served for eight years; now John Leach was in his second year, and they both represented a new generation of post-war clergy, formed from a very different mould than the pioneers and leaders of renewal who had been instrumental, under God, in the phenomenal growth since the 1960s. It was evident that glossy and slick presentation methods now current in the secular world were considered essential to any progress, and much of the modern presentational (and politically correct) jargon was firmly in place. To this I reacted negatively, until I realised they were doing precisely what I had advocated years earlier: relating to—and communicating with—the current culture. I realised that I am a creature of a bygone age, in a time warp and well past my 'sell-by date'.

We, and many others, received much spiritual benefit and enjoyment from the retreat and the ministry that was given there. However, during those three days I was given a rather disconcerting revelation about the future of Anglican Renewal Ministries. This was in the same pattern as many similar thoughts about what would happen that had come to me in past years, maybe quite irrational and only possible to verify by subsequent events. I felt that I was told that John Leach would be the last director of ARM, and that under his leadership it would come to an end. Whether this was to be in accordance with God's design, I did not know. Naturally, I suppose, given my original role in its formation, the vision I had received, and which, eight years later, God passed on to

Michael Mitton, I immediately construed that it could not be what God wanted to happen, and I shared my misgivings with the Turnbulls and others. This was in March 2000, two years before this predictive insight was actually verified by events. Clearly, over the years there had been a distinctive change of emphasis in the way ARM interpreted its role, and I sensed that some of the older 'originals' were not necessarily happy, but, that be as it may, God does not stay still and he often moves us in a new direction. After over ten years in a spiritual wilderness, it was not for me to criticise my successors, nor to question the seriousness of their motives.

A sad event took place in 2000. We still kept in contact with our friends Colin and Anne Oliphant, whom we believed God had brought in and used so positively for the consolidation of Lamplugh House, and who had been good guides and counsellors to us in its development. Their son Hamish was now living in Plymouth, where he worked as a marine architect, and they came down to visit him twice each year. This meant that we were able to meet up with them at Kingsbridge or enjoy together the beautiful coastal scenery nearby. We had seen them in May 1999, when Colin was the picture of good health. We were shocked when we learned at the end of the year that he had been struck down with a brain tumour. After several months of sustained and fervent prayer by many of their friends in different parts of the world, he died early in April 2000, at the age of fifty two. His funeral was attended by many people of different churches, who testified to the quiet and positive ministry for which he had been widely used. When thinking of how many former friends and effective leaders had died at a comparatively young age I was drawn to read Psalm 31. Verse fifteen registered with me: 'My times are in thy hand....'

Retirement gives much opportunity for reflection, and looking at the Anglican scene in the south west of England makes one realise how little it seems to have been affected by renewal, apart from a few notable exceptions. From these spiritual backwoods, however, I have come to realise that today's Church of England is very different from that wherein

I was ordained in 1955, not least because of new forms of service and inclusive language. At first, like many more, I was suspicious of the campaign to ordain women, though it did not come until after my retirement. Nevertheless, I have come to terms with it for the reasons that I have already expressed. I could see no theological objection to it, but I hated 'feminism', and had often joked that as the men were casting off their dog collars, the women were fast putting them on. I am very impressed with many of the women ministers I have seen in action, but why, oh why, must they wear male clerical dress? I like women to be women, not pretend men, and I wish some decent form of clerical attire, so long as such is deemed important, could be designed. The clerical gear of men is outdated enough, being as it is the stylised outdoor gear of the ancient Roman gentleman! Bishops, too, have changed from the magisterial, and autocratic, 'my lords' in gaiters that I remember. The diminution of such formality and deference has been a major change. Many younger clergy will refuse to move to pastures new because where they are situated their wives can earn more than they do, or they could not possibly disturb their children's education by moving them to another school. In the reviled old days, we trusted God to look after us over such considerations —and he did! Not so many clergy wives worked in those days, unless they were teachers or nurses, and stipends were very much lower than they are today. One gets the impression that clergy vocations are seen in much the same terms as secular 'jobs' nowadays. Patently, I am unreconstructed and politically incorrect! At my age it can be harder to adapt to some changes. We make jokes about 'political correctness', as though it was entirely a joking matter, but it is not; for as well as being a threat to the freedom of expression, to me it has satanic elements. What do I mean by that? For a start, the requirement that all 'faiths' be treated as equally valid is insidious, as it paves the way for disposing of the uniqueness of Jesus Christ as God's Son and the only Saviour. When the heir to the throne, by declaring he will consider himself 'defender of faiths' rather than defender of the Faith, seemingly backs such a syncretic abomination, some Christians might find it difficult to make the traditional oath of allegiance. Then there is the flouting of Christian marriage and family values, together with the acceptance of sexual deviance and its grossest desires as equally valid alternatives. Do many people remember how, years ago, it was said that satanists were praying against Christian marriage and morality? We were warned!

During the growth of the charismatic movement, the press and television had a field day; and its excesses, real or manufactured, were portrayed, ridiculed and regularly pilloried. Now the media interest has switched to the pronouncements and activities of the liberal unbelievers, whom one could easily deem to hold centre stage in today's church. An article in *The Times* (August 1st 2002) asked the question, 'Are the pulpits of Anglican churches occupied by closet atheists?' Judging by the apparent numbers who disbelieve vital doctrines of traditional faith, it might seem to be so. A contributor to the article, calling for more defenders of traditional faith, concludes: 'If the Church no longer teaches its historic articles of faith as true, then it is indistinguishable from any other humanistic pressure group. It might as well resign.' The liberal approach to moral issues such as those raised by homosexuality and sexual license are equally abhorrent, and confusing to those who would abide by traditionally accepted biblical values. Indeed, how the church has changed in the fifty years since I entered theological college in 1952. The question may be asked, 'Where is the Holy Spirit in all this?'

As Anglicans, Sunday by Sunday, we affirm our belief in 'the Holy Spirit, the Lord and giver of life' —but I wonder how often we believe that the Spirit also brings death into all that is not of God, and which does not conform to his perfect, holy will. The truth is that we can be cultivating and defending all sorts of things that are not of God; and, because they are not, no amount of prayerful tending will bring life into them.

...All men are like grass, and all their glory is like the flowers of the field. The grass withers and the flowers fall, because the breath of the Lord blows on them.[3]

We should face the fact that many things have been allowed to develop in the church which can scarcely be claimed as being of God. If some things are not of God, then possibly they should die. Considering there is much evidence of death in the church, we should allow those things to be buried. Rather than do this, however, the tendency instead is to try to administer any amount of artificial respiration to things in which God has no interest and are not part of the agenda that he has set for the church. In the debate regarding the future of Anglican Renewal Ministries, there has been talk of the need to die for there to be a future resurrection —though I find it difficult to identify ARM with the foregoing principle whereby the Spirit brings death to what is not of God. When problems and questions of relevance arise over the future of something manifestly of God and for the good of the church, I would think the first requirement should be to try and discover what has gone wrong, repent as needs be, change as may be required, and then start again.

Though forewarned, I was shocked, angry and bitter at the apparent demise of Anglican Renewal Ministries, and I quickly realised that was no condition from which I could attempt to make any objective comment on it. I repented of that, and I released it from my system, but I do feel that I should comment on these events as I have interpreted them, even though they are not in keeping with the apparent bland acceptance of it all by some with whom I have spoken. The ministry that ARM was to pursue began, in part, at Lamplugh House, several years earlier than its institution; and the clarification of the vision, and God's calling, was neither engineered nor was it sought by me, but was given to me in an unforgettable process of revelation that demanded obedience. It is not in a spirit of judgement or criticism of others, but in the sense of suggesting there might be another side to the story that I make my comments —outspoken, as is my temperament, but not designed to be intemperate or hurtful.

Because I had been given that word two years earlier, concerning its future, I was not surprised to learn that the trustees were set on ending ARM's current operations. Apart from that, even in our remote situation, I was aware that things were not going well. I had also been told that the director would not be applying for the renewal of his contract in September. Together with preposterous opinions being expressed in some quarters that ARM had successfully finished its role, I knew that some of the trustees were voicing the view that it was time to close it down. When I was told that early in January an *ad hoc* consensus meeting was being arranged 'to wait on the Lord', I was dismayed; my experience of consensus meetings was not good. In fact, had John Gunstone and I taken the consensus view of the 1980 meetings in London, ARM would never have emerged in the first place. Then, when I heard that this consensus meeting was to consist largely of 'younger' clergy, I was doubly dismayed. When the older generation show their lack of confidence in themselves and their given role, and idolise the young for their smart new ideas, then it says little for the biblical concept about the wisdom of age and experience. It seems that one or two pretty or sentimental 'pictures' that were produced at this meeting had the effect of convincing the trustees that ARM must be placed into a form of hibernation. The suggestion that, like Fountain Trust, it might need to die for something new to arise was offered as some justification. I do not agree, however, that FT had necessarily reached its sell-by date. I told Felicity Lawson, now heading the trustees, in reply to an advance notice of the forthcoming announcement, and in which she asked for comments, that, rather than having outlived its usefulness, Fountain Trust had lost its vision. At that time I could perceive that FT might adapt to the agenda ARM was to follow, but I felt that they were listening to more strident voices than the quiet one of the Holy Spirit. I suggested to her that perhaps the leadership of ARM was past its sell-by date. The seemingly silly proposal that ARM should be 'handed back to God' prompted the question, 'Who has it now, then?' One of the hazards of trying to listen to God in the rarefied intensity of charismatic get-togethers is that fantasies of the mind and/ or wishful thinking can be mistaken for the guidance of the Holy Spirit. Revelations and promptings of the Spirit need to be weighed and assessed by a more representative body of the constituency being addressed, as happened at the beginning, when ARM was established. The 'consensus' body was manifestly wrong when it decided in 1980 that there was no call for an Anglican renewal-servicing group. I have been asked by several people: 'Why has ARM closed down?' I have to say that I do not know.

My mind has pursued another thought: what about ERM in the United States, that had so ably assisted ARM's birth, and the other ARMs that had followed the Church of England and set up their own branches in Canada, Australia, New Zealand, Wales and elsewhere? Have they discovered that they have fulfilled their calling? How, I thought, could the representatives of the two most backward provinces of the Anglican Communion believe that they had done their job and God was satisfied, whilst the others were all still in harness? We were invited to attend the closing down service at Derby Cathedral, but apart from the fact that we did not wish in any way to be thought of as identifying with the decision, we could not have faced it emotionally. We are too aware of the years of agonising and prayer from which, eventually, Anglican Renewal Ministries came into being, to be satisfied with what I suspected might be a sentimental glossing of the reality behind the events. When I was invited to write an article on the early vision for ARM in the last issue of *Anglicans for Renewal*,[4] I refused. My ungracious thought was, 'It is a bit late now, if they have not yet discovered it!'

Following the service at Derby on 14th July we were sent copies of the form of service that had been used —ARM's custodians had become quite polished at producing services and liturgies, and this was no exception, though I looked in vain for any hint of penitence or the need for it. It was a well produced package in which, appropriately, given the decision and its reasoning, the corpse was laid to rest. It encouraged uplifting charismatic worship, and I expect a feeling of a job well done. One part of it that I found distasteful, though, was the suggestion that now it was in order for the director to hand his anointing for the role, 'back to God'. For anyone who has experienced the anointing of the Spirit in a special way, that is impossible. The anointing of the Spirit is not a badge of office bestowed by an appointing committee, even if that committee is the ARM trustees! My understanding, and I believe this is scriptural, is that it is God who bestows the anointing—the power with which to work for him—for a purpose or a task. He it is who withdraws it if, (a) the task or purpose is completed; or, (b) If the recipient is disobedient to God's will and requirements. Surely, to presume we can attempt to 'hand it back' to God is an improper and ungracious assumption.

I still find it difficult to accept that it is God who has applied his axe to this special tree of his planting, which has grown and flourished and produced much fruit; so I will make an effort to go along with the expressed expectation that God will create something new from the remains of Anglican Renewal Ministries. When the so-called 'pilot light' group gets around to turning the gas up, and a renewed vision is imminent, I believe it will be a vision to again reach out to the church and its individual members, and to enable and encourage them to receive the fullness of the Holy Spirit, so that as members of the Body of Christ, a community of *agape* —God's brand of love—they can be used to further the kingdom of God.

The word 'renewal' is a bit old hat now. The charismatic movement, certainly as we were understanding it in the institutional church, was to bring about a norm of Christianity that matches the New Testament description of apostolic faith and action. The ongoing life of the church ought to be in line with the Acts of the Apostles, for apostolic Christianity is real, normal Christianity. Perhaps the word 'restoration' may now be more appropriate to exemplify what God might do for ARM—and, through it, the church—once more at the grassroots, where the reality of faith belongs and from where it spreads. Another slogan has emerged: 'to be real it must be global.' If that implies that we can be too local in our concerns, I am not sure that I agree. By being truly local, and powered by the apostolic zeal that it inspires, the influence of the church moves out in often overlapping areas, whether it starts in Derby, Thwing or Timbuctoo.

Being 'global' in our thinking should not assume a Western, paternalistic attitude to other places in the world, especially toward Christians in developing countries. It is insulting to suggest that Christians of Africa and Asia are in greater spiritual need than we are, when patently they can show us much, where biblical faith and spirituality are concerned.

Several people have suggested to me that ARM lost its vision. Whether it did or not is not for me to judge. The calling and role of ARM has always been focussed as a mission to the local church. Can the question now be asked: In recent years did ARM move beyond the parameters wherein it was set? —seeking to tell the church 'how to do it', instead of constantly pointing to the spiritual resources that need to be appropriated, whereby the people of God are enabled to 'do the stuff' themselves, as John Wimber aptly put it? This is rhetorical, and I do not have an answer. But I believe it was never its role to produce fancy liturgies or adornments to public worship, like exotic offertory processions or artistic use of candles or anything else. The aim of ARM's eucharistic worship was to display how that which is sometimes boringly familiar could come alive in an exciting new way in the freedom of the Spirit. Again, do people need reminding that the church is in a process of change and how to deal with it? It is always in a process of change; our responsibility is to be sure the pressures of the world do not cause change to our raison d'être —instead seeking to be used to change the world itself through the gospel of Jesus Christ. That is a superhuman and supernatural task, and a church minus the powering of the Spirit is useless to change anything except the frontals and the flowers. I am concerned, as are others, that without ARM there will be no agency specifically teaching and encouraging Anglicans to seek the baptism in the Holy Spirit. If there is not, things will gradually fizzle out, just as movements of the Holy Spirit have sometimes done in the past.

Let us not write off the role that has been played by Anglican Renewal Ministries. We need to pray for the restoration of the vision that enabled it in the beginning, and that in God's timing a leader may be found who has gone through the refining fire and trauma of adversity, and has the ability to confront the spiritual enemy, in full confidence of God's will and workings. I also believe that, when such a person does emerge, there will be formulated a vision very similar to that which was beautifully revealed to Michael Mitton in those six fruits: 'prophecy', 'spiritual warfare', 'worship', 'prayer', 'great celebrations', and 'God's mighty Acts'.

Notes
[1] 1 Peter 2:9,10.
[2] 1 Peter 2:4,5.
[3] Isaiah 40:6,7.
[4] Sadly, the last issue reported the sudden and unexpected death of its founder, Trevor Marzetti.

Thirteen

The Tree

After nine years in South Devon and just over one year in South Wales, we are back again in the only area where we feel we have any real roots: Yorkshire —Scarborough, in fact. After a confusing two years, wondering what was happening to us and where we should go, we are now happily settled in a pleasantly situated ground floor flat, with lovely gardens and within two minutes walk of the Esplanade and its fine walks and scenic views. Not only have we met up again with many friends from our former days, we find that many people around here remember us. Also, we are not too far away from our daughters and their families.

Considering that most elderly people retire and then settle down somewhere more or less permanently, it may be wondered why we have to be so radically different! Why indeed? First, of course, we had the eighteen months back at Lamplugh, and in 1992 moved to Kingsbridge, where we thought we had settled for good, but it was not to be. Our son-in-law obtained a job with a telecommunications firm on the outskirts of Newport, South Wales, and so Jane and family moved to Magor, between Chepstow and Newport, towards the end of 2000. As that was 150 miles 'up the line' it was felt we should move too; we had hoped to find something in Ross-on-Wye, but were unsuccessful and ended up in a small, modern house in the next village to Magor. We were situated on the outskirts, a few miles from the Welsh end of the new Severn Bridge. It was not ideal, but once more I was becoming aware of health problems, and it seemed practical not to be too far away from family.

We began to settle into our new surroundings when the blow came. Ray was made redundant after only nine months, when the telecommunications bubble burst and his branch was closed down. There being few opportunities in South Wales, they began to look around on more familiar territory, and thus they moved to Scarborough, where Ray got a computer teaching job at the Yorkshire Coast College. Soon they found a house (an added bonus being that property prices were a little lower than South Wales) and moved north early in 2002. Margaret and I were in a quandary: we do not exactly like to keep moving house, but now I had eyesight problems, together with internal troubles requiring the usual long waits, several tests and eventual hospital treatment. The result was that in March 2002 I had an operation for the removal of a bladder tumour, followed three weeks later by an operation on my left eye. Over a very short period I had developed incurable macula degeneration in the right eye, thus reducing it to peripheral vision only. Margaret does not drive, and at that stage I faced the prospect of being unable to do so. We were a good distance from shops and facilities and faced the prospect of being more or less isolated in an unfamiliar place —very much 'under' the circumstances. Hitherto we had relied on Jane to chauffeur us when necessary, but now she was gone. The local vicar and his wife, Brian and Janet Parfitt, were most kind and helpful, as were our next-door neighbours, Norma and John Barry, driving me to and from the hospital at Newport.

Believe it or not, personally I was not at all keen on the idea of us moving north again, though Margaret thought we should go to Scarborough. The Church of England Pensions

Board, though understanding the reason for us wanting to move yet again, were not overwhelmed with excitement! Now, however, with interest rates being low, it was possible to obtain an ordinary mortgage at no higher rate than the Pension Board scheme, and that made things easier all round. The operation on my left eye, for the removal of a cataract, placing an implant and rectifying long-sightedness, had the effect of improving my general vision, so that when I was able to have an eye test I was pronounced fit to drive. I just hope and pray that the left eye does not go the same way as the other one.

Obviously I have overcome my earlier reservations about moving back to Yorkshire. We are happy and settled, convinced it is the right move, and the Lord has made it possible. It feels like a new lease of life and we have total peace with it. We are only twelve miles from Thwing, where it all began; and now often on Sundays we go there to worship; not at Lamplugh, where everything is happening and the dynamic work of the Holy Spirit proceeds 'under new management', and with which we have no problem, as I have already stated, but at Thwing Parish Church, where nothing has changed —still Lorna Coates playing the organ, faithful Arthur Berriman still ringing the bell, and quietly and without complaint keeping the churchyard as the neatest and tidiest for miles around; still many familiar faces, looking a bit older now, and a few new ones. Where the years have taken their toll, some old memorable faces are no longer there. But the Lord is there, as he always was, and we find the simple, straightforward Eucharist and a good biblical sermon is just what we need. We went there in the spring of 2002, to find an interregnum in progress. David Lunn, former Bishop of Sheffield, a warm, kindly and spiritual man, was looking after Thwing and the other churches within the enlarged benefice, and the parishioners have taken to him with great affection.

I have concluded it is these visits to Thwing Church that make me feel we have come back home after all our wanderings and wonderings. It is a beautiful and colourful little place, and still has that feeling of the numinous: as one of those special places where one is especially reminded of the closeness of the Lord (who, of course, dwells within the believer). It is good to see again some of the 'good yeoman stock', as the late Stanley Linsley described them: traditional, uncomplicated, friendly folk, whom we have known for over thirty years. Among them remain some who originally supported my scheme for the rectory and made it all materially possible at the outset. Did they believe God was using them? I do not know —in a sense, most of the dramatic happenings have occurred over their heads and apart from them. Do they realise that their little church is one specially blessed by God, and has been used by him in an extraordinary manner, not only in their lifetime, but also over many centuries? People now visiting Lamplugh House might be unaware of the amazing, true story of how God has been at work powerfully over such a long time. But he did, and he still does. So much has happened in our lives that began at Thwing—over all the circumstances; and it feels like being home again at last!

In the course of renewing old friendships and relationships we learned from Ron and Eliza Treasure, shortly after moving to Scarborough, that the York Diocesan Renewal Fellowship was holding a weekend at Wydale Hall, the York Diocesan Conference Centre, only a few miles away from our home. We decided we would like to attend this, not only for spiritual refreshment, but also in the hope that we might meet up again with more old friends. So off we went, in September 2002. Wydale Hall, it will be remembered, was the place we were supposed to have 'threatened' thirty years earlier, when we were seeking permission to set up Lamplugh House. Wydale is a beautiful, eighteenth century country house, formerly the home of the North Yorkshire Caley family, spacious and beautifully appointed, set in extensive grounds and gardens. It was ideal for a pleasant and reflective weekend in the country —which we imagined we were going there for. How wrong I was! Yes, it was all those things, but it turned out to be much more. The weekend was entitled *From Fountains to Floods*, and apart from two main addresses and the Eucharist sermon, it had several workshops on gifts of the Spirit, what they were, and how to use them for building up the body of Christ, which was all quite familiar stuff. One of the leaders was a vicar from a group of village parishes in East Yorkshire —youngish, a former RAF Chaplain, called John Hudghton. Nicely settled into a life of relative comfort and obscurity, I was a little disturbed when, following some discussion with him, he announced more or less that God was aiming to put me back into business! I could not see myself going around taking services occasionally, simply as an (ample) pulpit-filler. I thought I had finished with all that, given certain health considerations. I had, indeed, long since closed the door to such delights; however, it set me thinking and wondering.

Later that afternoon, I had put myself down for a session entitled 'Listening to God' and it was held in the lovely Wydale Chapel, designed, I believe, by the famous York architect George Pace. The East end of the chapel consists entirely of plain glass windows, and through it can be enjoyed wonderful views of countryside and woodland beyond the immediate gardens. Eliza gave a short talk, then encouraged the dozen or so participants simply to remain there in silence for the rest of the period that had well over an hour to run. I love silence and peace and quiet, and the chairs were quite comfortable! But I had already sensed that God was going to tell me something, so I sat with my thoughts and waited. Early that morning, Margaret and I had attended Morning Prayer before breakfast, and I had pointed out to her a tree with several dead branches on it, remarking that it looked as though it would need to come down. Actually, I have a bit of an aversion to trees left standing with lots of dead branches diminishing their tree-likeness. Now, sitting there in the silence, I began to look at this one particular tree.

The tree was some several hundred yards away, so one saw it as part of the landscape. It stood out above many more trees that were all very green and luxuriant. I began to notice that in fact it was far from dead; it had dead branches, yes, but it had a large area emanating from the centre that looked very much alive. I noticed also that birds were constantly gathering around the central greenness on the dead branches that were apparent around the sides, and seemed to be coming and going. It was then that God began to show me something about myself. First, as with the tree, he had in the past put me in a special position that had in time elevated me above the normal parochial level of ministry, in which I had previously served for many years. The dead branches represent the various health problems that had overtaken me as a result of the stress and strains, related in these chapters, that led in time to my retirement as Director of ARM in 1989. But of these I have been healed, and I believe I am at this time being healed of current health matters that have appeared in the last year. So that was it, I thought: a clear indication from God, and a confirmation of that word from John Hudghton that morning, that I can come out of the 'departure lounge', as it were, and be prepared to be of some use to him. I was thoroughly happy with this; all my previous experience told me that if God wants us for anything, all we need do is to say, 'Yes, Lord', and he equips us with all that is necessary for the task, so I was excited and happy at this prospect. Afterwards, I shared this revelation with Margaret, Eliza and several others.

The session that evening dwelt, among other important aspects, on obedience to God and the illustration of Moses striking the rock with his staff at God's command, followed by the living water. John Hudghton's address based on this scripture was dynamic and inspiring. But what I realised above all was that what he was saying I identified with absolutely, in that it was radical, clear and straight to the point on what was needed in the church and what is wrong with much of contemporary Christianity. It is absolutely no good whitewashing over the main failings in the church, that inhibit God's purposes for the spreading of his kingdom. God's work can only be done God's way, and so much of what happens in the church is designed only in human terms — and that gets no blessing from God. Later that evening, after the session, I chatted with John and told him of how, in the early years of ARM, we had tried to relate this sort of thing at local church level to people who do not go to charismatic gatherings —a task in which we had seen a good measure of God's blessing. It was refreshing to find someone with a passion for these basics actually 'doing the stuff' in the power of the Holy Spirit; a person who acknowledged that it must start with evangelism, and leading people to the baptism in the Holy Spirit. We found that we were equally sceptical of some of the independent big names who attract many to their meetings. So often, that does nothing to renew the local church. We were agreed that local ministry is the essential reality.

Off I went to bed, but I was awake a good part of the night, thinking over the events of the day, especially about the tree and God's message to me through it. Soon, however, a further word came to me about the tree. It was not just about me and any ministry I might have, it was also about the Church of England. Many people have given up on—or despair of— the old C of E, but the word to me was that God has not given up on it, and that it is still his lampstand to give light to this nation, and through it he will do just that in his good time. Like the tree, superficially observed, it appears to be dying. So, let us not be deceived: there is a lot of life left in it, and God has not finished with it yet! I had a strong feeling that the Church of England is to be used by God to reverse the tide of evil that appears to be swamping our nation, and that he will do it in an outpouring of the Holy Spirit such as we have only dreamt of. I have got to the stage now that this kind of revelation gives me no problem; I can (and we all can, if we listen) hear the authentic word from God. It is a prophetic word to Anglicans with conviction and openness to the Spirit. We are to get off our backsides, where we sit and watch the dreary predictability of the church's year around the major seasons, and from Harvest festival to the next jumble sale, never expecting that God will ever do anything about the state of the world, which we constantly deplore. If we want change in the world, we will get it if we are first prepared ourselves to be changed. Otherwise we will be changed by the world (as, sadly, some areas of the church seem already to have been). Neither is it much use complaining about the failures of the church unless we identify with those failures as our own and take responsibility, under God to reverse them.

It is time to begin to rejoice, even as we are faced with some of the current problems of the church, about which we usually moan. Like Parson Haslam in Cornwall, long ago, I am being converted by my own preaching in this respect! For centuries, our church has lived off its past: its wealth, its social prestige, and its privileged status in the nation as the Established Church. What we are now seeing is that all these things are being stripped away, it appears, by the force of social and economic conditions. This is not the really significant account of what is happening, and we need not look to newspaper articles for an explanation. The truth lies in the word of God, as it always has, that reveals his ways which never change. The Holy Spirit shows us how to apply the unchanging word to our situation today. As we have already observed, not only does the Holy Spirit bring life to the church, he also brings death to those things that are not on God's agenda, and I believe that in this respect he is at present doing a great deal of this so far as the Anglican Church is concerned —not to destroy or to punish, but in order that it may be restored to its true nature and purpose.

At the Wydale weekend, the Spirit spoke to us clearly through a reading of Psalm 74. The destruction of the Temple and the worship places seemed to give a parallel to our condition, so that we identified with the psalmist's cry to God: 'Remember how the enemy has mocked you, O LORD, how foolish people have reviled your name. Do not hand over your dove to wild beasts; do not forget the lives of your afflicted people for ever. Have regard for your covenant, because haunts of violence fill the dark places of the land. Do not let the oppressed retreat in disgrace; may the poor and needy praise your name.'[1] Inevitably, I suppose, my thoughts returned again to the recent demise of Anglican Renewal Ministries. I remain convinced that, somewhere down the line, someone had lost the plot and lost sight of the most important task it had been given: that of witnessing to the basic parochial grass-roots, and encouraging the people in the pews to receive God's power through the Holy Spirit. For if it does not happen there, the church remains in self-help mode, and is of little use in restoring our apostolic heritage and fulfilling God's agenda.

Since coming back to Yorkshire, the consciousness of God's call to me personally—and the assurance that again, in a sense, I must be prepared to be part of the answer to my own prayer—has returned; not to set up another ARM–like organisation, for those days are over; but, with God's prompting and the promised empowering of the Holy Spirit, it is my hope, together with John Hudghton and the York Diocesan Renewal Fellowship, to encourage the 'restoration' of our Anglican heritage, in the first instance through area conferences for clergy and laity at parish level —mostly folk who do not attend conferences and big meetings, but who long for there to be a fresh vision and purpose for the church, and have an unspoken feeling that there ought to be more to being a Christian, and an Anglican, than they are currently experiencing. Such events would initially be on the lines of what we did in the early years of ARM, and were the beginning of new life and purpose for many local churches. If this gets off the ground, and is seen to be of God, then it will develop, as more people are motivated to become involved. A small acorn indeed, but what potential for growth and development!

Not only is the South West something of a spiritual wilderness where the Church of England is concerned, so is Yorkshire and, I suspect, many other areas of the country. Nevertheless, there are also many green and refreshing oases providing spiritual sustenance to people, proving that the church is not dead—and the new life they have found is for all God's people everywhere. Let us all be encouraged: there is a promise and there is hope for today's church, as long as we are obedient to what God is saying and showing to us. This might be the prayer of many faithful Anglicans as they observe today's scene:

> My soul thirsts for God, for the living God. When can I go and meet with God? My tears have been my food day and night, while men say to me all day long, "Where is your God?"[2]

When we identify ourselves with the needs and the problems within the church, rather than distancing ourselves from them, in penitence we can then approach God, fully aware of our need of his power, and pray:

> Restore us again, O God our Saviour, and put away your displeasure towards us. Will you be angry with us for ever? Will you prolong your anger through all generations? Will you not revive us again, that your people may rejoice in you? Show us your unfailing love, O LORD, and grant us your salvation.[3]

God will answer such prayer when it is sincere and comes out of deep penitence, and he will restore the people whom he loves, who will then be fit to respond:

> When the LORD brought back the captives to Zion, we were like men who dreamed. Our mouths were filled with laughter, our tongues with songs of joy. Then it was said among the nations, "The LORD has done great things for them." The LORD has done great things for us, and we are filled with joy.[4]

> Restore us, O LORD God Almighty; make your face shine upon us, that we may be saved!'[5]

THE TREE

Notes
1. Psalm 74:18–21.
2. Psalm 42:2,3.
3. Psalm 85:4–7.
4. Psalm 126:1–3.
5. Psalm 80:19.